Out From Midtown

A Historical Walking Guide to New York City

Bob Swacker

DISRUPTION
BOOKS

Austin, Texas   New York, New York

Published by Disruption Books
Austin, TX, and New York, NY
www.disruptionbooks.com

Illustrated maps created by and used with permission
of Maggie McCaffrey Barnett.

Distributed by Disruption Books

For ordering information or special discounts for bulk purchases,
please contact Disruption Books at info@disruptionbooks.com.

Cover design by The Decoder Ring Design Concern

Print ISBN: 978-1-63331-037-7
eBook ISBN: 978-1-63331-038-4

First Edition

To my daughters,
Deborah Swacker Nussbaum and Hannah Swacker Kurnit

And to my grandchildren,
Ada and Sophia Nussbaum, and Oliver, Maisie, and Spencer Kurnit

CONTENTS

ACKNOWLEDGMENTS

Thanks to my friends, colleagues, graduate students, and neighbors who helped investigate, facilitate, and proofread this guide.

Brian and Kate Deimling
Elise Meslow Ryan
Leslie Jenkins
Henry Kandel
John McMorris
René Villicaña
Eli Forsythe
Nick and Kristin Fiori
Bob Rubin
Tom Dowling
Hugh Thornton
Jack McShane
Victor Marchioro
Bill Everdell
Carol Rawlings Miller
Jim Spivack
Toni Yagoda
Sarah Anderson Richards
Elizabeth Velikonja
Michael Parrella
David Turkel-Parrella
Drew Hill
Paul and Barbara O'Rourke
Liam Flaherty
Chris Richter
Chris Bertram
Phillip Deery

INTRODUCTION

For five decades, I have led tours through New York City's neighborhoods. As a field historian, I have researched in local institutions and on foot in all five boroughs. Local historical societies, neighborhood libraries, government statistics, and cemetery records have been my primary textual sources. Residents of each neighborhood have provided me with anecdotes and access to the hidden city. I delight in opening the unknown aspects of the city to my students, colleagues, foreign visitors, tourists, and New Yorkers.

The old canard "New York is a great place to visit, but I wouldn't want to live there" should be reversed. The complaint from frazzled tourists and suburbanites who have gotten out of touch with the city is directed at Midtown Manhattan. Fast-paced hordes crowd the streets, restaurants are expensive and you never know which is a good one, you rely on expensive taxicabs, and the cabbies' driving seems dangerous.

Very few New Yorkers actually live in Midtown, though many work there. It is a magnet for the 65 million visitors who come to the city yearly because it seems the essence of New York and is so different from most other places. Midtown is busy, exciting, fashionable, perpetually lit up, and packed with skyscrapers. Attractions include ebullient Broadway shows, world-class shopping opportunities, a plethora of museums, Central Park, superb restaurants, and some of the world's best-known buildings: Rockefeller Center, St. Patrick's Cathedral, the Plaza Hotel, the Empire State Building, and the Chrysler Building. New York City, however, is much more than these famous destinations.

Loosen your ties to Midtown! Leave those well-trodden sidewalks for real adventure and a sense of history. Get out and see the neighborhoods. The people who live in New York think it is a great place to live because they don't have to fight crowds or depend on taxis or expensive restaurants. A trip to some of the interesting areas outside well-known Midtown tourist spots rounds out a visit to the Big Apple. You can see how real New Yorkers live; examine the architecture; check out the local shopping, dining, and entertainment; and learn about neighborhood history, a source of pride to everyone. This guide breaks the mystique of the impenetrability of the Outer Boroughs and the more exotic parts of Manhattan.

New Yorkers, too, can benefit from broadening their outlook. It is easy to get in a rut, even in New York City. Extending yourself to unfamiliar areas will enrich your understanding of the whole. The architecture is waiting, the people are friendly, and the shopkeepers delight in showing their wares.

Traveling is not difficult, and this collection of short trips to interesting old neighborhoods can be made by subway, bus, car, bike, or ferry. Some are only a few minutes from Midtown. Once you are there, a map and explanations about several choice places to visit will make any of these adventures satisfying and give you a fuller sense of the city's life.

Each of the chapters has been chosen because it has a distinct story—historical, economic, or geographic. Some are single-ethnic enclaves, but mostly they are diverse. Change is the main constant. Each is a treasure and calls out for attention. Join me and become an urban adventurer. Let's explore all around New York City!

MANHATTAN

WALL STREET FINANCIAL DISTRICT

Original New Amsterdam & New York

Today's Wall Street Financial District is the original Dutch colonial New Amsterdam and English colonial New York. A good sense of imagination is needed to peel back the onion and picture previous iterations of New York City in an area where almost nothing is left of the Dutch period, and very little remains from the English period, the American Federal period, or even most of the nineteenth century.

The Great Fire of 1835 is one of the chief culprits; the other is the high cost of real estate in the most crowded section of the city where it always seemed financially sound to build more densely whenever possible. The successive buildings got progressively higher as the old buildings were destroyed.

When the Dutch arrived in 1624, they disembarked on Governor's Island (which they called Nutten Island) as a safe haven for man and animal until they scouted out a suitable spot for New Netherland's premier town, which they called New Amsterdam. They chose the narrow tip of Manhattan and relocated there a few months later in 1625.

By the time of the Revolution, New York City (just Manhattan's southern tip) was America's the fourth largest colony; Philadelphia, Boston, and Charleston were each larger. The United States Census of 1790 showed 33,131 people living in Manhattan. By 1860, over 800,000 residents were listed in the census figures. The city had expanded up to 42nd Street, though the financial, government, and court offices remained downtown.

Walking Trip Through Downtown Manhattan

> Begin at Bowling Green via #4 or #5 IRT Lexington Avenue express subway to Bowling Green Station, or M1 or M6 buses to Bowling Green. Other subways will get you close to Bowling Green: #1 IRT 7th Avenue local to South Ferry Station; #2 or #3 IRT 7th Avenue express to Wall Street Station; BMT W or R to Whitehall Street Station; BMT J, Z, or M to Broad Street Station; or IND A train to Broadway-Nassau Station.

Bowling Green

Lower Broadway at Battery Place in front of the Custom House

The Dutch used the small open space as a cattle market and later as a hay market. In 1733, the English colonial government rebuilt the half-acre public space for lawn bowling. It was a private concession leased to operators for the token yearly fee of one peppercorn. The British authorities erected a gilt equestrian statue of George III in 1770, which was pulled down by American patriots in 1776 and melted down for bullets after the first public reading of the Declaration of Independence in New York State. In 1819, it became a private park for use by the owners of town houses that had been built around it. Around 1850, it was transformed into a public park and was restored to its English colonial appearance. The iron fence is original, though the royalist crown finials were broken off in 1776. A large bronze statue of a bull (representing financial market optimism) dominates the northern end of Bowling Green. In a case of wishful economics, there is no bear in sight! The statue was entitled *Charging Bull* by its sculptor, Arturo Di Modica, who placed it there in 1989 without securing permission. *Fearless Girl*, a feisty-looking, determined young girl was installed in front of the bull in 2017. Kristen Visbal, the sculptor, had secured permission for her installation, though the city government moved *Fearless Girl* in 2018 and plans to eventually move *Charging Bull*.

United States Custom House

At the foot of Broadway, south of Bowling Green

Built on the site of the east end of Fort Amsterdam, the Custom House occupies a prime geographic space. The present monumental grey granite structure built in 1907 was designed in a triumphalist Beaux Arts style. The offices of the Collector of Customs of the Port of New York vacated the imposing building in 1974 to move into the World Trade Center. Since 1994, it has housed the Smithsonian Institution's collection of the National Museum of the American Indian. The enormous importance of the role of customs collector is underscored by both the imposing architecture and the realization that before the imposition of the federal income tax (Sixteenth Amendment in 1909), customs were the main financial source of the federal government's income. In front of the building are large statue clusters, each with a domineering enthroned European figure in the center. Called *The Continents*, they represent Asia, North America, Europe, and Africa. Representations of a Chinese laborer, an American Indian, and an African slave are trophies for the seated figure. The facade has twelve Corinthian columns, each topped with the head of Mercury, the Roman god of commerce. Higher up are a dozen statues representing centers of the Greco-Roman European world: Greece, Rome, Phoenicia, Genoa, Venice, Spain, Netherlands, Portugal, Denmark, Germany, England, and France. At the center of the top balustrade is the Great Seal of the United States, flanked by heroic female figures of war and peace and crowned by an American federal eagle. Inside, the immense central rotunda has six oil murals depicting scenes of 1930s New York City harbor commissioned by the Works Progress Administration. The paintings are placed on panels high above a huge marble-topped oval containing fifty-six workstations for tariff-collecting clerks. While gorgeous inside and out, the Custom House glorifies the global economy and the triumph of America's Manifest Destiny. Perhaps this is not the best location for a collection of the National Museum of the American Indian.

The Battery
South tip of Manhattan where the Hudson River and East River merge to form New York Harbor

The Battery, now a park, is named for forts that originally dominated the southern tip of Manhattan. Fort Amsterdam, built in 1625 to protect New Amsterdam, housed four gun batteries and was built of logs, mud, and stones, and was located just west of the US Custom House. It contained a windmill, barracks, and a Protestant (Dutch Reform) church. From the fort, Governor Peter Stuyvesant reluctantly surrendered the town to the English in 1664. Reconstructed and renamed Fort George, it was demolished in 1788 and its remnants, along with other landfill and garbage, were dumped into the harbor to extend Manhattan southward. The circular fort near the harbor and about one hundred yards west of the Custom House is called Castle Clinton. It was built by the United States federal government in 1811, on an islet thirty yards offshore to defend the harbor. A two-hundred-foot wooden causeway linked the fort to Manhattan. In 1823, the fort was demilitarized and given to the city; the city added more landfill to the harbor to envelop the islet into Manhattan. The squat, rough-faced brownstone fort was outfitted with a roof and renamed Castle Garden. P. T. Barnum and others regularly leased it as an entertainment center. Barnum's highlight was the debut of the Swedish Nightingale, Jenny Lind, who sang to packed audiences in 1850. Between 1855 and 1890, it became the main East Coast immigration center; and from 1896 until 1941, it housed the NYC Aquarium. Presently called Castle Clinton again, its center holds a small bookstore and postcard kiosk and a ticket booth for ferries going to Ellis Island and Liberty Island.

Shrine of St. Elizabeth Ann Bayley Seton and Rectory
7 and 8 State Street, across from the Staten Island Ferry Terminal

The two attached buildings comprise a rectory and the church-shrine to the first American-born Roman Catholic saint. The rectory, originally the James Watson House, was finished in 1806 and is the last of the town houses formerly surrounding Bowling Green and extending south to the harbor. The tall slender building is a mix of Georgian and Federal styles. Mother Seton, for whom the chapel is named, was born on Staten Island in 1774, converted to Roman Catholicism in 1805 two years after the death of her husband, founded the American Sisters of Charity in 1809, and in 1975, was canonized in Rome.

 From the Rectory, walk east on State Street one block, left (north) on Whitehall Street one block, right (east) on Pearl Street two blocks.

Fraunces Tavern

54 Pearl Street, corner of Broad Street

Built as a private house in 1719, it was transformed into an inn by Samuel Fraunces after he purchased it in 1762. The Sons of Liberty met there and General George Washington bid farewell to his officers in 1783 in the Long Room:

> *With a heart full of love and gratitude, I now take leave of you. I most devoutly wish that your latter days may be as prosperous and happy as your former ones have been glorious and honorable.*[1]

In 1785, the national government (under the Articles of Confederation) began to move into Fraunces Tavern; and by 1789, under the US Constitution, it housed the Departments of Foreign Affairs (State), War (Defense), and the Treasury. President Washington rented a suite upstairs for the beginning of the single year when the federal government's capital was in New York City. In 1904, the Sons of the Revolution purchased the red and yellow brick building and remodeled what had been altered beyond recognition. The new plans, however, were based mostly on romantic conjecture. It reopened in 1907 as a restaurant and bar with a museum upstairs.

 Walk east on Pearl Street two blocks past several early nineteenth-century commercial buildings; turn left (north) on William Street.

India House

1 Hanover Square, between Pearl Street and Stone Street

This handsome 1853 three-story brownstone Florentine palazzo seems isolated among the twentieth-century office buildings. It serves as a historical reminder that a good part of the city was once covered with brownstone-faced buildings.

---

[1] Lynn Price, "'With a Heart Full of Love and Gratitude I Now Take Leave of You': George Washington's Farewell Toast." *The Washington Papers*. January 19, 2018. gwpapers.virginia .edu/heart-full-love-gratitude-now-take-leave-george-washingtons-farewell-toast.

Abraham De Peyster Statue
Hanover Square

Opposite the India House is the Abraham De Peyster statue in half-acre Hanover Square Park. Dutch-born De Peyster (1657–1728) was a wealthy merchant and gold trader; he held a host of municipal jobs, including alderman and mayor. He is shown seated with enormous boots and a brimmed cavalier's hat. Originally, the statue was at Bowling Green. *Note:* Hanover Park has no grass, just the De Peyster statue with several rows of benches to accommodate the lunchtime crowds.

 Detour: turn left (west) for fifty yards on Stone Street.

The Dutch-style, stepped gable roof at 57 Stone Street attempts to recover the seventeenth-century Dutch ambiance when some buildings copied architecture in Amsterdam.

 Continue north on William Street one block.

Delmonico's (building and restaurant)
56 Beaver Street, corner of Beaver Street, William Street, and South William Street.

Orange terra-cotta and brick alternate in a rich design on a building with great visibility given its narrow rectangular shape squeezed between two converging streets. Built in 1891, the office building was converted into a condominium in 1996. The restaurant has been at this location since 1982. It was founded by Italian-Swiss brothers in 1827 and occupied several locations from William Street to 26th Street and back again to the Financial District. It was the best-known restaurant in the United States for more than a century, offering fresh quality produce, dairy products from its farm in Brooklyn, fish from the nearby Fulton Fish Market, and specializing in innovative dishes such as Baked Alaska and Lobster Newburg. Delmonico steak, a boned steak from the front of the short loin of beef, took its name from the restaurant.

Left (southwest) on South William Street two blocks; turn right (north) on Broad Street three blocks.

Broad Street

The way George Washington walked to work when he resided at Fraunces Tavern

Shadowed by tall buildings housing banks and other financial service institutions, Broad Street has no resemblance to any century but the one in which its buildings were built: the twentieth. You need historical imagination to follow President Washington's steps leading to his office in Federal Hall.

New York Stock Exchange

8 Broad Street, at the corner of Wall Street

The present home of the New York Stock Exchange is a richly decorated 1903 Roman Revival building of grey granite. The economics textbook story of the 1792 Buttonwood Agreement signed under a buttonwood tree by twenty-two stockbrokers is largely apocryphal. While trading had gone on since Dutch days, it was informal and generally took place in offices or taverns. In 1817, the New York Stock Exchange was organized by twenty-eight stockbrokers to provide membership criteria and set days and hours for trading. Companies listed on the Big Board, as the NYSE is sometimes called, achieve an enhanced level of prestige as well as accessibility to the public. The balcony of the Trading Floor was formerly open to visitors on days and hours when the stock market was open until the September 11, 2001, attack on the World Trade Center.

Federal Hall (formerly US Subtreasury Building and originally US Custom House)

28 Wall Street, at the corner of Nassau Street

This is not President Washington's Federal Hall, but the site of the old Federal Hall where George Washington was inaugurated from the second-floor balcony in 1789. The original edifice had been the second New York City Hall, built in 1699 and remodeled in 1788 by Pierre Charles L'Enfant, who later planned the street grid of Washington, DC. (The first City Hall, called Stadt Huys by the Dutch, was in a tavern on Pearl Street facing

opulent building became a monument to brazen graft and corruption netting the Tweed Ring at least $12 million in thievery and kickbacks. The interior, for example, was rebuilt three times to generate more opportunity for theft of public funds. Boss Tweed ended up dying in prison in 1878 after conviction for fraud and theft; estimates of the total cost of his rule from 1863 until 1872 range from $50 million to $200 million. The stately Victorian structure was constructed between 1858 and 1878 and was used as a courthouse, then as a storage facility for municipal records. It suffers from the Tweed connection and its odd, undignified placement: a grand front overlooking a narrow street. The front stairway, removed to widen Chambers Street in 1942, left the anterior portico an ungainly stump for six decades. In 2001, Chambers Street was constricted from four lanes to three in the middle of the block to rebuild the lower portion of the stairway. It was part of an $85 million restoration. The building is now the headquarters of the Department of Education.

Municipal Building
One Centre Street at the east end of Chambers Street

East of the Tweed Courthouse at the approach of the Brooklyn Bridge is the twenty-five-story majestic civic skyscraper that was finished in 1913 and had its fanciful rounded wedding cake top crowned by the gilt *Civic Fame*. It holds the offices of the Manhattan borough president, comptroller (treasurer), public advocate, and city clerk. A small shop selling items relating to New York City is on the ground floor of the north end. It offers postcards, playing cards, neckties, scarves, paperweights, books, and municipal publications, including the *Green Book* (a theoretically accurate list of prominent city government positions along with their names, addresses, and phone numbers). Unsubstantiated rumor had it that Joseph Stalin was impressed by photographs of the Municipal Building and used it as a model for Moscow's eight famous skyscraper wedding cake buildings constructed in the 1930s.

Surrogate's Court (originally the Hall of Records)
31 Chambers Street, between Centre Street and Elk Street

The exterior of the 1911 Surrogate's Court is arguably the most ornate public structure in the city. Built to express civic pride, the eclectic French

Renaissance edifice is splendid inside and out. The mansard roof is decorated with tracery and green terra-cotta designs. Eight flowery Corinthian columns are clustered toward the center of the facade. High on the balustrade stand eight figures representing New York City's history. The most recognizable by his Dutch clothing and peg leg is Peter Stuyvesant. The interior lobby is a grand palace of shiny marble: stairs, columns, archways, and a curved central balcony. Presently, the building houses both the Surrogate's Court (probate of wills and settlement of estates) and the Hall of Records (birth, marriage, death). An unexpected treasure can be found in the basement offices of the Municipal Archives: 720,000 photographs documenting every building in the five boroughs from 1939 to 1941 as part of a New Deal WPA program to aid the Department of Finance (then called the Department of Taxes) with property assessments, but also to help employ out-of-work photographers during the Great Depression. At least thirty-two anonymous photographers worked on the program, which methodically captured plain front views of each building identified by address, block, and borough. Useful to architects and historians, individual photographs may be purchased as mementos.

The Sun Building (formerly A. T. Stewart's Department Store)

280 Broadway, between Chambers Street and Reade Street

A. T. Stewart's Department Store, founded across the street in 1823, opened his seven-story marble palace at this site in 1846. It was New York City's first marble-faced commercial building. Lavish and elegant on the inside, it offered reasonable prices and encouraged browsing, the prototype of a century of department stores. *The Sun*, founded in 1833, was the nation's first successful penny paper distributed by newsboys. It was a generally conservative newspaper heavy on political news and police stories. *The Sun* published the most famous editorial in American journalism in 1897 in response to a doubting letter from an eight-year-old girl. "Yes, Virginia, there is a Santa Claus . . ." began editor Francis P. Church. In 1950, *The Sun* was absorbed into *The New York World-Telegram*. Two large four-sided Roman numeral clocks were added by the newspaper and adorn the building's corners. They are engraved in Old English lettering: THE SUN, IT SHINES FOR ALL.

Negroes Burial Ground
Duane Street and Elk Street

This was the burial ground outside the Wall for free and enslaved blacks, Native Americans, white paupers, and prisoners. Its five acres were located on the southwest slope of the Collect Pond. It is unclear when the burials began; they may date from the late Dutch period, though earliest official records to mention the cemetery are not found until 1712. When burials ended is also unknown. Draconian laws prohibited evening burials (common in Africa) and graveside funeral gatherings of more than twelve mourners. Further indignity came as eighteenth-century body snatchers periodically raided the cemetery to obtain skeletons or corpses for medical schools. Slavery lasted from 1626 in the Dutch period, through the English period, and was not wholly abolished in New York State until 1841. In 1795, the burial ground was subdivided and sold as lots for houses. Houses were constructed over the graves. Between 1991 and 1994, during construction of a new thirty-four-story federal building, more than four hundred skeletons were uncovered. Archaeologists noted African-style burial practices: corpses buried facing east accompanied by cowry shells and shroud pins. Presently, a small corner of the land has been preserved and a memorial has been built.

Cross Elk Street and walk downhill toward the open space.

Collect Pond, the Freshwater, or *Kalch*
Foley Square area

The Collect is well named in English. It may have received its Dutch name from a corruption of the word for pond: *kolch*. But *kalch*, which means lime in Dutch, could have referred to the heaps of oyster shells left by the Lenape Natives around the perimeter of the pond. It was the largest source of freshwater for the early colonists. Perhaps eighty acres and sixty feet deep, it was a valuable asset, which both the Dutch and English colonists degraded by using it as the town dump and by building tanneries, breweries, and slaughterhouses along its banks. Eventually, it became a foul menace and was filled in between 1803 and 1813 during the Federal period. The pond's outline can still be seen, as the land in and around Foley Square forms a sloping depression of several feet. The large black granite sculpture in the center of Foley Square, *Triumph of the Human Spirit*, memorializes all enslaved Africans and celebrates their will to survive. Special mention is made on the dedication plaque to those interred in the Negroes Burial Ground. Inspiration came for the striking monument from the tall West African Chiwara headdresses. At the north end of Foley Square is diminutive Thomas Paine Park, named to honor the Revolutionary War figure and author of *Common Sense*.

> When exiting Foley Square, walk east on Pearl Street, between the New York State Courthouse and the taller United States Courthouse, two blocks to Park Row, turn left and walk another one hundred yards. As you feel yourself walking out of the low spot that was once the edge of the Collect Pond, watch on the left for a small sign posted just before the block's only apartment building. It reads: DANGER: SINKING GROUND—DO NOT ENTER. The enigmatic sign and the slight depression of the land are the only visible reminders of Manhattan's lagoon dating from the Dutch and early English colonial periods.
>
> Proceed to Chatham Square; turn right down St. James Place.

Jews Burying Ground
St. James Place off Chatham Square

This is the first of three small extant cemeteries outside the Wall operated by the Spanish and Portuguese Congregation Shearith Israel, formed in 1654 by Sephardic Jewish immigrants from Recife, Brazil. Jews were denied permission to build a cemetery within the walled city or to build a synagogue until 1729. (The other two cemeteries are in Greenwich Village and in Chelsea. The synagogue is at Central Park West at the corner of 70th Street.)

St. James Roman Catholic Church and School
32 James Street, between St. James Place and Madison Street, just around the corner from the Jewish Cemetery

Al Smith, the first Catholic to be nominated for President (1928), went to church and school here, as did hundreds within the Five Points Irish neighborhood. This is the area where the Democratic club, Tammany Hall, originated. The church, built in brownstone-covered Greek Revival Doric style, rises magnificently from the middle of the narrow block. Inside the almost square building is a white altar and an imposing altarpiece with three large scalloped areas featuring paintings from the life of Jesus with a central crucifixion scene. Positioned high on the walls are stained-glass windows, mostly of saints, with St. Patrick and St. Brigid at the front places of honor. (The street's secondary name is Ancient Order of Hibernians.)

Restaurant Recommendation

Fraunces Tavern

54 Pearl Street, corner of Broad Street

This may be one of America's original theme restaurants. Through several incarnations, beginning in 1907, Fraunces Tavern has served what is generally perceived as late-eighteenth-century American fare. Though the food is poked fun at regularly by critics, the experience of eating at the venue where all the Founding Fathers gathered remains attractive.

GOVERNORS ISLAND

New Amsterdam's Temporary Settlement, Military
Installations, and Popular Recreation Venue

T he island just off the coast of Manhattan's southern tip attracted
the first wave of Dutch and Walloon settlers in 1624 because it
offered natural protection from the Native Americans and a safe
place for their cattle to graze. They called it Nutten Island because of the
presence of nut trees, presumably bearing chestnuts and acorns. Nutten
Island was to be a place to reconnoiter while they prepared to establish a
permanent settlement in Manhattan.

The island is actually closer by half to Brooklyn than Manhattan.
The Red Hook section of Brooklyn lies just across the narrow Buttermilk
Channel from Governors Island. All the islands around Manhattan,
including the three in the inner harbor, are politically part of Manhattan,
though Ellis Island and Liberty Island remain part of the federal
government's National Park System.

In 1625, the colonists moved to Manhattan and established New
Amsterdam. Nutten Island was left under the control of the Dutch West
India Company. Ownership of land was an unknown concept to the
Lenape American Indians; but to the Dutch, who *bought* it from the Native
Americans in 1637 for some axes, nails, and colored beads, it was legal
and permanent.

In 1698, during the English colonial period, the state legislature set
the island aside for the use of the royal governors and changed the name
to Governors Island, which was intended for residential use by governors
while the colonial capital was in New York City. New York State turned the
island over to the federal government in 1800. Forts were constructed as
part of a series of fortifications to protect New York Harbor.

Governors Island served military purposes during the nineteenth and twentieth centuries. After the American loss at the Battle of Long Island (in Brooklyn) in 1776, Governors Island was held briefly by the retreating troops of General Israel Putnam. British Admiral Richard Howe soon recaptured the island, but the diversion helped give General George Washington time to evacuate from Brooklyn across the East River to Manhattan.

The British evacuated in 1783 and New York State resumed ownership. State and federal officials cooperated in building two major defenses on the island. Though war with Great Britain commenced in 1812, New York Harbor was not attacked. Military use of Governors Island included protection that the two forts offered during the War of 1812 and the Civil War, a recruitment station and later a prison camp for captured Confederates during the Civil War.

During World War I, the island was a supply depot for soldiers sailing for Europe, a pilot training center, and a coastal defense center. The United States Army used it for a regional headquarters during World War II. The Coast Guard received Governors Island from the United States Army in 1966 and used it for its East Coast regional headquarters. At its height, 3,500 Coast Guard personnel and dependents lived on Governors Island. As a cost-cutting measure, the Coast Guard withdrew in 1997, leaving the pear-shaped island uninhabited.

Beginning in 1901, landfill from the Interboro Rapid Transit was dumped off the southern end of the island, which nearly doubled its size, from 90 acres to 172 acres. In 1909, aviator Wilbur Wright used the level, treeless southern end of Governors Island to take off on the first flight over water, a brief trip which ended with a safe landing at the edge of Riverside Park near Grant's Tomb.

President Bill Clinton offered to sell the island to New York City for $1 in 1995 if the city and state came up with a land-use plan that included public access. Nothing happened until President George W. Bush reiterated the offer in 2002. Governor George Pataki and Mayor Michael Bloomberg accepted the second offer. They suggested a new City University of New York (CUNY) campus specializing in teacher training and the sciences. Ample dormitory space, classrooms, and some laboratories already existed. Ultimately, the focus changed, dormitories and classroom spaces used by the military were demolished, more landfill was added, and

Governors Island was fully transformed into a park and cultural center. Before he left office, President Clinton declared both forts and the surrounding historic buildings, about twenty acres, to be a national monument so that, whatever would happen to the remainder of Governors Island, the historic core would be protected and eventually open to the public by the National Park Service. Fort Jay and Castle Williams remain under the oversight of the National Park Service. Governors Island is now open to the public, with a ferry running throughout the year to the Battery Maritime Building in Manhattan and an additional weekend ferry running to Brooklyn's Atlantic Avenue in the summer.

Ferry Trip to Governors Island Ferry Terminal

Take the IRT #4 or #5 train to Bowling Green Station, walk four blocks southeast on State Street to the Governors Island Ferry Terminal; or take the IRT #1 train to South Ferry Station, walk east past the Staten Island Ferry Terminal to the Governors Island Ferry Terminal; or take the BMT N or R train to Whitehall Street Station, walk one block southeast on Whitehall Street to the Governors Island Ferry Terminal; or take the BMT M train to Broad Street Station, walk five blocks southeast on Broad Street to the Governors Island Ferry Terminal.

Governors Island Ferry from the Battery Maritime Building

The Battery Maritime Building is used as the Manhattan terminal for the Governors Island Ferry. The Beaux Arts structure, completed in 1909, has a large waiting room with slender cast-iron columns and stained-glass windows. The building was originally built as the terminal for a ferry to 39th Street in Sunset Park, Brooklyn, whose service ended in 1938. It is next to the Whitehall Ferry Terminal of the Staten Island Ferry.

Depart the small white ferry to Governors Island and walk fifty feet ahead to the Visitors Center to obtain a free map of the island. There are several books and souvenirs for sale and information about event planning and reserving camping sites on this 172-acre island.

Walking Trip Through Governors Island

Governors House

Completed in 1708 by British Governor Lord Cornbury, the two-story Georgian brick house was used by English colonial governors. In 1797, following American independence, the state capital was moved to Albany, and the island's military commander used the house as his residence.

Castle Williams

The semicircular three-story red sandstone fort built at water's edge was a companion of Castle Clinton, initially built off the Battery in Manhattan. Castle Williams was constructed between 1807 and 1811 and served as a military prison for American military convicts, except during the Civil War, when it was used as a prisoner of war camp for Confederates.

Fort Jay

More a series of low earthwork bunkers built behind a star-shaped dry moat than a fort, it was constructed in the island's center between 1794 and 1808. By the Coast Guard period, it served as the officers' club. The brownstone arch entrance is topped by a striking triumphal sculpture of cannons and flags. Built in 1812 to protect the harbor and Buttermilk Channel from foreign invaders, it was eventually converted to serve as quarters and storage facility. A string of illustrious American generals have lived there: Winfield Scott, John Pershing, Omar Bradley, and Walter Bedell Smith.

Chapel of St. Cornelius the Centurion (Episcopal)

Trinity Church parish on Broadway sponsored a small chapel here in 1847. The present Gothic Revival chapel replaced the initial Protestant church in 1905. It is decorated with battle flags representing key struggles in American military history. The chapel is named for a patron of the military, Cornelius, who appears in the Acts of the Apostles as a centurion from the Italian Regiment posted in Caesarea. Cornelius was the first pagan baptized by Peter.

Four Hills

A recent addition has been four man-made seventy-foot hills, one with three slides of varying lengths, two for climbing with superb panoramic views of New Jersey, Manhattan, Brooklyn, and Staten Island, and one with a flat grassy top for relaxing.

Urban Camping Site

In 2018, several large tents placed on wooden platforms were set up at the southwest portion of Governors Island for a glamorous overnight camping experience. Tents are equipped with electric outlets and lamps inside and on the wooden decks surrounding the tents. Running hot and cold water are supplied. Toilets are a short distance away. Each tent has real beds, comfortable chairs, and rugs. The campground affords wonderful views of the harbor, and especially the Statue of Liberty and Ellis Island. Reservations are necessary.

Interesting Experience

If you choose to rent bicycles to bike around the island, you will find the roadway flat and wide and just a few feet from land's end. It will provide opportunities to stop and rest, or explore periodic places to obtain drinks or enjoy different views. There are play areas for children, including a tree house, a children's community garden, miniature golf, and various games placed in the grassy section between two rows of officers' houses next to the Chapel of St. Cornelius.

Opportunities for Refreshments

Island Oyster

Island Oyster is near the ferry dock on the north shore. They serve shellfish and cocktails on a faux beach with sand and artificial palm trees.

Governors Island Beer Company

The Governors Island Beer Company offers beer and light food at Liggett Terrace, a complex of buildings in the south-central part of the island. Also in Liggett Terrace is a food court with food trucks and stationary cafés, including a Starbucks.

migration to New York City came from the Carolinas and Virginia. (Migration from the Deep South generally went straight north to Baltimore, Philadelphia, St. Louis, Chicago, Milwaukee, and Detroit.) By the mid-1920s, there were eighty thousand African Americans in Harlem. In the 1930s, the black population topped two hundred thousand.

Harlem became the largest concentration of blacks in any American city, north or south, and was quickly catapulted to national prominence. It became the focal point of black independence and cultural achievement, and residence for many black politicians, intellectuals, writers, and musicians.

Adventurous whites in search of new forms of entertainment or novelty visited Harlem regularly. The idea of *prestige from below* was powerful among some avant-garde whites, and they filled many of Harlem's clubs from the 1920s through the 1950s. But white residents continued to move out of Harlem as blacks moved in, a situation that transformed many institutions, especially places of entertainment, churches, and synagogues.

From 1914 until 1934, the Apollo Theater featured burlesque and played to a whites-only audience. New owners opened its 1,500-seat auditorium with a program featuring black musicians, dancers, and comedians to entertain mixed audiences. Over the years, Billie Holiday, Bessie Smith, Louis Armstrong, Duke Ellington, Charlie Parker, and Dizzy Gillespie were featured onstage.

White religious institutions, following their congregations, migrated to other parts of the city or simply closed their doors. The churches and synagogues were eventually sold to black congregations, as the buildings were recycled. Among the most influential black Harlem churches were the Abyssinian Baptist, Canaan Baptist, and St. Philip's Episcopal, which had active middle-class congregations and prominent ministers. The Prince Lodge of the Masonic Order was another strong middle-class voice in the community.

Even as concentrations of blacks developed after World War II in Brooklyn, Chicago, Detroit, St. Louis, Memphis, Los Angeles, Cleveland, Baltimore, Philadelphia, Boston, Atlanta, and Washington, DC, Harlem remained the symbolic capital of Black America. It had earned its preeminence by being in the largest American city where many of the most influential black opinion leaders had settled.

Cultural and political issues during the Harlem Renaissance were often combined in single personalities. The poet and playwright Langston Hughes raised political consciousness by focusing on the lives of everyday characters with problems and aspirations common to many African Americans. Countee Cullen, poet, novelist, and teacher, also examined the struggles of blacks in their neighborhood subculture. The respected research library in Harlem is named for him. Painter Romare Bearden organized exhibitions promoting the work of young black artists who portrayed themes drawn from the African American experience. Paul Robeson, Columbia University football player, lawyer, actor, and opera singer, struggled for progressive causes during the bleak days of the Great Depression and during the Cold War. Adam Clayton Powell Jr., Harlem's delegate to the House of Representatives and copastor at the Abyssinian Baptist Church, was the leading national congressional voice on issues of importance to African Americans throughout the country.

The rise of suburbs hurt all cities, especially inner cities, by emptying them of significant portions of their residential and commercial bases. The remaining whites in Harlem who could afford to leave did leave for the suburbs, and many businesses and nightclubs closed or moved downtown. An exception was retail stores, which generally remained in the hands of Jewish and Italian proprietors until the 1970s. Deprivation, poverty, welfare, unemployment, drug dealing, addiction, violence, alienation, and isolation were the maladies that began to characterize Harlem. The rapidly decreasing population left boarded-up buildings scarring the urban landscape. Bus tours showing decay and social disorganization became a staple of tourist incursions in Harlem.

Through the 1960s and '70s, boycotts and demonstrations were staged to protest against white shopkeepers, especially those who refused to hire blacks. The effect was to drive more merchants from the neighborhood. Drug addiction and crime reached epidemic proportions in those years, which dissuaded new businesses, black or white, from opening. Banks redlined the area as unprofitable and refused loans to start-up businesses. Harlem became something akin to a commerce-free zone. During the 1970s and '80s, Harlem, with two hundred thousand residents, did not have a single supermarket, and shoppers had to pay higher prices for groceries at small mom-and-pop stores.

There were also some proud moments in the 1950s and 1960s. Churches continued to hold services and organize efforts to aid senior citizens, students, and the poor. Bookstores became intellectual centers where new ideas were shared during readings and receptions. Radio stations opened, and the gutsy, controversial, "tell 'em like it is" weekly, the *Amsterdam News,* published a newspaper read by blacks throughout the city. Clubs continued to feature cutting-edge musicians. Political leaders represented the neighborhood at City Hall, Albany, and Washington, DC. By 1970, the main avenues of Harlem, streets that earlier developers designed to emulate the broad avenues of Paris, had their names changed to honor Adam Clayton Powell Jr., Martin Luther King Jr., and Malcolm X.

Three of the key north–south avenues now have names instead of numbers. With one partial exception, they are named for important figures in African American history. Lenox Avenue, conamed Malcolm X Boulevard (6th Avenue), received its first nonnumbered name in honor of James Lenox, a collector of books and art and founder of the Lenox Library, which in 1895 merged with the Astor Library and Tilden Trust (a bequest of books owned by Samuel J. Tilden) to form the New York Public Library. Its second nonnumbered name honors Malcolm X, the Black Muslim leader who was assassinated in 1965 shortly after he left the Nation of Islam (Black Muslims), made a pilgrimage to Mecca, and became an orthodox Sunni Muslim. Unlike 6th Avenue, which was conamed Avenue of the Americas in 1945 but which name is rarely used by New Yorkers, the names Lenox Avenue and Malcolm X Boulevard are both used to refer to 6th Avenue north of Central Park. Adam Clayton Powell Jr. Boulevard (7th Avenue) was renamed in 1974 to honor a Harlem community leader who was concurrently pastor of the Abyssinian Baptist Church and an eleven-term United States congressman. He was an outspoken fighter for civil rights and was well known across the nation. Frederick Douglass Boulevard (8th Avenue), in Harlem, was named for the enormously influential antislavery crusader, author, and speaker. He escaped slavery in Maryland and later made powerful speeches in the North, giving dramatic performances about the horrors of the slave system. He was editor of *The North Star*, an abolitionist newspaper published in Rochester, New York. During the Civil War, he met with President Lincoln in the White House on several occasions.

Radicals like Paul Robeson stirred emotions with hard-hitting analyses of the general suffering of black Americans and the particular problems of Harlem. A. Philip Randolph, president of the Brotherhood of Sleeping Car Porters, was an active voice in the labor movement during the 1930s, '40s, and '50s, and a civil rights leader with a national following during the tumultuous 1960s. W. E. B. Du Bois, who had authored *The Souls of Black Folk* in 1903, was a fiery opponent of Booker T. Washington's ideas of economic gains first, a policy calling on blacks to forgo civil rights. Du Bois was active in the leftist American Labor Party, and, with Paul Robeson, operated the Council on African Affairs. In 1961, disillusioned with the United States, Du Bois joined the Communist Party, and shortly after went into voluntary exile in Ghana, where he remained until the end of his life at the age of ninety-five. The Nation of Islam, and Malcolm X in particular, raised the issue of black nationalism and self-segregation to a new level of acceptability. Black nationalism and communism had considerable appeal in Harlem. The Communist Party had many prominent blacks in its ranks and had stood up against racism in the labor movement and segregation in the South and in the armed forces since the 1920s.

In 1975, 60 percent of Harlem's housing was owned by New York City, which had become the city's biggest landlord through default. Owners had walked away from unprofitable buildings or had had them seized for nonpayment of taxes. The city had neither the resources nor the political will to engage in a broad program of housing development. Small programs existed and the city dutifully cleared burned-out hulks and left them as incongruous meadows among the remaining buildings.

Harlem moved from impoverished ghetto to early gentrification in the 1980s as the city began to attract suburbanites (or their children) returning to New York City. Escalating housing prices caused New Yorkers to look in areas they had previously dismissed out of hand. In the 1990s, gentrification became a word used to describe Harlem. The proximity to three subway lines, one railroad line, numerous highways, a housing stock that, while degraded, had great promise, and the panache of living at the edge in a neighborhood that was recognized, for whatever reasons, by all Americans were some of the reasons blacks (and a few whites and

Hispanics) got involved in gentrification. Some of the city's African immigrants began settling in Harlem.

The process has been accelerated by a potent combination: the buoyant economy of the 1990s, an activist Greater Harlem Chamber of Commerce, development-oriented churches and mosques, banks finally willing to lend, politicians focused on helping their neighborhood, and government agencies, such as Housing and Urban Development, Upper Manhattan Empowerment Zone, and Small Business Administration, getting involved. In the 1990s, city-owned buildings in receivership were transferred to private developers and homeowners.

Encouraging signs of new economic life include row house and apartment renovations, new stores and restaurants, and more jobs. Every block in the neighborhood has a construction project. People are moving into Harlem rather than fleeing from it. Now bus tours focus on the building boom, and so many tours want to attend gospel services at churches that they need to be limited by reservations. Sylvia's is no longer the only nice restaurant in Harlem. The 1990s brought the advent of the gospel brunch, though most of the restaurants are more interested in serving good food than promoting traditional African American music.

The benefits of Harlem's gentrification are spread unevenly. Some people get forced out through evictions and others are priced out of their apartments. The economically impoverished and socially vulnerable are at risk, and some long-time Harlemites worry that the area will evolve into the upper-middle-class neighborhood it was once designed as by speculators more than a century ago. It may look better now and in coming years, but it might lose its place as the heart and soul of Black America. Change, of course, is the one constant in New York City neighborhoods.

Walking Trip in Central Harlem

 Take the IND local subway B or C train to West 135th Street Station.

Walk east on West 135th Street one short block; turn left (north) on Frederick Douglass Boulevard (8th Avenue).

St. Charles Condominiums

Both sides of Frederick Douglass Boulevard from West 136th to West 138th Streets

Built in 1997, the development sponsored by St. Charles Borromeo Church (Roman Catholic) has 120 units of subsidized housing. The new buildings succeed in emulating the spirit of Strivers' Row, though the metallic front steps detract from the endeavor. Upgrading or replacing Harlem's housing stock has been on the top shelf of projects to enhance the community and improve the lives of Harlem's residents.

 Turn right (east) on West 138th Street and walk two blocks.

Strivers' Row

West 138th Street (and West 139th Street) from Frederick Douglass Boulevard (8th Avenue) to Adam Clayton Powell Jr. Boulevard (7th Avenue)

Constructed as the King Model Houses between 1891 and 1893, the grouping reflects different styles but fits together harmoniously. The block is vaguely Georgian architecturally, and the original white owners hoped others would emulate their refined taste and commitment to the northern reaches of Manhattan. The patronizing term *Strivers' Row* became attached to them in the 1920s once African Americans had purchased most of the houses. W. E. B. Du Bois, Eubie Blake, and W. C. Handy lived on the block.

Abyssinian Baptist Church

132 West 138th Street, between Frederick Douglass Boulevard (8th Avenue) and Adam Clayton Powell Jr. Boulevard (7th Avenue)
212-862-7474

American University Gothic in appearance, the church was built in 1923 and became the most important black pulpit in the United States. The charismatic orator Adam Clayton Powell Jr. was copastor and concurrently a member of the House of Representatives (1944–1970). He was expelled from Congress in 1967 on a legal technicality, but really for upsetting the majority of his colleagues by being too arrogant and uppity, having well-publicized dalliances, and marrying a white entertainer. Powell was reelected in 1968 and exonerated by the Supreme Court in 1969, but was defeated the following year by Charles Rangel. The latest pastor, Calvin O. Butts III, is a well-known advocate for Harlem. Abyssinian Baptist was named for Ethiopia, an early Christian kingdom in Africa, which successfully held off colonial powers until defeated by Mussolini in 1936. The church, originally chartered in 1808 when it was housed in a building near City Hall, has been an institutional leader in agitating for social reform and organizing neighborhood housing projects through the Abyssinian Development Corporation. The church's gospel choir draws worshippers and guests to the 11:00 a.m. Sunday service.

 At Lenox Avenue-Malcolm X Boulevard (6th Avenue), turn right (south).

Harlem Hospital

506 Lenox Avenue-Malcolm X Boulevard (6th Avenue), between West 135th and 136th Streets

This large public facility is the primary health care provider in the neighborhood. City budget allocations for Harlem Hospital often become political struggles over how much the community needs. Among the City of New York's municipal hospitals are Bellevue Hospital in Manhattan, which traces its lineage to the Almshouse Infirmary in 1736 (essentially a prison for the poor with chronic illnesses), Kings County Hospital in Brooklyn, which dates from 1831, Bronx Municipal Hospital, which opened in 1954, and Harlem Hospital, founded in 1877 as Reception Hospital. Since 1965, both city and private (religious and nonreligious) hospitals have received indirect aid from the state in the form of reimbursements from Medicare and Medicaid programs. State regulators monitor all hospitals in New York State, and the New York Health and Hospitals Corporation, a city department, governs municipal hospitals.

Schomburg Center for Research in Black Culture of the New York Public Library

515 Lenox Avenue-Malcolm X Boulevard (6th Avenue), between West 135th and 136th Streets
212-491-2200

The Schomburg is New York City's premier research facility for black literature and history. Arturo A. Schomburg, a black Puerto Rican, originally organized the collection in the 1920s. Its staff of sixty maintains the archives containing over one hundred thosand books on the *black experience*. There are five million photos, video and audio recordings, letters, and manuscripts by W. E. B. Du Bois, Langston Hughes, and many others. The Schomburg Center sponsors over sixty public programs each year, which utilize its archives.

Jungle Alley

Block of 133rd Street, between Lenox Avenue-Malcolm X Boulevard (6th Avenue) and Adam Clayton Powell Jr. Boulevard (7th Avenue)

This was the center of white people's fantasy of African American culture. White-owned and black-owned clubs along the block hosted *jungle shows,* where white-only audiences could see scantily clad black women dance to erotic beats of *jungle music*, always heavy on percussion.

Former Site of Liberation Book Store

421 Lenox Avenue-Malcolm X Boulevard (6th Avenue), corner of West 131st Street
212-281-4615

This popular bookshop opened in 1967 during the Black Power Movement. It carried a wide variety of books on numerous subjects concerning

African Americans and Africa. Until it closed in 2002, it served as an unofficial gathering place for many Harlem intellectuals.

Muhammad's Mosque #7

106 West 127th Street, just off Lenox Avenue-Malcolm X Boulevard (6th Avenue)
212-865-1200

This is a Nation of Islam mosque, the successor to the one opened in 1946 by the Chicago-based group under the leadership of Elijah Muhammad. Malcolm X led Mosque #7 from 1954 until 1964 when it was located on 116th Street and Lenox Avenue-Malcolm X Boulevard (6th Avenue). Malcolm X broke with the Nation of Islam (Black Muslims) after his pilgrimage to Mecca when he accepted orthodox Sunni Islam and opened a small mosque in the Theresa Hotel. For a brief time, Louis Farrakhan led Mosque #7. Since 1976, the 116th Street mosque has been known as the Masjid Malcolm Shabazz and is associated with the orthodox Sunni Islam movement led by Wallace D. Muhammad. (Malcolm X was assassinated in 1965 while addressing a group at the now-razed Audubon Ballroom, located at Broadway and West 165th Street.)

 At West 125th Street, detour one half block to the left (east).

Lenox Lounge

288 Lenox Avenue-Malcolm X Boulevard (6th Avenue), just off West 125th Street
212-722-9566

Just around the corner from 125th Street is a popular jazz club where patrons come to hear some of the finest instrumentalists and vocalists performing in the center of Harlem. The sleek art deco Zebra Room has hosted Billie Holiday, Miles Davis, John Coltrane, and others. Malcolm X sometimes visited the Lenox Lounge. When there are no live artists performing, disc jockeys play underground disco, hip-hop, reggae, and jazz. Though jazz has lost much of its importance as an American cultural icon, it still has devotees in the neighborhood and throughout the world.

Many of the successful New York jazz clubs are now located downtown, especially in the West Village. The Lenox Lounge features a busy musical schedule, which also includes cabaret vocalists and comedy routines. The food ranges from crab cakes and fried whiting to barbecue ribs and broiled chicken.

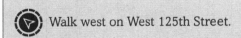 Walk west on West 125th Street.

North General Hospital, Paul Robeson Center (originally Koch & Company)

132–140 West 125th Street, between Lenox Avenue-Malcolm X Boulevard (6th Avenue) and Adam Clayton Powell Jr. Boulevard (7th Avenue)

A premature move in 1893 by a famous downtown dry goods store to cash in on the upscale neighborhood fizzled when Harlem's sustainable middle class failed to materialize. The building is brick and terra-cotta with rounded limestone-framed windows. The health center was named for Paul Robeson (1898–1976), the football star, lawyer, singer, actor, and left-wing political activist who strongly and persuasively advocated labor causes and civil rights. He is well known for his role in *The Emperor Jones*.

Studio Museum of Harlem

144 West 125th Street, between Lenox Avenue-Malcolm X Boulevard (6th Avenue) and Adam Clayton Powell Jr. Boulevard (7th Avenue)
212-864-4500

The small museum has a permanent collection as well as temporary exhibits showing the work of black painters, sculptors, photographers, and craftsmen. The accent is on local artists, though artists from beyond Harlem are also exhibited. There is a sculpture garden in the back and a gift shop at the front.

Harlem State Office Building

163 West 125th Street, at the corner of Adam Clayton Powell Jr.
Boulevard (7th Avenue)

Built in 1973, the architectural monstrosity was a testament to the growing political power of Harlem. It did provide government office access and new jobs in the community when the neighborhood was at its lowest point economically. Government bureaus, the congressional home office, and several local officials are located here.

Theresa Towers (originally Hotel Theresa)

2090 Adam Clayton Powell Jr. Boulevard (7th Avenue), corner of West
125th Street

Cuban President Fidel Castro stayed at this hotel in 1960 during a visit to the United Nations. Cheering crowds below delighted as he appeared at the balcony with Soviet Premier Nikita Khrushchev. The building now holds offices and Malcolm-King College, a two-year community college of the City University of New York. Theresa Towers was built in 1913 and significantly altered in 1971. The white brick building has a series of balconies on the top floors.

Apollo Theater (originally Hurtig & Seamon's New Burlesque Theatre)

253 West 125th Street, between Adam Clayton Powell Jr. Boulevard
(7th Avenue) and Frederick Douglass Boulevard (8th Avenue)
212-749-5838

From 1914 until 1934, this 1,500-seat theater featured burlesque. New owners opened it up to black performers and mixed audiences. Billie Holiday, Bessie Smith, Charlie Parker, Dizzy Gillespie, Gladys Knight, Aretha Franklin, and countless other well-known singers and musicians have entertained at the Apollo. Shows continue in the down-at-the-heels romantic theater, with the raucous Amateur Night each Wednesday being a big hit. Performers from around the country, and individuals called up from the audience, dance or sing to some harsh reviews. Pearl Bailey, Luther Vandross, Dionne Warwick, Leslie Uggams, the Jackson Five, and the Shirelles all got their starts by winning first prize on Amateur Night.

The audiences attract whites from the United States and Europe, and significant numbers of people from Japan. Contestants compete with rock presentations as well as jazz, R&B, gospel, and rap.

United House of Prayer for All People (now Pentecostal)

2320 Frederick Douglass Boulevard (8th Avenue), at the corner of West 125th Street
212-864-8795

This is the former home church of Daddy Grace, who was a flamboyant self-ordained minister of the Holiness and Pentecostal style who began preaching in 1925. He taught divine healing, morality, obedience to his leadership, and racial separatism, advocating the deliverance of black people from white rule. He eventually substituted himself for God with congregants genuflecting and praying to him. He advanced a line of healing products to sell: soap, toothpaste, facial cream, hair tonic, and talcum powder. The church is now owned and operated by a Pentecostal congregation. The second floor offers a public cafeteria operated by the new church; it specializes in soul food.

 Turn left (south) at Frederick Douglass Boulevard (8th Avenue); turn left (east) at West 123rd Street and walk three blocks to Mount Morris Park West.

Commandment Keepers Ethiopian Hebrew Congregation (originally and presently a private home)

1 West 123rd Street, at the corner of Mount Morris Park West

This is the former synagogue of the Black Jews of Harlem, who believe Africans are descendants of the Lost Tribes of Israel. They believe American blacks are really Ethiopian Falashas who were stripped of the knowledge of their past by slavery. The group, made up largely of West Indians, appeared in 1915, was incorporated in 1930, and moved into this building in 1962. In the 1930s, there were eight Black Jewish groups in Harlem; not unlike the Nation of Islam, Black Judaism represented giving up the idea of integration. This congregation has moved to Newark, New Jersey.

Continue south on Mount Morris Park West.

Mount Morris Ascension Presbyterian Church

15 Mount Morris Park West, at the corner of West 122nd Street
212-831-6800

Oz-like eclectic architecture is surprising for a Presbyterian church, a denomination generally favoring more restrained architecture. Built in 1905, this church is topped by a small dome over a many-windowed boxlike frame with a wraparound balustrade.

Marcus Garvey Memorial Park (originally Mount Morris Park)

Bounded by East and West 120th Street, East and West 124th Street, Mount Morris Park West, and Madison Avenue

Set aside by the city as a park in 1839, it still has its original cast-iron fire watchtower, one of a chain of many that guarded nineteenth-century New Yorkers from conflagration. The housing stock around the park, always notable, sunk into decades of disrepair, but has been largely renovated. Two ugly 1960s park buildings intrude on the rocky terrain at the bottom of the hill. Originally named for British landowner Colonel Roger Morris, it was renamed for black nationalist leader and founder of the Universal Negro Improvement Association Marcus Garvey (1887–1940) in 1973. Garvey was a Back to Africa proponent who proclaimed the Empire of Africa in 1921, organized the Black Star Line, and began raising money for a transatlantic exodus. Prosecuted and convicted of mail fraud in 1925, Garvey went to prison for two years and was subsequently deported to Jamaica. Always opposed by church leaders, the press, and civil rights organizations in the black community, he had a strong following among those who felt working within the system had been fruitless.

 Turn left (east) on East 120th Street.

Apartment Building

2 West 120th Street, at the corner of 5th Avenue

This unusually detailed and elegant corner apartment building possesses a striking cornice and interesting terra-cotta designs adorning the numerous windows. The building underwent significant restoration in 1998.

 Turn right (south) on 5th Avenue; turn right (west) on East 118th Street.

Bethel Way of the Cross Church (Nondenominational Protestant), originally Congregation Shaari Zadek of Harlem (Jewish)

25 West 118th Street, between 5th Avenue and Lenox Avenue-Malcolm X Boulevard (6th Avenue)
212-534-9236

The building, erected in 1900, has phantasmagorical windows and doors seemingly borrowed from *1,001 Arabian Nights*. Elongated cornices grace the top. Religious institutions in Harlem shifted from Jewish synagogues and Roman Catholic churches to Protestant churches reflecting the population change. (In the Lower East Side, the reverse can be seen: former Protestant churches are being used as Jewish synagogues.)

Children's Aid Society (Dunlevy Milbank Center)

14–32 West 118th Street, between 5th Avenue and Lenox Avenue-Malcolm X Boulevard (6th Avenue)
212-996-1716

This new building is one of many social centers in New York City operated by the Children's Aid Society, which was organized by Charles Loring Brace in 1848. He was shocked at the misery of street children and decided to do something about it. To him, the problem was an embarrassment to our industrial system and to democracy. Brace came up with a completely new plan, which he thought would solve the problem. He wrote, "As Christian men we cannot look upon this great multitude of unhappy, deserted, and degraded boys and girls without feeling our responsibility to God for them."[2] He called his idea the Emigration Plan. Between 1854 and 1929, a quarter of a million children, many from New York City, were sent to live with rural families. About half the children were sent by the Children's Aid Society; the rest by other reform groups. The Children's Aid Society has changed enormously during recent decades. Today, it provides after-school, counseling, and tutoring programs. It gives free dental, eye, and medical exams, and operates a shelter across the street at 17–21 West 118th Street.

 Turn left (south) on Lenox Avenue-Malcolm X Boulevard (6th Avenue) to West 116th Street.

Masjid Malcolm Shabazz (Sunni Islamic Mosque)

102 West 116th Street, at the corner of Lenox Avenue-Malcolm X Boulevard (6th Avenue)
212-662-2201

The three-story renovated building with an aluminum orientalist dome houses an orthodox Sunni Islam congregation. Formerly, this was Muhammad's Mosque #7, led by Malcolm X until he split from the Nation of Islam. Today the mosque and its effusive leadership are prominent in political life in New York City. The mosque is active in sponsoring housing renovations and establishing increased neighborhood commercial activity. Reflecting its African American base, the mosque does not use a curtain, movable divider, or balcony for women. They pray separately, but in the same prayer hall as the men.

Malcolm Shabazz Harlem Market

Corner of West 116th Street and Lenox Avenue-Malcolm X Boulevard (6th Avenue)

African fabrics, statues, baskets, decorative gourds, dashikis, shoes, hats, handbags, cosmetics, books, and greeting cards are found in the market operated by the mosque to encourage neighborhood entrepreneurial activity. There are ninety-six stalls offering goods for sale.

---

[2] United States of America. Senate of the State of New York. *Documents of the Senate of the State of New York*. By New York State. Vol. 3. Albany, NY: James B. Lyon, 1891.

Return via IRT #2 or #3 subway train at 116th Street Station at the corner of West 116th Street and Lenox Avenue-Malcolm X Boulevard (6th Avenue). Or continue walking east on West 116th Street, which at 5th Avenue becomes East 116th Street-Luis Muñoz Marín Boulevard, to IRT #6 subway train at 116th Street Station at the corner of West 116th Street-Luis Muñoz Marín Boulevard and Lexington Avenue.

Restaurant Recommendations Offering Traditional Soul Food

Sylvia's

328 Lenox Avenue-Malcolm X Boulevard (6th Avenue), between West 126th Street and 127th Street

212-996-0660

Sylvia's serves soul food: comfort food from the South. Almost since it opened in 1962, this was the preeminent restaurant in Harlem, and politicians and cultural notables could be spotted here. Many have their pictures are on the walls. Now, they have many other choices. The kitchen doles out large portions of filling food in a friendly atmosphere: deep-fried chicken and fish, spareribs, corn bread, candied yams, and sweet potato pie. Lots of sugar, salt, and fats are used; even the collard greens, turnip greens, and black-eyed peas are flecked with lard. Of special interest: the Saturday jazz and Sunday gospel brunches.

Miss Maude's Spoonbread Too

547 Lenox Avenue-Malcolm X Boulevard (6th Avenue), between West 137th Street and 138th Streets

212-690-3100

The restaurant is named for the great-aunt of the genealogy-minded proprietress, who will be glad to tell background stories to her family photographs, which line the walls. North Carolina barbecue ribs, fried chicken, pork chops, oxtails, and Louisiana catfish are the cholesterol-filled features in this comfortable eating establishment. Also available is Sugar Hill Golden Ale, produced by the new Harlem Brewing Company, which presently brews in Saratoga Springs, New York, but plans to ultimately open its own brew pub in Harlem. Spoonbread, a Southern specialty, is made of flour, milk, eggs, and butter, like a moist, rich soufflé meant to be eaten with a spoon.

United House of Prayer for All People

2320 Frederick Douglass Boulevard (8th Avenue), at the corner of West 125th Street
212-864-8795

The second floor sports a public cafeteria operated by the Pentecostal Church and specializing in Soul Food. The large dining room is directly across from the sanctuary. Trays brimming with chicken, ribs, fish, collard greens, corn, okra, and corn bread give the customer an overview of the whole menu.

CHINATOWN

Before the arrival of the Europeans, a band of Lenape American Indians known as Werpoes had a small village on top of a hill where Mott Street now bends and intersects with Pell Street. For some time after the Native Americans disappeared, presumably from Old World diseases like smallpox, the area was called Werpoes Hill. In the Dutch colony, the area now known as Chinatown included the undulating hills that had given shelter to the Werpoes clan and a stretch of sloping fields with a large freshwater pond called the Collect Pond at its western end. Its presumed natural beauty was ignored by the settlers of New Amsterdam, who used the site as a garbage dump and nearby slopes as burial grounds for those barred from interment within the confines of the walled town. In the eighteenth century, the elevated area, with its good views and breezes, was an alluring location for housing, and a number of fine homes were built by the wealthy. As more people constructed townhouses and multidwelling buildings, the area became overcrowded and slid into disrepair, developing a reputation for crime. Centuries before zoning laws, mixed residential and industrial areas lowered the area's desirability for housing. Breweries, tanneries, and slaughterhouses proliferated on the hillside, where they could dump their waste into the pond below. (Three of the main streets were named after butchers: Mott, Pell, and Bayard.)

The population in Europe doubled between 1750 and 1850, and many chose relocation in America. The late eighteenth century saw the start of an immense German migration from the Rhineland-Palatinate to the United States, and many who came to New York City settled in this area on the northeast edge of the city. Before the Civil War, 1.7 million Irish emigrated to the United States. Those choosing New York City often found housing in the swampy low area just south of Chinatown's present location. In time, as English and Germans exited and after Ireland's potato famine, the area became overwhelmingly Irish.

Absentee landlords quickly converted their dwellings into rookeries, a name applied to subdivided houses, warehouses, or factories with jerry-built additions. Some buildings were built as rookeries, and whole families were packed into small, cramped rooms with little or no ventilation.

Tenement is a term applied to structures built in a routine form to cash in on the rush of immigrants. In the early nineteenth century, the typical pattern was to construct two tenements (front and rear) on a standard city lot (twenty-five by one hundred feet). These were Spartan four-story buildings with four apartments on each floor. A small courtyard divided the two buildings and was the site of outhouses and rainwater cisterns. Tenement life, dark and poorly ventilated, was a breeding ground for cholera, tuberculosis, typhoid, and smallpox. Reformers managed to get a number of changes enacted by state law and city ordinance shortly after the Civil War.

Legislation was first enacted in 1867, and subsequent laws were passed in 1879, 1901, and 1929. Each added a few amenities to squalid tenement life: space between front and rear buildings (just eleven feet), minimum room size (seventy square feet), indoor toilets, air shafts, fire escapes, running water, electricity, and heat. None of the earliest rookeries exist in Chinatown, though an 1824 tenement still stands at 65 Mott Street. Most extant tenements were built after the 1879 legislation.

Manhattan had no public parks or playgrounds before Central Park opened in 1859. The Five Points–Chinatown area desperately needed open space and recreation areas. Children played in the narrow streets. Jacob Riis, a Danish immigrant who became a prominent photojournalist, published his award-winning *How the Other Half Lives* in 1890. He became friends with police commissioner Theodore Roosevelt and was able to obtain support for his pet project, tearing down two rectangular blocks of particularly bleak slums on Mulberry Street and constructing Mulberry Bend Park (now Columbus Park). The park provided breathing space for the neighborhood as well as a site for recreation and relaxation.

By the Jacksonian period, gangs like the Short Boys, Dead Rabbits, Roach Guards, Plug Uglies, and Bowery Boys periodically rampaged through Five Points. Some exaggeration by the *Police Gazette* was natural, since gang activity ranked high on the list of topics about which even respectable New Yorkers enjoyed reading. Even Charles Dickens, an authority on London slums, called the area "loathsome" after a visit prior to the Civil War. Though it is true that the area had become overcrowded, disease-laden, and often raucous by the 1830s, the Five Points was a popular whipping boy for the press and probably got more bad publicity than it deserved.

Tammany Hall began as the middle-class professionals' and artisans' answer to the rich men's clubs from which they were excluded. Formed in 1788 as the Society of St. Tammany or the Columbian Order, it lionized the legendary Delaware Valley Native American chief Tamanend and chose American Indian-inspired names for its clubhouses and officers. Meeting halls were called *wigwams*, leaders were *sachems*, and members were *braves*. In parades, they marched single file and each carried a tomahawk. By the 1850s, the fraternal organization had become politicized, and after the Civil War, the society became a disciplined Democratic Party political machine.

Tammany built its strength in poor immigrant neighborhoods by swapping votes for services at a time when the government offered none. So if a widow needed a bucket of coal or a returned veteran needed a job, the organization would oblige. Tammany politicians are sometimes remembered as lovable rogues. In truth, they were neighborhood oligarchs with no appreciation for democracy. Tammany Hall was a collection of thieves, embezzlers, and swindlers. They provided bread and circuses for the masses, especially the poorest immigrants, but granted no long-term relief for the needy. Even so, Tammany also included hardworking honest politicians and was a symbol of pride to the working class, Roman Catholics, and Irish. Tammany seemed to them a protection against the rich and powerful elites of the city. The pinnacle of Tammany influence and fame came in the years surrounding Governor Alfred E. Smith's candidacy for president in 1928.

Al Smith grew up in Five Points and spent most of his life on South, Madison, and Oliver Streets. Smith represented the progressive wing of Tammany and agitated for rent regulation, workers' compensation, public housing, and more effective building and fire codes. He represented Five Points in the state assembly from 1904 to 1915 and also served as sheriff of New York County, president of the Board of Aldermen, and governor. In 1928, he became the first Roman Catholic nominated by either party for president, but was defeated by Herbert Hoover and Republican charges that Smith stood for *Rome, Rum, and Rebellion*. After his defeat, he dedicated himself to private and Catholic charitable projects.

The Bowery, the main artery through Five Points–Chinatown, passed through several stages in its history from a rural road to an avenue of upper-middle-class homes to a street of rookeries, bars, transient hotels, and honky-tonk entertainment. When the Chinese first established a presence in southern Manhattan, the Bowery was at the eastern edge of Chinatown; now it runs through the enclave as the major north–south axis. As Chinese immigrants moved into the area, the Bowery began to lose the character it had assumed as a housing preserve for men from the underclass. By the end of World War II, the Bowery had one hundred flophouses providing sleeping cubicles for ten thousand men. Thirty down-and-out Bowery bars dotted the street. These were the gin mills so often featured in lurid dime novels and religious tracts. None are left, though a few flophouses remain.

The transcontinental railroad completion in 1869 made it much easier for Chinese immigrants seeking the *Gold Mountain* (America, or the American Dream) to move to the East Coast of the United States. Prior to that, most Chinese Americans lived on the West Coast or in the mountain states. Early Chinatown was huddled along Mott, Pell, and Doyers Streets. Commercial specialties included chop suey–chow mein restaurants, laundries, and gift shops.

By 1900, New York Chinatown's population was about five thousand. Jacob Riis knew Chinatown well, as it was just fifty yards from his pet project at Mulberry Bend. He portrayed the neighborhood as quiet compared to the Irish, Italian, and Jewish sections, saying, "Chinatown as a spectacle is disappointing." But the noted reformer meant it as a backhanded compliment:

> One thing about them was conspicuous: their scrupulous neatness. It is the distinguishing mark of Chinatown, outwardly and physically. It is not altogether by chance the Chinaman has chosen the laundry as his distinctive field. He is by nature as clean as the cat, which he resembles in his traits of cruel cunning and savage fury when aroused.[3]

Faulting immigrants in *How the Other Half Lives*, Riis represented the contradictions of reformers, mostly upper-middle-class people with

---

[3] Jacob A. Riis, "Chinatown." In *How the Other Half Lives*, 2nd ed., 127. New York: Bedford/St. Martin's, 2010.

antecedents in northwestern Europe, who decried the tenement neighborhoods but blamed the inhabitants. Despite Riis's moving photographs of poverty, the text of his book leaves no doubt that his reformist instincts emanated from racial, ethnic, and religious bigotry: "Ages of senseless idolatry, a mere grub-worship, have left him without the essential qualities for appreciating the gentle teachings of a faith whose motive and unselfish spirit are beyond his grasp." [4]

The 1892 *King's Handbook of New York City* was also unkind: "The district is a veritable Chinatown, with all the filth, immorality and picturesque foreignness, which the name implies." [5] For decades, Chinatown struggled to overcome this kind of negative publicity.

Until World War I, 60 percent of all Chinese in New York came from one county in southern Guangdong province: Toishan, near Canton. Most of the others came from counties in the same province. Born of the fear of cheap labor and revulsion of the cultural habits attributed to Chinese people, the Chinese Exclusion Act of 1882 kept Chinese immigration low. Furious prejudice was directed against the supposedly deviant habits of the Chinese: opium, gambling, prostitution, even baby eating. Franklin Delano Roosevelt signed the bill ending the Chinese Exclusion Act in 1943, and the immigration of Chinese could begin again. However, the yearly limit placed on the Chinese amounted to just 105 immigrants per year. The entire immigration law was liberalized by John F. Kennedy, which gave immigration from China and Overseas Chinese a real boost. Today, about half of Chinatown's residents refer to themselves as "ABC": American-born Chinese.

Chinatown's population is about sixty thousand today, making it one of the largest Chinese communities in the United States. Initially, it was just a tiny enclave on the border of two other immigrant neighborhoods: Irish and Italian. Now it dominates the section and has moved into surrounding areas, especially Little Italy and the Lower East Side. By the end of the twentieth century, other Chinese neighborhoods had established themselves in Brooklyn, along 8th Avenue in Sunset Park, and in Flushing and Elmhurst, Queens. By 2018, the most populous Chinatown was Sunset

---

[4] Ibid., 124.

[5] Moses King, "Thoroughfares and Adornments." In *King's Handbook of New York City*, 144. Boston: Moses King, 1892.

Park, followed by Flushing, and then Manhattan. Most young Chinese Americans choose not to live in Chinatowns.

Chinatown has been a haven from the hostile outside world as well as a place for some to postpone assimilation. For most, it has been a stepping-stone to middle-class life in other, less cramped parts of New York City. The Tong Wars, 1896 to 1925, between two powerful commercial organizations (tongs), were disruptive to the community. They were violent and were always reported in lurid detail in the press. The Hip Sing controlled the Pell Street–Doyers Street area, and the Ong Leong dominated Mott Street. These business associations were involved in legitimate as well as criminal activities. Control of gambling and drug trafficking led to the violence and negative publicity.

Despite problems, an attempt at a unified public face was orchestrated by the Chinese Consolidated Benevolent Association from its formation in 1883 until the 1970s. It is a kind of nongovernmental organization town council and an umbrella organization of many fraternal, occupational, business, and family groups. Chinatown split into two factions as immigration increased. On the surface, the dispute seems to be about political orientation either to the People's Republic of China (Communist regime in Beijing mainland) or the Republic of China (Nationalist regime in Taipei on the island province of Taiwan). But the dispute also is about how Chinese Americans see themselves in the United States: passive or activist. Chinatown's two statues, only a hundred yards from each other, speak volumes about this schism. *Confucius* (at the Bowery and Division Street) represents quietude and self-cultivation; *Lin Zexu* (at the Bowery and East Broadway) represents forcefulness and public demonstrations.

There are two National Day celebrations: October 10 (Ten-Ten) along Mott Street for the Taiwan regime (the Republic of China), and October 1 along East Broadway for the mainland regime (the People's Republic of China). The four Chinese language dailies and several weeklies are highly politicized and aligned with one or the other group.

Lion dances and dragon dances proliferate at Chinese New Year (late January or early February) on Chinatown's primary streets. Long bodies of cloth trail the elaborate heads of lions or dragons, usually made of brightly colored papier-mâché, carried by several energetic dancers. A man ritualistically teasing the animal with a head of lettuce on a string leads each ensemble accompanied by drummers. Eventually the lion, amid bursts of exploding firecracker strings, gets to eat the lettuce, which symbolizes a pearl. The streets are clogged with dancers and onlookers. Shopkeepers give donations to dancing teams willing to stop and perform in front of their stores, which brings good luck to the sponsors. Various martial arts schools or clubs sponsor most of the troupes. Interestingly, the ensembles are composed of New Yorkers from every background, not just Asians.

Walking Trip of Four Key Streets: Canal Street, Mulberry Street, Mott Street, the Bowery, and Elizabeth Street

Take the subway to any Canal Street subway station (#1, #2, #6, A, C, E, M, J, Z, N, or R), proceed east along Canal Street toward the large arched stone entrance of the Manhattan Bridge. Turn right (south) on Mulberry Street. Walk south on Mulberry Street, which is three blocks before the Manhattan Bridge. Proceed three blocks toward Worth Street.

Hai Cang Trading Inc.
71 Mulberry Street, between Canal and Bayard Streets
212-385-0981

Fresh fish from around the world are neatly displayed in this small seafood shop. There are tuna, salmon, bluefish, flounder, red snapper, mackerel, porgies, butterfish, croakers, and the long flat beltfish found at all Chinatown fishmongers. This is one of the few Chinatown fish shops to have several varieties of fish already filleted, though most are sold whole, and some, like eels, carp, lobsters, and hard-shell and soft-shelled crabs, are sold alive.

Chinatown Community Center
70 Mulberry Street, at the corner of Canal and Bayard Streets

This building is home to several social service organizations, including the Chinatown Senior Center. On the sidewalk around the hulking red building, formerly a public school, elderly people set up stalls to sell jewelry, tell fortunes, and repair watches and shoes.

Chinatown Senior Center

70 Mulberry Street (entrance around the corner on Bayard Street at the end of the building down a narrow walkway)

Canton Opera Concerts with traditional Chinese musical instruments are presented free each day at about 1:30 p.m. Most of the elderly who attend this day program sit in a large room playing mah-jongg or cards. Some read newspapers or books, chat with friends, practice tai chi, or engage in calligraphy. Each day, they receive lunch from the cafeteria kitchen.

Columbus Park (originally Mulberry Bend Park)

Between Bayard and Worth Streets

This park was the result of a slum-clearance vision of photojournalist Jacob Riis with help from police commissioner Theodore Roosevelt. Two blocks of slum buildings were demolished in 1892 to gain some breathing space for the crowded neighborhood. The land had previously been part of the Five Points, a legendary slum recently made famous by Martin Scorsese's *Gangs of New York* (2002). Today, it is a beehive of activity: women playing mah-jongg, groups of men walking their caged songbirds, other men huddling around portable tables set up for dominoes, checkers, and card games. Early in the morning, individuals go through the slow moves of tai chi exercises.

Wah Wing Sang Funeral Home

28 Mulberry Street, between Mosco and Worth Streets

This was once one of several Italian funeral homes to line this block. The baroque facade is not all that is left of the Italian influence. (The building was originally built in 1881 as Antonio Cuneo's Bank.) A part of immigrant Italian culture that is no longer found in Italian neighborhoods is alive and well in Chinatown. Both Chinese funeral homes on the block employ the same small band of Italian Americans, dressed in funereal black, to play music and briefly march behind the hearse as it begins to make its way through Chinatown's narrow streets. A Chinese custom is to drape a large black-framed photograph of the deceased atop the hearse labeled with the name written in Chinese characters.

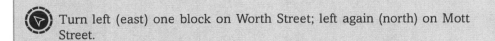

Turn left (east) one block on Worth Street; left again (north) on Mott Street.

Transfiguration Roman Catholic Church and School (originally Zion English Lutheran Church, 1801)

29 Mott Street, at the corner of Mosco Street
212-962-5157

Fr. Félix Varela, an expatriate Cuban priest, founded Transfiguration Roman Catholic Church, the city's fourth Catholic congregation, in 1827. It initially served mostly Irish, then Italian, and now Chinese parishioners. Of the children presently attending the parochial school, 90 percent are Buddhists. The exterior Georgian walls and Gothic windows were built of fieldstone with an interesting jerry-built octagonal wood and copper steeple added in the 1860s. The edifice towers over most of the nearby buildings. Inside, it retains older stained-glass windows with saints dear to Ireland (Patrick, Columba, Brendan, and Brigid), though the wall space has the look of a typically ornate Italian church with the usual statues of Italian favorites: Francis, Lucy, Theresa, Anthony, Jude, Ann, Victor, and Rocco (two). The high altar has been removed and replaced with an elaborate wooden chair with a side table. The reconfigured interior almost takes on the look of a Baptist church. The only Chinese addition is a wood polychrome statue of Jesus and Mary with vertical ribbons of classical Chinese couplet characters on either side proclaiming the name of the church ("Transfiguration," i.e., *To Show His Face*) and the following: SHOWING HIS FULL MIGHTY POWER HE CREATED HEAVEN AND EARTH (on the right); MAKING HIS MERCIFUL LOVE GIVE LIFE TO ORDINARY PEOPLE (on the left). Transfiguration Church contains architectural and design elements reflecting the Irish, Italian, and Chinese stages in the neighborhood's history.

Chung Chou City

39 Mott Street at Pell Street
212-285-2288

Chung Chou City is a fascinating dried food shop selling everything from inexpensive (dried baby shrimp, seaweed, mushrooms) to costly ($500 per pound shark fins or $800 per pound abalone) delicacies.

Golden Fung Wong Bakery

41 Mott Street at Pell Street
212-233-7447

Golden Fung Wong Bakery is where to get the glazed big Buddha and fish cookies. They have various buns and cakes filled with bean paste, plum paste, lotus seed paste, and custard. All items are marked in English.

Chinese Consolidated Benevolent Association

62 Mott Street, between Bayard and Canal Streets

For many years, this 1950s white brick building with balconies on five stories was the unofficial Chinatown City Hall. Prominently displayed on rooftop flagpoles are three flags of Taiwan (Republic of China). The power of this businessmen's association, organized in 1883, has been partially eclipsed by rival groups politically loyal to the mainland (People's Republic of China).

Eastern States Buddhist Temple of America

64 Mott Street, between Bayard and Canal Streets
212-966-6229

Located on the ground floor of the Chinese Consolidated Benevolent Association, this temple is often called the tourists' temple because of the groups trotted through by tour leaders. It is a legitimate Buddhist temple, featuring two altars and periodic neighborhood supplicants offering prayers. The main altar has two primary statues: Shakyamuni, the historical Buddha, and, in front, a smaller statue of the popular deity Guanyin, a bodhisattva. An interesting four-faced Buddha is in a glass case on an altar in the center of the small room.

Oldest Existing Tenement Building in New York City

65 Mott Street, between Bayard and Canal Streets.

This seven-story brick walk-up tenement towered over the surrounding two-story wooden houses and rookeries when it was constructed about 1824. At the time, most apartments in 65 Mott Street were tiny two-room suites holding as many as a dozen people. Half the rooms had no windows. All occupants used outhouses in the backyard. Since then, 65 Mott Street has been renovated many times, and, while still not a palace, has heat, running hot and cold water, and a toilet in each apartment. Today its size fits in, since nearby buildings are the same height. The featureless structure is without the usual large ornamental cornice or decorative window lintels. Access to the apartments is through a long narrow hallway on the left side of the building.

 Turn right (east) on Canal Street one block toward Manhattan Bridge; turn right (south) on Elizabeth Street.

Oriental Culture Enterprises

13–17 Elizabeth Street, 2nd floor, just off Canal Street
212-226-8461

This store sells books, art and calligraphy supplies, stationery, gifts, and paintings imported from the People's Republic of China. Oriental Culture Enterprises carries magazines and newspapers from the mainland and has a filled side room, exhibiting fine porcelain and pottery. In the school supply section, they feature a music area with Western guitars and traditional Chinese wind and string instruments.

 Reverse directions on Elizabeth Street; turn right (east) on Canal Street; cross the intersection of Canal Street and the Bowery.

Mahayana Buddhist Temple

133 Canal Street at the intersection with the Bowery and the entrance to the Manhattan Bridge

This building was a former movie theater and is painted the traditional yellow and red, which distinguishes Buddhist buildings throughout China. Inside is a very large gilt Buddha, the historical Shakyamuni (c. 563–483 BC) on an altar with the five gifts: flowers, fruit, oil, pure water, and fire (candles). On the sides are scenes from the life of the Buddha. Two small shrines, each with a tiny statue on an altar, stand at the worship hall's entryway. On the right is an altar to the Medicinal Buddha, where prayers for the sick are recited. On the left is an altar to the Pure Land Buddha (also called the Amitabha), where prayers and incense for the dead are offered. Behind the altar, about four hundred small yellow memorial plates hang on the wall. Each two-inch-by-five-inch strip of plastic has a passport-size picture and name (in Chinese characters) of an ancestor to be remembered. In the narthex is a shrine to Guanyin, the highly regarded and beloved Bodhisattva of Compassion. A bodhisattva is a Buddha-to-be who has chosen to stay in the Sentient Being Realm to help the inhabitants achieve higher states. Buddhist chants are piped in softly, and it is quite possible to discern the subtle striking of wooden fish drums and animal hide drums, which punctuate and direct the prayers. A Taoist element is the chi mirrors (over faux windows) pointing up toward the ceiling to reflect possible bad chi flowing from the real windows across the room. This element of Taoism is known as feng shui.

 Proceed south on the Bowery from Canal Street three blocks to Chatham Square.

Chi Bong Wong Da Sheen Taoist Temple
6 Pell Street, at the corner of Bowery

Taoist practices influence many aspects of traditional Chinese life, yet there are few Taoist temples anywhere, even in China. Taoism, a folk religion practiced at home more than in temples, is often fused in some of its customs and rituals with Buddhism, if the Buddhist monks are obliging. This syncretism can be seen in almost all Buddhist temples in Chinatown. The Chi Bong Wong Da Sheen Taoist Temple is named for one of the great immortals (celestial beings) who is well known in Taoist stories: the Red Pine Yellow Celestial Being, often associated with the accumulation of wealth.

Edward Mooney House
18 Bowery, at the corner of Pell Street (undergoing restoration)

While not the oldest house in Manhattan, this is the oldest row house. Completed in 1789, the year the US Constitution went into effect, its form combines elements of the new Federal as well as the older Georgian style.

If you look at the landscape, you can see that this house was one of those built on the east end of Werpoes Hill, the high ground favored by the wealthy in the eighteenth century.

Lin Sisters Herb Shop
4 Bowery, between Doyers and Pell Streets
212-962-0447

Like an old American apothecary, this traditional Chinese pharmacy has all kinds of remedies in scores of carefully marked wooden bins. After a consultation with an herbal specialist, each prescription is individually prepared by combining and grinding powders, herbs, and sometimes dried animal parts. The powder is put in an envelope, and at home the patient dissolves the contents in hot water and drinks it as a soup. Some commonly prescribed ingredients are ginseng, loquat, dandelions, centipedes, ground deer antlers, turtle jelly, and powdered seahorse. There are several traditional pharmacies in Chinatown.

Confucius Plaza Apartments
33 Bowery, at the corner of Division Street

The curved redbrick apartment building can be seen prominently for miles up 2nd Avenue and across the East River from the Brooklyn Heights Promenade. It is Chinatown's highest building. Finished in 1976, the large edifice, a welcome addition to a neighborhood short of housing, contains apartments on the upper floors and Public School 124 on its lower floors.

Statue of Confucius (Kong Fuzi or K'ung Fu-tzu)
Corner of Bowery and Division Street

This ornate but squat statue was erected in 1976 to honor both the American bicentennial and Confucius (551–479 BC), the conservative social philosopher from Qufu, in Shandong province. Put up while Mao was proclaiming his 1974 Campaign against Lin Biao and Confucius on the mainland, Confucius became an icon of the anticommunist, pro-Taiwan faction in Chinatown's polarized political and cultural world.

Chatham Square

Memorial Archway to Honor Chinese American Veterans of World War II

A subdued grey arch of modernistic design with only a hint of Chinese elements honors Chinese American war dead. The inscription reads: IN MEMORY OF THE AMERICANS OF CHINESE ANCESTRY WHO LOST THEIR LIVES IN DEFENSE OF FREEDOM AND DEMOCRACY.

Statue of Lin Zexu (Lin Tse-hsu)

PIONEER IN THE WAR AGAINST DRUGS proclaims the inscription below the name Lin Zexu (1785–1850), commissioner plenipotentiary of the emperor to Canton who precipitated the Opium War. Lin is viewed as a great patriot who fought against British imperialism (drugs, too). He was a native of Fujian (Fukien) province. His statue, erected in 1997 after the Confucius statue, was put up facing down East Broadway, where most immigrants from Fujian, loyal to the People's Republic of China, work and shop. Lin stands as counter-presence to Confucius, the hero of the pro-Taiwan faction.

 Walk northwest from Chatham Square up the Bowery toward Canal Street.

Sweatshops along East Broadway

Look up. You can't miss them. On the higher floors of some buildings on East Broadway, Market Street, Mechanics Alley, Chrystie Street, and others are sweatshops producing finished apparel at very low prices. Long hours, poor working conditions, and minuscule pay are the rule. Steam from the machines is regularly emitted through the windows, and the lights are on until late at night.

Restaurant Recommendations

Great New York Noodle Town

28 1/2 Bowery, at the corner of Bayard Street
212-349-0923

Noodle Town is a real find. It is an inexpensive eatery with delicious dishes and an exceptionally popular takeout component in the front specializing in soups and roasted meats. The noodles are commendable, but this is much more than a noodle shop. Salt-baked shrimp, chicken, scallops, squid, and soft-shell crabs are signature dishes; roast pork, goose, duck, and whole fish in any of several sauces are also specialties. The shrimp dumpling soup is exceptional. You may see a whole roast pig brought up to the front counter from the back kitchen.

New Yeah Shanghai Deluxe
50 Mott Street, at the corner of Bayard Street
212-566-4884

There are several outstanding dishes at Yeah's and many are seafood. Chrysanthemum fish, visually enchanting, is cross-cut like flower petals, with its lightly dusted fillets placed together to resemble the elegant flower. The sliced and sautéed yellow eel, a staple of Shanghai cooking, is served braised in brown sauce and garnished with chives. Roast chicken northern style comes in a mound of thin slices mixed with a ginger and garlic sauce. The large meatballs in Lion-Head Casserole contain rice instead of bread. Beef, not usually a signature item in Chinese restaurants, is redeemed at Yeah's with orange-flavored beef, a crispy sweet and spicy dish served with chili peppers and broccoli.

Wo Hop
17 Mott Street, between Chatham Square and Mosco Street
212-267-2536

Discovering 24-hour Wo Hop's is almost a gnostic experience. Friends tell friends about this cheery old-fashioned downstairs Cantonese eatery dating from 1938. There is nothing fancy at Wo Hop's and some plates are too much like what Chinese miners out west reputedly ate in the nineteenth century. The best bet is the superb wonton soup. The simple homestyle noodle dishes (lo mein, chow fon, chow mai fon come with sliced duck, pork, chicken shrimp, or vegetables) are dependably excellent. Don't confuse this place with the Wo Hop's at 15 Mott Street; the intriguing one is down a flight of steep stairs.

Peking Duck House

28 Mott Street at Mosco Street
212-962-8208

Swanky new digs with mirrored walls are home to this Chinatown standby, the first restaurant where you could get Peking Duck (slow roasted over a fire) without 24-hour notification. Come with friends or family, sit around a large round table, and share whole roasted Peking duck, sea bass in chili sauce, and an assortment of succulent shrimp dishes. The waiter comes to the table with the cooked duck and carves it, ensuring that each morsel of meat has some of the crispy skin. Thin crepes are filled with pieces of duck, a slice of cucumber, a scallion, and some Hoisin sauce. The richly filled but taste-balanced crepe is then folded and eaten.

Nam Wah Tea House

13 Doyers Street at the crook of the picturesque elbow-shaped lane
between Pell Street and Bowery
212-226-3553

Nam Wah seems right out of a movie set. It is a teahouse, dim sum parlor, and restaurant all in one. Established in 1920, it was the first place in Chinatown to serve dim sum, which remains its culinary appeal. The decor is bare bones: red leather booths with Formica tables under a pressed-tin ceiling. On the side is a small counter with several stools. Steamed or fried, the morsels served at Nam Wah come packed with uncomplicated combinations of meat and vegetables. The restaurant excels in longevity and simplicity. It is a perfect spot to catch the ambiance of Chinatown fifty or seventy-five years ago.

Jing Fong Restaurant

20 Elizabeth Street, just south of Canal Street
212-964-5256

This is a Chinese wedding palace, an opulent banquet and party restaurant, which can seat 1,500. The motifs are double happiness (marriage) and dragon and phoenix (emperor and empress, but also male and female). Traditional murals, silk screens, and tasseled lantern-chandeliers decorate screened-off sections for receptions. Regular decorations feature lighted photographs of Hong Kong. Despite the banquet hall ambiance, there is usually space set aside for diners uninvited to lavish nuptial parties. The dining style can be a several-course banquet, buffet, dim sum, or selections from a menu. Among the best dishes are taro nest special (shredded chicken with beef tenderloin), salt-baked squid, prawns in rich garlic sauce, and deep-fried bean curd stuffed with whole shrimp.

Hwa Yuan

In the three-story former home of Bank of China, 42 East Broadway, between Catherine and Market Streets
212-966-6002

Chen Lien Tang opened Hwa Yuan in 2017; his father, Shorty Tang, was the legendary chef who brought his version of dan dan noodles to New York City. The father's restaurant, which operated through the 1980s in the space next to this iteration, was one of the first Sichuan restaurants in the city. The spacious, well-appointed restaurant uses the old safe deposit box room in the basement for private dinners and parties. Whole fish, Peking duck, cold noodles in sesame sauce, dumplings, and grilled baby squid have made the new restaurant a popular destination.

LOWER EAST SIDE

ost of the area was garden and dairy farms outside the city in
1830 when large-scale German immigration brought thousands
of people to the city's edge where new construction was under
way and old houses were being enlarged or divided into small apartments.
Kleindeutschland, the enormous German quarter, stretched from Grand
Street to East 23rd Street and from the Bowery to the East River. About
250,000 Germans lived there by the Civil War. Its southern end became
the basis for the German Jewish immigration in the 1870s. Germans, both
Christian and Jewish, progressively migrated uptown, north of East
Houston Street; and by 1890, their places had been taken by Eastern
European Jews and Italians.

Jacob Riis, friend and advisor to police commissioner Theodore
Roosevelt, gained his credibility among the white Anglo-Saxon Protestant
reformers by taking shocking photographs of tenement squalor and
successfully advocating for slum clearance and the construction of Mulberry
Bend Park (now Columbus Park) in the Five Points area. He harshly
chastised immigrants in his 1890 book, *How the Other Half Lives*, blaming
them for their misfortunes and surmising that their religious, ethnic, and
racial backgrounds were the problem. Riis lumped the new inhabitants of
the Lower East Side together as he lambasted them for their poor housing:

> Hardly less aggressive than the Italian, the Russian and Polish
> Jew, having overrun the district between Rivington and Division
> Streets, east of the Bowery, to the point of suffocation, is filling
> the tenements of the Old Seventh Ward to the river front, and
> disputing with the Italian every foot of available space in the back
> alleys of Mulberry Street. The two races, differing hopelessly in

much, have this in common: they carry their slums with them wherever they go, if allowed to do it. . . . Between the dull gray of the Jew, his favorite color, and the Italian red, would be seen squeezed in on the map a sharp streak of yellow, marking the narrow boundaries of Chinatown.[6]

Russian-born Abraham Cahan, editor of *The Jewish Daily Forward* from 1901 to 1951, portrayed the Lower East Side much differently than Danish-born Jacob Riis. Cahan had his protagonist in the vaguely autobiographical 1917 novel, *The Rise of David Levinsky*, muse about the Lower East Side:

> The great thing was that these people were better dressed than the inhabitants of my town. The poorest-looking man wore a hat (instead of a cap), a stiff collar and a necktie, and the poorest woman wore a hat or a bonnet.[7]

Each group assimilated quickly, usually in a generation. Newspapers such as *The Jewish Daily Forward* and *Il Progresso Italo Americano* urged readers to adopt American ways. That generally meant leaving the neighborhood. The earliest groups of Dutch and English dispersed quickly and did not re-create ethnic enclaves. While the other groups assimilated, they had to wait for generations to pass before they achieved integration. The Germans moved to the upper part of the neighborhood, now called the East Village (and from there to Yorkville), before truly integrating. Italians went to the West Village, Brooklyn, or the Bronx on their way to integration. Jews did likewise but separately chose Brooklyn or the Bronx. Some Jews and Italians still live in the Lower East Side, but they tend to be older people. Hispanics and Chinese now comprise large portions of the area. Ironically, the newest group to move into the northern blocks are the completely assimilated young Americans of varying backgrounds who are held together as a group by nothing more than their shared youth; enjoyment of the trendiest eating, drinking, and entertainment

---

[6] Jacob A. Riis, "The Mixed Crowd." In *How the Other Half Lives*, 77. 2nd ed. New York: Bedford/St. Martin's, 2010.

[7] Abraham Cahan, "Chapter II." In *The Rise of David Levinsky*, 63. Mineola, NY: Dover Publications, 2002.

establishments; and an outwardly iconoclastic hipster style. The center of their neighborhood presence is the area between East Houston and Delancey Streets.

Robert Moses had plans to tear down almost all buildings in the Lower East Side and replace them with modern residential towers owned by the city or labor unions, or organized as independent cooperatives. He managed to transform about half of the area. Though the old structures are more interesting, most of the residents were happy to leave them and move into apartment buildings with elevators, modern bathrooms, hot water, buzzer systems, and resident superintendents.

The urban renewal (removal) policy that destroyed existing housing and commercial buildings created a skinny park seven blocks long between Canal Street and Houston Streets and only one short block wide between Chrystie and Forsythe Streets. In ironic coincidence, or just spite on the part of Mayor Fiorello La Guardia, the park was named for Sara Delano Roosevelt, the snooty patrician mother of President Franklin Delano Roosevelt, who no doubt would be appalled to learn that her memorial is located in a gritty neighborhood surrounded by people she had always avoided. Further, one of the demolished buildings was the Tenth Ward Hotel, at Forsythe and Broome Streets, where Karl Marx relocated the International Workingmen's Association (or First International) from 1872 until 1876.

Walking Trip of the Lower East Side

 Take the F train to Second Avenue Station, exit at 1st Avenue. Begin walking east on the south side of the Houston Street.

Russ & Daughters

179 East Houston Street, between Allen Street and Orchard Street
212-475-4880

Four generations ago, this family began with a pushcart. Today the store is decidedly upscale; the immigrant roots must be imagined. People arrive from all over New York City to buy the unique stuffed trout (trout meat mixed with mayonnaise and stuffed back into the bulging golden skin of a smoked trout), smoked salmon varieties, caviars, cream cheeses, breads, dried fruits, nuts, and pickles. The cheese counter has superb French and Italian selections, while Eastern Europe's humbler cheeses are at the deli counter. Russ & Daughters Cafe is located three blocks south at 127 Orchard Street. (212-475-4880)

 Turn right (south) on Ludlow Street at Katz's Delicatessen.

Esther Apartments (1930)
126–128 Ludlow Street, at the corner of Rivington Street

Showing its Jewish pride, this moderately decorated six-story pink brick building has its name and address proudly written in Hebraized English letters over the entrance.

Site of former Shaarey Shomayim, First Roumanian-American Congregation
89 Rivington Street, between Ludlow Street and Orchard Street

Built in 1860 as the Allen Street Methodist Church, the 1,600-seat sanctuary became a synagogue when the neighborhood changed and a Jewish congregation bought it and named it Shaarey Shomayim (Gates of Heaven). The facade was rebuilt, giving the former Protestant structure what came to be a Jewish look: neo-Moorish windows and brick designs. Famous cantors Jan Peerce and Richard Tucker sang there on the High Holy Days. In 2006, the roof collapsed from water damage and the building was razed shortly after.

 Turn left (east) at Rivington Street.

Economy Candy Store
108 Rivington Street, between Essex Street and Ludlow Street
212-254-1531

This small old-fashioned Lower East Side candy shop sells stacks of affordable penny candies, like Mary Janes and Tootsie Rolls. Dried fruit, nuts, seeds, and chocolate are sold by the pound or in bags or boxes. Grandmothers once kept such treats in dishes in their living rooms. In the back are large wheels of halvah.

 Continue east on Rivington Street; turn left (north) on Norfolk Street.

Shul of New York

172 Norfolk Street, between Rivington Street and East Houston Street
212-420-0364

Built in 1850 for Anshe Chesed (People of Kindness), a German Reform Jewish congregation now on the Upper West Side, the Gothic Revival structure is the oldest surviving synagogue building in New York City. Abandoned in 1977 by Congregation Anshe Slonim (People of Slonim), the Belarus congregation that had owned it since 1921, it was empty until 1986, when Spanish sculptor Angel Orensanz acquired it and began restoration work while using it as an arts center. In 1999, the Shul of New York began holding religious services in the historic building.

Statue of Lenin

View of the only statue of Vladimir I. Lenin in the United States

Cross the street and look up to view the founder of the Soviet Union on top of an apartment building at 178 Norfolk Street. Lenin has his right hand extended as in most of his statues, pointing to the future. The eighteen-foot-high statue was originally placed on top of Red Square, an apartment building on nearby Houston Street constructed in 1989 when the Soviet Union began to fall, hence the ironic statue and name.

 Turn around, back to Rivington Street and turn left (east).

Public School 160

107 Suffolk Street, at the corner of Rivington Street

This 1897 Dutch Gothic building represents the height of public support for education. It is a five-story light brick structure with terra-cotta trim in disrepair, but with promise.

Turn around, walk back to Essex Street, and turn left (south) on Essex Street.

Essex Street Market
From Rivington Street to Delancey Street

This bleak institutional *civic moderne* building is the fruit of Mayor Fiorello La Guardia's drive to get pushcarts and itinerant peddlers off the street and into sanitary indoor spaces. He banned all pushcarts in 1938. The Essex Street Market is clean, light, and well kept, though only moderately busy. In 2019, the market plans to move south of Delancey Street to the ground floor of the Essex Crossing Development.

Vista Note: View of the Williamsburg Bridge from Delancey Street

Though it looks like a hulking Erector Set monstrosity, the Williamsburg Bridge was enormously significant when it opened in 1903. Jewish and Italian immigrants saw it as an escape route from the crowded Lower East Side to the comparative openness of Williamsburg, Brooklyn. It also gave more commercial possibilities to both the Lower East Side and to Williamsburg, though it destroyed Williamsburg's downtown district by intruding into its center. There is a pedestrian walkway and three subway lines that share the bridge with cars, trucks, and buses.

 Continue south on Essex Street.

Site of Eastern Dispensary (later the Good Samaritan Dispensary)
75 Essex Street, at the corner of Broome Street

The abandoned building, last occupied by Eisner Brothers Sporting Goods, is an 1895 four-story salmon-colored brick edifice in the Florentine style. Dispensaries predated hospitals in the nineteenth century, when patients were normally treated at home. Protestants generally organized dispensaries and hospitals. Jewish and Roman Catholic communities eventually established their own health care systems as a response to government-sanctioned Protestant proselytizing in private and public hospitals.

Seward Park High School
Essex Street, between Broome Street and Grand Street

Long the pride of the Jewish community, the large five-story U-shaped high school was the most massive building in the area and was a beacon of possibilities for education-minded youth and their parents. Still a well-managed school, its population is about 85 percent foreign-born, mostly from various regions of China. It no longer has the same prestige, since area students who achieve well academically take citywide tests in the hope of getting into special schools outside their neighborhood, notably Stuyvesant High School and Bronx High School of Science. (The front entrance is on Ludlow Street.)

Founding Site of B'nai B'rith
Marked by a very small plaque placed high on the brick wall of an apartment building yard and playground on the east side of Essex Street between Broome Street and Grand Street

The Jewish Anti-Nativist, Self-Protection, and Mutual Aid Society was established by secular Jews from Germany in 1843 who met in Sinsheimer's Saloon, located at 60 Essex Street, to organize a community response to anti-Semitism.

Straus Square
Confluence of Essex Street, East Broadway, Canal Street, and Rutgers Street

This was the hub of Lower East Side Jewish communal life and the site of the Daily Forward Building, Seward Park Public Library, Garden Cafeteria, and the still-vibrant Educational Alliance.

The Daily Forward Building
175 East Broadway

Under the large electric Yiddish sign, journalists throughout the eleven-floor structure produced a daily paper that was the heartbeat of the Jewish settlement. It began publication in 1897 and, under the editorship of the legendary Abraham Cahan, from 1901 to 1951, *The Forvertz* was a democratic socialist paper with many nonpolitical features: book and theater reviews, serializations of new writers, and the popular column *A Bintel Brief* (*A Bundle of Letters*), where Cahan exhorted Jews with reason and humor to Americanize and leave behind many Eastern European customs, prejudices, and superstitions. Americanization succeeded too well for the newspaper. By 1990, *The Forward* was being printed in English as a weekly from offices in New Jersey, and in 2019, it moved to digital publication. After a few years housing garment factories, the Forward Building was converted into a Chinese condominium, though the Yiddish sign will stay because it is landmarked.

 Stay on Essex Street one short block south beyond Strauss Square, turn left (east) on Henry Street.

Apartment House

165 Henry Street, between Essex Street and Jefferson Street

The former Rabbi Jacob Joseph School is now converted into apartments. Above the door is a decorative shield with a torch flanked by Ten Commandments tablets, each topped with a Star of David. The building inscription records the date as 5672 (1912). Rabbi Jacob Joseph (1840–1902) was called from his post in Vilna (then Russia, now Lithuania) in 1888 to serve the Orthodox Russian Jewish community in New York City as their chief rabbi. He was a colorful figure, a noted homilist, fundraiser, and organizer. Thousands attended his funeral procession, which was marred when workers at a nearby factory pelted the mourners with nuts and bolts. The school was named in his honor.

 Turn left (north) on Jefferson Street one block, then right (east) on East Broadway.

New York Public Library, Seward Park Branch

192 East Broadway at Jefferson Street
212-477-6770

This three-story library provided one of the chief means of upward mobility (or escape) by remaining open seven days a week until late in the evenings, even during the Depression.

Educational Alliance

197 East Broadway, at the corner of Jefferson Street
212-780-2300

The five-story Renaissance Revival building dates from 1889 and holds one of the main settlement houses in the Lower East Side. The Educational Alliance was formed by wealthy assimilated German Jews to Americanize the new wave of Eastern Europeans. In time, the Russian and Polish Jews predominated and it widened its offering of legal, employment, medical, and linguistic aid to newcomers. The variety of immigrant services also included free milk, subsidized lunches, warm showers, and classes in art, music, theater, and citizenship. Today it offers Hebrew and Yiddish language education, health and fitness programs, after-school activities, two summer camp facilities, mental health programs, and residential housing for senior citizens. They operate another center on East 14th Street. The facility is open to people of all backgrounds, and program participants reflect the present diversity of the area. (The other noted settlement house is the nearby Henry Street Settlement at 263, 265, and 267 Henry Street, between Montgomery Street and Gouverneur Street, and a new building at 466 Grand Street between Willett Street and Pitt Street.)

Iglesia Cristiana Primitiva

207 East Broadway, between Jefferson Street and Clinton Street

This egregious eyesore is an attempt at modern architecture. Nothing could be more jarring to the block's look than this monstrosity with a hodgepodge of colored stones set in a panel above the doorway to separate two massive areas of serrated brickwork.

Shul Block of Tiny Synagogues

Between Clinton Street and Montgomery Street

The Shul Block features eight small Orthodox synagogues (*shteiblech*) and the offices of the Yiddish newspaper *Algemeiner Journal*, which serves an Orthodox and Hasidic readership.

 Turn left (north) on Pedestrian Street past Bialystocker Plaza and Grand Street, continuing on Willett Street.

Bialystoker Synagogue

7 Willett Street, off Grand Street
212-475-0165

Immigrants from Bialystock in Russian Poland founded this Orthodox Jewish synagogue. The large, airy structure was built out of native mica-schist fieldstone with brownstone and limestone trim. It was formerly the Willett Street Methodist Episcopal Church, built in 1826, and has curious zodiac figures in the ceiling, including the very unkosher (and unconventional) symbol for Cancer, a scorpion that looks like a lobster! The Jewish Museum on 5th Avenue at 92nd Street has a sixth century BC mosaic tile floor from the remains of the Beth Aleph Synagogue in Israel featuring a zodiac with a scorpion (*akrav*), as well. The museum description states: *Rabbinic discussions from the period indicate that pagan decorative imagery was allowed as long as it was not worshipped.* The museum's scorpion actually looks like a scorpion, unlike the symbol at the Bialystoker Synagogue.

 Return from Willett Street to Grand Street and walk west.

St. Mary's Church (Roman Catholic)

440 Grand Street, between Pitt Street and Clinton Street
212-674-3266

Built in 1833, St. Mary's is the second-oldest Roman Catholic Church building in New York City. (Old St. Patrick's Cathedral on Mott Street between Prince Street and East Houston Street was constructed in 1815.)

It replaces the previous St. Mary's, which was burned by anti-Catholic nativists in 1831. The 1871 addition of the many-windowed facade in red brick with two tall conical towers of black shingle and green bronze trim and twelve front windows and three doors were a busy, ambitious attempt to give the church elevated architectural status as Catholics became more numerous due to increased migration from southern Germany and Ireland. Originally, this church was less grandiose: simple grey ashlar blocks. The white-walled interior is a large space unencumbered by columns. Bright stained-glass windows flood the space with light. The altar area is under an interesting double-rotunda ceiling. A statue of Mary presides high above the congregation, perched on an oversized sanctuary tabernacle on the high altar.

Kossar's Bialys

367 Grand Street, just off Essex Street
212-473-4810

The bialy is a bread from Bialystock (now in Poland, then in Russian Poland), which, while not as popular as the bagel, is a genuine treat. These are chewy round rolls with a puffy rim and a depressed center sprinkled with flakes of onions. Kossar's also sells bagels and a variety of breads.

Federal-Style Houses

Grand Street on two blocks between Essex Street and Orchard Street,
one by itself and four adjacent

Five Federal-style houses from the early nineteenth century survive on this end of Grand Street: house numbers 357, 339, 337, 335, and 333. These distinctive three-story brick buildings, with the front half pitched gently up and the back half pitched sharply down, were in great evidence before the arrival of tenement buildings. Unfortunately, most have been radically and clumsily altered to serve commercial needs.

 Turn left (south) on Orchard Street.

This is the south end of the main section of the Orchard Street Shopping District.

Apartment Building

14–16 Orchard Street near Canal Street

The twin-entrance apartment building is prominently decorated with two rows of eight large Stars of David carved out of terra-cotta and surrounded by intricate finials and tracery. The six-story redbrick building has elaborately decorated, oversized, hooded cornices on the top, one high over each entrance. Such cornices became a kind of residential tenement heraldry. Intricate carvings painstakingly chiseled by Italian artisans made their buildings more valuable. In this case, the carvings also showed religious pride. Whether viewed as pulchritude or ostentation, complex designs found throughout the Lower East Side helped landlords get a little more rent for their apartments.

S. Jarmulowsky's Bank Building

Southwest corner of Orchard Street and Canal Street

The imposing eleven-story building with neoclassical features on the bottom two floors was built in 1912 to house Sender Jarmulowsky's thriving immigrant bank, which had been founded in 1873. The panic ensuing from the start of World War I in 1914 caused a run on the bank and it failed. Previously, a small domed and columned temple stood on the roof at the northeast corner of the building.

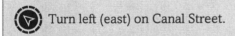 Turn left (east) on Canal Street.

Hong Kong Funeral Home

41 Canal Street and 5 Ludlow Street

The decorative neoclassical L-shaped building is the major Chinese funeral parlor in the Lower East Side. Earlier, it had been the home of the Kletzker Brotherly Aid Association, the largest Jewish funeral home in the area, which was operated by one of the three thousand landsmanshaften— mutual aid societies—in New York City. They provided sick benefits, gave loans like credit unions, helped secure jobs and apartments, and operated sections in cemeteries. The Kletzker Building was one of the few that operated a funeral home. Its Jewish sign and Star of David are intact and can be seen high above the doorway around the corner from Canal Street at the side entrance, 5 Ludlow Street.

 Turn right (west) at the intersection on Division Street, then left (south) on Pike Street (Allen Street below Division Street).

Sung Tak Buddhist Temple (*Limitless Virtue*)
15 Pike Street, just east of East Broadway

Built in 1903 as the Sons of Israel Kalwarie Synagogue in the Rundbogenstil style (German neo-Romanesque), the brightly decorated Buddhist interior combines in a syncretistic way elements of both major schools of Buddhism: Mahayana and Hinayana (or Theravada). It has Mahayana bodhisattvas, including Guanyin and a military guardian bodhisattva, and the eighteen Hinayana arhats, nine to the right and nine to the left of the front altars. Bodhisattvas represent Enlightened Ones who, rather than progressing to Nirvana (becoming one with the universe instead of continuing on the Wheel of Life), linger as spirits in the Sentient Being Realm to help humans achieve perfection. Arhats represent Enlightened Ones who linger to more passively serve as models for perfection-seeking humans. Each represents an attribute such as compassion or benevolence. In the front center is the Historical Buddha (Shakyamuni); to the right is the Medicinal Buddha; and to the left is the Pure Land Buddha. The swastikas on the chests of the three Buddhas on the front altar may be unsettling to non-Asian visitors. Buddhism and Hinduism use the swastika (facing either direction) along with the wheel as symbols of transmigration of souls (reincarnation).

 Turn around back to Division Street.

Major Draft Riot Site
Along Allen Street and Chrystie Street

This was a site of devastation after the 1863 Draft Riot (July 13–16) following Lincoln's Emancipation Proclamation and the Federal Conscription Act, which inflamed tempers among poor Irish who feared competition from black workers. The issue had been exacerbated by federal troops sent by Lincoln to protect black strikebreakers during a largely Irish longshoremen's strike in June. The enraged crowd lynched eleven black men and burned the Colored Orphan Asylum. Lincoln sent five Union Army regiments from Gettysburg and 105 rioters were shot dead; numerous buildings burned during the street fighting.

 Turn left (west) on Division Street, then right (north) on Eldridge Street.

Eldridge Street Synagogue (K'hal Adath Jesurun)
12 Eldridge Street, between Canal Street and Hester Street
212-219-0888

Completed in 1887, this Gothic structure with Moorish arches is the first synagogue in the Lower East Side (or anywhere in the United States) completed by Eastern European Jews. The synagogue was closed in 1951 as the largely Russian and Polish congregants left the area. The Eldridge Street Project has raised funds to repair and restore the building, which it now shares with the completely Chinese block, including a small storefront Buddhist temple. (Tours may be arranged by calling 212-219-0302.)

Dr. Sun Yat-sen Intermediate School (I.S. 131)
100 Hester Street at Eldridge Street

Though it looks forbidding, this large curvilinear building with beige coloring and small riot-modern fortress windows is a lively community center as well as a school. Sun Yat-sen actually stayed not far from here very briefly in 1910 as he was traveling from an American speaking and fundraising tour to Nanking to accept the presidency of the new Republic of China.

 Continue north on Eldridge Street.

Vista Note: Looking north on Eldridge Street offers a superb view of the shining Chrysler Building in Midtown framed by the tenements of the Lower East Side.

Turn right (east) on Broome Street.

Kehila Kedosha Janina Synagogue

280 Broome Street

Distinct from both Ashkenazic and Sephardic traditions, the Romaniotes of Greece descended from Jews escaping the clutches of Roman slavery after the destruction of the Second Temple in 70 AD and the expulsion of Jews from the province of Judea in 130 AD. Later, the name and tradition referred to most Jewish communities in Byzantium, especially in Greece. They were greatly influenced by Hellenism and adopted Greek names and used Greek in synagogue services. Different ethnic and religious customs developed, and in New York City, the Romaniotes organized their own house of worship. This is the only Romaniote synagogue in the Western Hemisphere. The synagogue's museum holds a unique Torah written in Greek. (To arrange visits, call 212-431-1619.) The diminutive two-story brown brick structure has some decorative features: several Stars of David and two sets of Ten Commandments, the lower one flanked by lions.

 Turn left (north) on Orchard Street.

Orchard Street Shopping

From Canal Street to East Houston Street

The seven-block stretch of more or less traditional Lower East Side stores has partly survived the postwar period. Apparel hangs from thin metal bars extended out over the sidewalks of many shops. North of Delancey Street, Hispanic hawkers call their wares; the more sedate Orthodox Jews to the south beckon with signs advertising bargains. Orchard Street shops sell all manner of goods: antiques, apparel, fabrics, handbags, luggage, hats, hosiery, linens, lingerie, jewelry, leatherwear, shoes, and umbrellas. Costly hip stores have been replacing the bargain shops that once predominated.

Lower East Side Tenement Museum

Office at 90 Orchard Street, at the corner of Broome Street; museum at
97 Orchard Street (guided tours only)
212-431-0233

This is a popular and interesting history museum. Conceptually, the craze for information about immigrants who came at the turn of the last century was a reaction to the enormous emphasis previously put on the importance of Mayflower and other very early arrivals. The children and grandchildren of Eastern and Southern Europeans struck back; the results include the Ellis Island Museum and the Lower East Side Tenement Museum. The museum is an 1863 five-story redbrick tenement house, which, from the time it opened until its abandonment in 1935, housed over ten thousand people from twenty-five countries. Most have been carefully registered and catalogued from records of the US Census, New York State Census, and Municipal Directories. Professors and graduate students at Columbia University did much of the initial research. Four apartments have been meticulously restored and are historically connected with families that once lived there (i.e., Gumpertz in 1874, Confino in 1916, Rogarshevsky in 1918, Baldizzi in 1935). Their descendants were located and each apartment has incorporated articles of clothing, furnishings, and photographs from the obliging relatives. Some tours include dramatizations with museum staff dressed in period clothing and speaking to visitors as characters who once lived in the building.

Restaurant Recommendations

Katz's Delicatessen

Houston Street west of Avenue A at Ludlow Street
212-254-2246

Still hanging is the World War II vintage sign, *Send a Salami to Your Boy in the Army*, which rhymes only when the old Lower East Side accent is used to say *Ahmy*. There is a scene in *When Harry Met Sally* in Katz's dining room where she fakes an orgasm and gets at least some looks from a jaded crowd. Once primarily a Jewish eatery, the restaurant serves a completely multicultural crowd, essentially reflecting the diversity of the area. Although it is not completely kosher—because it opens on Saturdays, serves cheeseburgers, and is unsupervised by a rabbi—the food is certainly kosher-style. Overstuffed meat sandwiches, franks, fries, soups, and the full line of Dr. Brown's sodas are popular. The large matzoh ball in the matzoh ball soup is made with interestingly coarse grain, which provides a different but appealing taste.

Sammy's Roumanian Restaurant

157 Chrystie Street, between Delancey Street and Rivington Street
212-673-0330

This is the unabashed king of cholesterol; dishes are served with a container of chicken schmaltz (liquid fat) in case the large portions of garlic-crusted meat aren't Herculean enough for your system. Some dishes come with gribenes (cracklings from chicken fat and skins fried with grated onions), or solid schmaltz. (They provide seltzer as an antidote. In fact, a bottle of seltzer adorns the sign in front of the door.) Favored entrées range from rib eye steak to veal chops to skirt steak, though fish and chicken are available. Two appetizers or side dishes of note: juicy karnatzlach, a Romanian garlic sausage, and seared kishka, a sausage of matzoh meal and onions held together with chicken fat. A klezmer band plays on the weekends, adding to the cacophony of the noisy, friendly atmosphere.

El Castillo de Jagua Restaurant

113 Rivington Street, at the corner of Essex Street
212-982-6412

Spanish American food is a mixture of Puerto Rican, Dominican, and Cuban specialties. This popular diner, where everyone seems to know each other, serves full-bodied stews made of goat, oxtail, pigs' feet, and tripe (beef stomach), as well as chicken and pork. Avocado salad, seafood soup, octopus in hot sauce, pepper steak, and fried chicken are big numbers. Their Cuban sandwiches are deliciously juicy. A Cuban sandwich is ham, Swiss cheese, mortadella, mustard, and pickles pressed in something that resembles a waffle iron so that the four sides are sealed. El Castillo de Jagua also serves American diner fare: BLT, tuna fish salad, grilled cheese, and omelets.

Wu's Wonton King

165 East Broadway, at the corner of Rutgers Street on Straus Square
212-477-1111

Originally the Garden Cafeteria, offering Eastern European Jewish fare and a place to sit and talk over coffee, with a WPA mural on its west wall, it is now a bustling Chinese restaurant. In both cases, most of the clientele have been neighborhood residents. The restaurant offers Cantonese fare, including dim sum, noodles, congee (porridge made from leftover rice), baked or steamed buns with meat filling, as well as Shanghai and Sichuan specialties. You do not need to call ahead to order Peking duck, though you must call a day ahead to order a whole roast piglet.

Yonah Schimmel Knish Bakery and Restaurant

137 East Houston Street, between Forsythe and Eldridge Streets
212-477-2858

This knishery retains its nineteenth century look: crowded counters and rough wooden tables. Knishes are Eastern European snack foods made of mashed potatoes inside a thin baked (or, heaven forbid, fried) pastry shell. Alternatively, some knish varieties are stuffed with cabbage, ground meat, or kasha (groats). Yonah Schimmel's also sells potato and noodle kugel (pudding), and pretzels.

EAST VILLAGE

The North Portion of the Lower East Side

Dutch governor Peter Stuyvesant was not fond of the crowded conditions and filth that characterized New Amsterdam. He built his country house, a working farm, a convenient ride north from the town wall, though far enough away to afford some isolation. He chose a tract of land that stretched from the marshes along the East River to the Bouwerie (meaning farm in Dutch)—the rural road running north on Manhattan's east side, approximately along the route of today's 4th Avenue. Using the present street grid, Stuyvesant's estate stretched from the East River to 4th Avenue and from East 5th to 20th Streets. For almost two centuries, the Stuyvesant holdings remained farmland and were held by the family. Some of the fields were leased to others.

Cereal crops, vegetables, fruit, dairy products, and livestock were raised in farms close to the city. The demand from grocers, butchers, restaurants, and ships traveling to the Caribbean looking for cargo kept seventeenth- and eighteenth-century Manhattan farmers occupied. Ultimately, the expanding city drove up land prices and farms were converted to lots for row houses and tenements.

Soon after Daniel D. Tompkins came to the city from Scarsdale, New York, he entered politics and real estate. Tompkins purchased the southern portion of the Stuyvesant estate and began selling lots for residential housing. He was elected governor of New York State (1807–1817) and vice president of the United States under James Monroe (1817–1825). His political success gave a high profile to his real estate projects. Tompkins left land undeveloped at the center of his estate to allow farmers from across the river in Williamsburg to sell their wares from carts. Tompkins Square was eventually transformed into a park by the city and has borne his name since 1833.

Tompkins sought to take advantage of New York's growth as a commercial center by planting a seven-hundred-acre suburb on the south side of the Inner Bay. He quickly grasped that a suburb would be dependent on steam power, which alone could provide dependable, scheduled ferry service to Manhattan. Consequently, he organized the first scheduled steamship service between Tompkinsville, Staten Island, and Manhattan in 1817.

In Staten Island, Tompkins overextended himself. By 1820, acutely short of money, he borrowed large sums and was unable to pay his debts. His creditors sought judgments against him, he turned to drinking, his health declined rapidly, and he died at age fifty-one in 1825 at his home in Tompkinsville. The funeral service was held in St. Mark's Church-in-the-Bowery at 2nd Avenue and 10th Street, where he rests with two other governors, Peter Stuyvesant and Henry Sloughter.

Tompkins was perceptive, but the vision of a suburban Staten Island was 150 years premature. His development of the Stuyvesant estate was successful because it was much closer to the city, which by the time of his death was approaching Canal Street.

As the land Tompkins bought from the Stuyvesant heirs began to sprout housing, Broadway became increasingly commercial, and a corridor along parallel Lafayette Street developed into housing for the rich. Astor Place, at the western edge of today's East Village, became a center where the wealthy shopped and enjoyed entertainment. Socially, it marked a separation between well-to-do establishments and those left behind on lower Broadway near City Hall, which increasingly attracted a poorer and often rowdy clientele. Astor Place was surrounded with theaters and opera houses by 1830.

Astor Place theater life was also the tinderbox for one of the worst riots in New York City's history. On the surface, the Astor Place Riot pitted the supporters of American actor Edwin Forrest against the followers of English actor William C. Macready. Forrest's partisans interrupted Macready's performance at the Astor Opera House in May 1849, fights erupted, and the streets were filled with brawling rioters. The police and the state militia fired on the crowd when they refused to disperse. Twenty-two died and forty-eight were wounded. The underlying causes were the raw ethnic and class tensions in the rapidly growing city.

Most of the area was still garden and dairy farms in 1830 when large-scale German immigration brought thousands of people to the edge of the city where much new construction was under way and old houses were being enlarged. Kleindeutschland, the emerging German settlement, stretched from Grand Street to East 23rd Street and from the Bowery to the East River. About 250,000 Germans lived there by the Civil War. Its southern end became the basis for the German Jewish migration uptown in the 1870s. Germans, both Christian and Jewish, were always in the process of migrating uptown and leaving their apartments to the next wave of Europeans. By 1890, the Germans had vacated the southern end of Kleindeutschland (the Lower East Side) and Eastern European Jews and Italians moved into their apartments.

At the turn of the last century, the upper part of the Lower East Side, now called the East Village, was unmistakably German. Demographics changed rapidly, and as the Germans prospered and were being pushed from the south by new immigrants, the *General Slocum* ship disaster radically changed the ethnic equation. The Germans were utterly devastated by the loss of 1,021 of the 1,331 passengers aboard the paddle-wheel excursion vessel heading toward the Bronx for a picnic outing sponsored by St. Mark's German Lutheran Church in 1904. The community migrated almost en masse to Yorkville. Ukrainian, Russian, and Polish Christians, and Eastern European Jews replaced the Germans. Even churches moved, and the congregation of St. Mark's German Lutheran Church on East 6th Street relocated uptown and sold their building to an Orthodox Jewish Congregation.

Economic problems faced by Germans in Europe had fostered their immigration. By 1880, similarly plagued Eastern Europeans and Italians were moving into the neighborhood. Ethnic maps show how closely each group stayed together in settlement patterns. Italians lived along a narrow strip from 2nd Avenue to Avenue B between East 10th and 12th Streets. Jews settled the eastern part of the area, while Ukrainians, Russians, and Poles lived in the western segment of the neighborhood. Census tract reports and placement of stores, churches, and synagogues tell the same story.

By numbers, Ukrainians dominated the Eastern European community in the East Village. Ukrainian Christians were divided almost equally by religious affinity, Eastern Orthodox and Byzantine Rite Roman Catholic. While Russians and Poles also came to the East Village, most who came to New York City settled in Brooklyn. The neighborhood of choice for Polish people was Greenpoint, and for Russians it was Williamsburg or Brownsville. In fact, while many Eastern European Jews settled in Greater New York, the metropolitan area received a relatively small portion of the large Eastern European Christian immigration, who were more likely to go to Buffalo, Cleveland, Detroit, St. Louis, Chicago, and Milwaukee.

The small Italian enclave's population left the East Village decades ago, yet a few signs of their community can still be found: one remaining Italian spaghetti house (1908), a pastry shop (1894), and a grocery store (1909) represent the former Italian presence. A labor hiring hall at 231 East 14th Street is long gone, but the sign remains chiseled in granite above the second-floor windows: ITALIAN LABOR CENTER.

As Eastern European Jews began exiting the eastern part of the East Village in the 1940s, their apartments were often rented to Puerto Ricans. By the 1960s, Avenues C and D were largely Hispanic, both Puerto Rican and Dominican.

Cheap rents attracted cultural Bohemians and a large and diverse foreign population made it easy to fit in. Emma Goldman, Alexander Berkman, John Reed, and Max Eastman characterized the two decades after 1900. Goldman and Berkman were anarchists, John Reed wrote *Ten Days That Shook the World*, a favorable journalistic account of the Russian Bolshevik Revolution, and Eastman edited *Masses*, an unaffiliated socialist magazine, from 1911 until 1917.

Leon Trotsky, who as a Bolshevik was to lead Soviet Russia's Red Army, lived in an eighteen-dollar-a-month apartment on East 164th Street near the Grand Concourse in the Bronx from January through March 1917, and coedited a Russian language newspaper, *Novy Mir* (New World), with socialist theoretician Nikolai Bukharin from a basement office on St. Mark's Place. He spent free time addressing workers and articulating his political views, Menshevik at the time, in neighborhood cafeterias along 2nd Avenue.

In the 1950s, the area played host to a small group of influential young people challenging societal conventions in the early Cold War period. The Beats expressed themselves at art shows, poetry readings, theater performances, coffeehouse concerts, and wherever people gathered to read and discuss books and magazines.

St. Mark's Church was an important center for the Beats in the 1950s and early 1960s. The twenty-two used bookshops that formerly lined 4th Avenue and the dingy bars underneath the 3rd Avenue El also attracted Beatniks. The 3rd Avenue El, a steel monstrosity that darkened the street from 1878 until it was demolished in 1956, drove down rents along its route, which drew countercultural people.

The Electric Circus, head shops, and *The East Village Other* (an alternative newspaper) epitomized the later Bohemians of the mid-1960s and early 1970s. It was a hippie culture with an edge. In the 1960s, the East Village was shedding the immigrant cultures it had sheltered for 130 years.

Imperceptibly, the northern part of the Lower East Side began to be called the East Village. It signaled and reflected a terminological and physical divorce from the better-known immigrant culture of the Jewish area below East Houston Street. The dominant culture of the East Village, despite the presence of Hispanics in the eastern half and Ukrainians and Poles in the western part, was an in-your-face youth culture. The brash new culture ignored race, ethnicity, and religion and focused on the common denominators of music, clothing, and drugs.

Culturally, there was a closer affinity between the East Village and Greenwich Village than with the Old World culture personified by the East Village's Catholic and Eastern Orthodox religious processions and the restaurants and shops specializing in Eastern European fare.

The youth culture of the East Village romanticized the down-and-out feeling of Greenwich Village, an area increasingly known as the West Village. Greenwich Village was also going through changes. The neighborhood received landmark designation, real estate prices skyrocketed, and countercultural people who lacked rent-stabilized apartments gravitated to the East Village or Chelsea. Greenwich Village became solidly middle class.

Cheap rents, funky buildings, avant-garde music and art, and easily scored drugs were the hooks for many who gravitated to the East Village in the 1970s and 1980s. Similarly, long-time residents left for those reasons. From 1988 to 1991 a series of violent confrontations centering on Tompkins Square Park seemed to point toward a neighborhood future as a slum. The police won the confrontations and squatters were removed from the park and many abandoned buildings. Gentrification began, and every block had a few renovations. Restaurants flourished, boutiques opened, and bars and clubs that stay open until 4:00 a.m. drew tourists and people from all over Greater New York. The streets became safe and new rents hit all-time highs.

Today, the culinary promiscuity of its restaurants and scores of bars, which hint that something bad may be going on inside, draw thousands of people into the neighborhood each evening. Unlike the West Village, however, subway transportation is poor and the housing stock is old and small. The East Village was never middle class and its tenements and apartment buildings lack pulchritude and amenities. The strategy of many developers has been to buy old buildings, demolish them, and build luxury apartments, cooperatives, or condominiums. The East Village will continue to change but slower than other gentrifying neighborhoods.

Walking Trips Around Astor Place and up and down the Avenues

Many of the East Village's points of interest are on the street grid's north–south avenues, so a methodical way of seeing the neighborhood is to choose one or more avenues to walk up or down. Sites are arranged by avenue in this section. The Gateway to the East Village from the West Village is Astor Place, formerly the elegant center of a coveted residential area and high-end shopping district.

 Walk #1: Start at the intersection one block west of 3rd Avenue at the confluence of Astor Place, Lafayette Street, East 8th Street, St. Mark's Place, 4th Avenue, and Cooper Square.

Recreated Subway Kiosk
On a traffic island in Astor Place Square

This cast-iron and glass subway kiosk was re-created and added in 1985. The Metropolitan Transit Authority scrapped the original subway entrance coverings in the first two decades after World War II. Below ground, the Astor Place Station is decorated with strikingly beautiful terra-cotta beaver plaques to recall an important landlord in the area, fur trader John Jacob Astor.

Cube

On the main sidewalk widener at Astor Place Square

Bernard Rosenthal created the cube sculpture, officially named *Alamo*, and it was installed in 1967. It actually turns if enough people are recruited to give it a large sustained push.

The Cooper Union for the Advancement of Science and Art

At Cooper Square

Cooper Union's Great Hall has been at the center of many of our nation's great debates. It is where Abraham Lincoln delivered the speech that gained him support of East Coast Republicans as he sought his party's 1860 presidential nomination. The speech was enormously important. Lincoln took a definitive stand against slavery in his remarks, which had immediacy, since many of the Abolitionist Republicans in attendance were veterans of the struggle against slavery in New York State, which had ended with the abolition of slavery nineteen years earlier in 1841.

Peter Cooper, noted engineer, landlord, glue factory owner, and general entrepreneur, established and endowed Cooper Union so that, to this day, it is a tuition-free college. Construction was completed in 1859. Inside, the low ceiling and obstructive pillars give the windowless Great Hall, located a few steps below street level, an inelegant appearance. Cooper Union has three schools: engineering, architecture, and art. The classrooms, studios, workshops, and galleries are upstairs to take advantage of natural light. Divining the future, Peter Cooper installed a cylindrical shaft in the building to hold an elevator, which was finally installed once Elisha Graves Otis developed the safety elevator. For more than a century, a square elevator operated inside the shaft until 1972, when John Hejduk designed a tubular stainless steel carriage to fit as Peter Cooper intended. Take the elevator to the eighth floor to see the simple mechanical workings that drive the large clock facing the south side of the building.

Statue of Peter Cooper

In Cooper Square south of Cooper Union

The engineer and glue magnate sits regally in a chair on top of a pedestal flanked by two Ionic columns holding up a granite covering. It was installed in 1897, and became a popular outdoor meeting place.

Wanamaker Building

Northwest end of Cooper Square

Once part of the largest department store in the United States, this Wanamaker annex (the original store was on the next block north) was a profitable outpost of the Philadelphia-based chain. It finally closed its doors in 1955, long after the department store district had gravitated to 5th Avenue north of 34th Street. The fifteen-story building sits diagonally across from Cooper Union and is bounded by Broadway, 4th Avenue, East 8th Street, and Wanamaker Place. Presently occupied by various offices, its ground-floor commercial space houses Kmart, Ann Taylor, and Chase Bank.

Colonnade Row

428–434 Lafayette Street between Astor Place and East 4th Street

These stately worn remnants of nine four-story Greek Revival town houses with magnificent Corinthian columns erected in 1831 on what was then LaGrange Terrace (named for the country estate of the Marquis de Lafayette) give a glimpse of the elegance of the area in the early nineteenth century as the wealthy moved up from lower Broadway. At disparate times, Astors and Vanderbilts lived here. Only four of the attached houses remain. The southern five were demolished in 1902 for a truck garage, a reminder of how fast neighborhoods rise and fall.

Joseph Papp Public Theater (formerly Hebrew Immigrant Aid Society, originally the Astor Library)

425 Lafayette Street, just south of Astor Place
212-539-8778

Constructed in stages between 1853 and 1881, this magnificent Romanesque Revival building (in a style sometimes called Rundbogenstil) was a free public library erected and stocked by John Jacob Astor. Presently, it is home to five live performance spaces, including Joe's Pub, a cabaret, and one movie theater. It's not unusual to see people lined up around the block to buy tickets for events here.

St. Mark's Place

Between East 2nd and 3rd Avenues

The block's north side is dominated by a large building made from three fused 1833 brownstones at 19–23 St. Mark's Place. It once housed the Dom, an early 1960s trend-setting, late-Beat nightclub featuring a house band, the Fugs, who specialized in radical lyrics and hilarious obscenity. Their songs included "Slum Goddess," "Group Grope," "Kill for Peace," and "Coca Cola Douche." The Electric Circus, a hippie icon offering light shows, music, and theater, occupied the site and continued to feature the Fugs, as well as the Family Stone, and the Mothers of Invention. Mirroring an unfortunate effect of the drug culture, the building became a rehabilitation center from 1971 until 2000. Two years later, three new floors were added on top of the four-story edifice, which has reverted to its original residential use, this time as an apartment complex.

St. Mark's Place, along with nearby Stuyvesant Street, was once one of the two most elegant blocks in the area. Presently, it is a bustling street of trendy and trashy shops catering to young tourists and suburban weekenders. It is filled with tattoo and body-piercing parlors, CD and DVD shops, and clothing stores, with almost every place selling sunglasses, T-shirts, and postcards. Most of the bars and downscale restaurants are inexpensive and packed with unadventurous teenyboppers who believe the entire East Village scene can be experienced on this block.

 Walk #2: Walking down 3rd Avenue at the Bowery (the lower four blocks of 3rd Avenue is the Bowery).

Former Site of CBGB-OMFUG

315 Bowery at Bleecker Street

This was the famous rock club where punk was born and slam dancing started. For thirty years, it tried to stay at the cutting edge. In the 1970s, patrons could hear the Ramones, Debbie Harry and Blondie, and Patti Smith at CBGB-OMFUG. The acronym signifies the original music of the club: Country, Blue Grass, Blues, and Other Music for Uplifting Gourmandizers.

Merchant's House Museum

East 4th Street, between the Bowery and Lafayette Street
212-777-1089

This spectacularly well-preserved row house was built in 1832 just around the corner from fashionable Astor Place and Lafayette Street. From 1835 until 1933, it housed Seabury Tredwell, a wealthy hardware importer, and his descendants. It has the greatest collection of original furnishings of any of the historic houses in New York City. Of special note is the basement kitchen with a beehive oven and brass servant call bells. Upstairs are chairs and sofas with horsehair upholstery, period prints, mahogany furniture, and chinaware. The Merchant's House Museum affords a window into the lifestyle of the privileged in mid-nineteenth-century New York.

Former Home of *The Village Voice*

36 Cooper Square, between East 5th and 6th Streets

The pink brick edifice houses the offices of *The Village Voice*, a feisty tabloid founded in 1955 to battle Cold War conformity, McCarthyism, and cultural sterility. It promoted the civil rights movement, mutual disarmament, and reform politics in New York City. It provided crucial coverage and reviews of avant-garde events: poetry readings, music and dance concerts, and Off-Broadway and Off-Off-Broadway performances. Important *Voice* contributors were Norman Mailer, Jack Newfield, Joe Flaherty, Andrew Sarris, Nat Hentoff, Alexander Cockburn, Erika Munk, and James Ridgeway. Jules Feiffer provided editorial cartoons. Once the preeminent newspaper of the Greenwich Village and surrounding areas, it had been buffeted in recent years by gentrification and by the *New York Press*, a more hip but also more conservative newsweekly read by more of the twentysomethings downtown. *The Village Voice* ceased publication in 2017. The building is now home to the Grace Church High School.

St. George Ukrainian Catholic Church

16–20 East 7th Street, east of 3rd Avenue at Taras Shevchenko Place
212-674-1615

This Byzantine-style Roman Catholic church is a polychrome granite building with a high central dome. The congregation formerly referred to itself as Ruthenian (borderland of Slovakia and Ukraine), but a name change came with the new building in 1977.

Sunrise Market (Japanese)
4 Stuyvesant Street, just off 3rd Avenue, 2nd floor
212-598-3040

The hidden anchor of Little Japan, a block with several Japanese restaurants, bars, hair stylists, and boutiques, is a second-floor grocery store that stocks everything necessary to cook the cuisine of Japan. It offers Japanese vegetables and dried seaweed, dried fish, rice and rice flour, soy sauces and other condiments, sodas, candies, junk food, and canned goods. A side room has plates, bowls, cups, and chopsticks. Many of the young Japanese people living in the East Village are involved in design and graphics.

Undergraduate Dormitory, New York University
33 3rd Avenue at East 9th Street

This wins the contest for ugliest building in the neighborhood. Built in 1986, it horrified neighbors with its out-of-scale proportions, complete lack of detail, and truly hideous color scheme of alternating sections of pink and grey bricks. The roof sports a space-hangar dome open at two ends. At least once inside, the students don't have to look at it.

Site of Peter Stuyvesant's Pear Tree
Northeast corner of 3rd Avenue and 10th Street

A reminder of Dutch days is the seldom-noticed quaint plaque placed by the Holland Society of New York in 1890. It marks the spot where a pear tree stood that the governor-general of New Amsterdam brought back as a sapling from the Netherlands and planted on return following his temporary recall in 1664. He intended it to be his memorial: *By which my name may be remembered.* The old fruit tree lasted more than two centuries and died shortly before the plaque was erected.

Emma Goldman's Former Apartment

6R, East 13th Street, just east of 3rd Avenue

A plaque marks the building where Emma Goldman, the Russian-born anarchist and feminist, lived from 1903 until 1913. Goldman championed free speech, birth control, and free love. She was arrested for opposing American entry in World War I and deported to the Soviet Union in 1919. Unhappy with the Bolshevik regime, she spent the rest of her life espousing radical politics and feminism in various countries in Western Europe. She died in 1940 in Canada.

Kiehl's

109 3rd Avenue, between East 13th and 14th Streets
212-677-3171

This shop is one of the last connections to the neighborhood's German period. Since 1851 when this was Kleindeutschland, Kiehl's has been a popular presence, selling its own high-end line of cosmetics, lotions, and shampoo. The picturesque and pricey shop has long lines that go out the door by weekend afternoons.

Restaurant Recommendations

McSorley's Old Ale House

15 East 7th Street, west of 3rd Avenue
212-473-9148

McSorley's claims to be the oldest bar in Manhattan and has seen generations of Irish, German, Slavic, and eventually multiethnic crowds enjoying the old ambiance. Now more of a tourist attraction than a neighborhood saloon, it has long lines forming in front on weekend evenings. Weekday lunch draws the neighbors with burgers, hash, chili, soups, and sandwiches. The interior is dignified and well preserved: a light sawdust covering on the wood-planked floor, walls covered with old photos and lithographs, and a marvelous coal-burning potbellied stove. This is not a place to sit at the bar; following the old saloon tradition, there are no barstools. But there are plenty of tables in both of McSorley's two rooms, including two next to the stove. McSorley's makes and serves its own ale. Two strange customs hang on at McSorley's. There is only one restroom, a consequence of the days when no women were allowed—a restriction ended in 1970 by federal law. And patrons often order two small mugs of beer—one light, the other dark—each time they order.

Competition to be the oldest bar in town is strong. The tavern claims to have been in business since 1854, but three bars predate it: Bridge Cafe (1794), destroyed by Hurricane Sandy in 2012; Pete's Tavern (1851); and Fanelli's (1857). McSorley's does not show up in any city records until 1862, despite the 1854 claim. For an evocative discussion of McSorley's initial eighty-eight years and its first four owner-bartenders, read "The Old House at Home," a 1940 short story by Joseph Mitchell, the lead narrative in a set called *McSorley's Wonderful Saloon*, available in the collection of Mitchell's New York City writings entitled *Up in the Old Hotel*.

Grassroots Tavern

20 St. Mark's Place, between 2nd and 3rd Avenues
212-475-9443

A couple of steps down from street level is the Grassroots, a low-ceilinged tavern with worn wood everywhere. The wood chairs and tables along the side and the scuffed-up bar seem never to have been polished. The floral pattern on the paint-covered tin ceiling dates it to the turn of the last century. The mood at Grassroots is convivial. Late afternoon regulars, who are older than you find at most East Village hangouts, talk about literature, politics, and sports. At night, a much younger, college-age set dominates.

 Walk #3: Start at 2nd Avenue—the corner at Houston Street is the secondary Gateway to the East Village (from the F train).

Anthology Film Archives

32–34 2nd Avenue, at the corner of 2nd Street
212-505-5181

Only avant-garde films are shown in the small viewing rooms of this former courthouse structure. Anthology Film Archives was organized in 1969 and has a renowned library and several thousand films and videos in storage. There are not too many locations in the United States where a place like Anthology Film Archives could survive.

New York Marble Cemetery
2nd Avenue, between East 2nd and 3rd Streets

This is a tantalizing hidden treasure, but difficult to get inside or even to see into. Established in 1831 as a private nonsectarian cemetery, New York Marble Cemetery served primarily as a burial place for Protestants from Episcopalian and Dutch and German Reformed denominations. Now it is open to the public only once a year. The fact that it was built in an innovative fashion that never caught on elsewhere makes it a truly exceptional cemetery. It is situated in the core of a fully square, not rectangular, city block, and has a high brick wall surrounding it. Embedded in the wall are marble markers denoting the interred who are buried in 156 individual crypts below the plain grassy lawn. A solid black metal gate on an alley leading from 2nd Avenue is the only access, but it is locked and offers no possibility to see inside. (Consult www.marblecemetery.org for dates and times of the periodic public openings.)

New York City Marble Cemetery
52–74 East 2nd Street, midway between 1st and 2nd Avenues

Established in 1831, just a few months after its neighbor around the corner, the New York City Marble Cemetery was built by the same corporation. It has its entire south side exposed to the public view through a cast-iron fence. Underground family crypts hold coffins, but tombstones are allowed and many are interspersed throughout the well-kept yard. One eye-catching name on a stone toward the front marks the interment site of New York patrician Preserved Fish, who must have had enough respect for his parents, or fear of them, never to have changed his name. Another interesting case is James Monroe, fifth president of the United States, who rested here for twenty-seven years. Monroe expired while living with his daughter in a house, no longer standing, at the corner of Lafayette and Prince Streets. The former president died impoverished after selling his Virginia plantation, Ash Lawn, to pay his debts. He was interred in the New York City Marble Cemetery from his death on July 4, 1831, until

1858, when his body was reinterred in Richmond, Virginia. (Monroe shared the same patriotic month and day of death as Thomas Jefferson and John Adams, and the same exhaustion of funds at life's end as Thomas Jefferson and James Madison.)

Russian Orthodox Cathedral of the Holy Virgin Protection (originally Mount Olivet Memorial Church, German Reformed)

59 East 2nd Street, between 1st and 2nd Avenues, across from the cemetery
212-677-4664

Until 1970, this was a Russian Orthodox cathedral. The congregation is now affiliated with the autocephalous (self-governing) Orthodox Church in America. The priests and monks have re-created a bit of Old Russia in this church by strictly observing traditional Orthodox canon law; hence there are no pews or instrumental music. Worshippers stand or kneel amid scores of icons and the smell of liberal doses of incense. In 2001, a new iconostasis (icon screen) was installed to separate the chancel from the nave. A smaller Georgian Orthodox congregation also worships here at a side chapel dedicated to St. Innocent of Irkutsk.

Maryhouse

55 East 3rd Street, between 1st and 2nd Avenues
212-777-9617

Maryhouse is the center of the Catholic Worker movement in the United States, and around the corner, at St. Joseph House (36 East 1st Street), is the headquarters of their bimonthly journal, *The Catholic Worker*. Founded in 1933 by Dorothy Day and Peter Maurin, the Catholic Workers are a utopian anarchist lay organization of pious Catholics unaffiliated with the Roman Catholic Church. They are active in promoting the causes of peace, affordable housing, nonviolence, ecology, social justice, diversity, manual labor, and voluntary poverty. An important component of their beliefs is introspective spirituality, and they sponsor periodic retreats, often in silence, at Peter Maurin Farm, their upstate outpost in Marlboro, New York.

Off-Off-Broadway Theater Row

East 4th Street, between 2nd Avenue and the Bowery

 Duo, 62 East 4th Street (with front exterior circular fire escape)

La Mama Experimental Theater Club, 66 East 4th Street

New York Theatre Workshop, 79 East 4th Street

The Theater Red Room, 85 East 4th Street

Scores of experimental theater groups in various incarnations have thrived on this block for fifty years. The theaters are intimate and the tickets are inexpensive. The theaters provide thespians with the opportunity to act in serious, often experimental plays.

Former Site of Ratner's Kosher Dairy Restaurant

111 2nd Avenue, between East 6th and 7th Streets

Now a Met Food grocery store, Ratner's was a popular hangout for the Beats in the 1950s and the hippies in the 1960s. Bill Graham's Fillmore East, often the scene of Grateful Dead, Jefferson Airplane, and Janis Joplin concerts, was next door at 105 2nd Avenue, and after shows, the concert crowd filled up Ratner's tables and booths.

Middle Collegiate Church (Reformed Church in America)

112 2nd Avenue, between East 6th and 7th Streets
212-477-0666

The rough light granite facade cuts a striking figure on 2nd Avenue. This is the former Dutch denomination that was the dominant Protestant religion in New Amsterdam. This building was constructed in 1892, and the diversity-welcoming congregation, which dates from 1628, differs markedly from its earlier restrictive and judgmental Calvinism. A jazz quintet, brass quintet, steel drummers, modern dancers, and gospel choir are frequently featured at informal East Village–style Sunday and holiday services.

Orpheum Theater

126 2nd Avenue, between East 7th Street and St. Mark's Place
212-477-2477

Known for a string of long-running shows such as *Little Shop of Horrors*, Eric Bogosian's shows, and *Stomp*, this small theater, where everyone gets a good seat, has long been a neighborhood favorite for avant-garde fare. In the first half of the nineteenth century, the stretch of 2nd Avenue between East Houston and 14th Streets was called the Jewish Rialto, and in its earlier years, the Orpheum was a Yiddish theater.

Porto Rico Importing Company (since 1907)

40 ½ St. Mark's Place, just east of 2nd Avenue
212-533-1982

The overpowering aroma of a large stock of coffees and teas is the olfactory introduction to this popular shop. Many coffee varieties are sold in four basic categories: with caffeine, without caffeine, flavored, and organic. Coffees range from lightly roasted to dark espresso style, and are sold as whole beans or ground to specification. There is a modest assortment of teas, and the shop sells various coffeemakers, grinders, and filters. Brewed coffee and coffee-based candy is sold at the front counter. Coffeehouses have been associated with the East Village for more than a century. Porto Rico Importing Company gives customers a broad selection of quality beans to brew at home.

Ottendorfer Branch, New York Public Library (originally Freie Bibliothek und Lesehalle)

135 2nd Avenue, between St. Mark's Place and East 9th Street

The German Free Library and Reading Room is magnificently housed in an 1884 edifice made of red brick with imaginative terra-cotta tracery featuring shells and globes to signify armchair travel. It memorialized Oswald Ottendorfer, publisher of the *New-Yorker Staats-Zeitung*, the leading German language newspaper. Today it is a branch of the New York Public Library.

Stuyvesant Polyclinic Hospital (originally Deutsches Poliklinik)

137 2nd Avenue, between East 9th Street and St. Mark's Place

Once the downtown affiliate of the German Hospital (now Lenox Hill Hospital), it is presently affiliated with Cabrini Medical Center. The 1884, red terra-cotta masonry facade has a similar eclectic style as the Ottendorfer Library next door, including head finials of classical figures in medicine: Hippocrates, Celsius, Asclepius, Galen. The name was changed in 1917 at the height of anti-German sentiment at the time the United States entered World War I.

Baczynsky's East Village Ukrainian Meat Market

139 2nd Avenue, between East 9th Street and St. Mark's Place
212-228-5590

This Old World butcher shop was established in 1970 when there were six other Eastern European butcher shops in the East Village. Pork is the specialty at Baczynsky's, especially ham, which is cured on the premises. They also sell beef, lamb, turkey, chicken, and prepared foods: kielbasa, soups, stuffed cabbage, and breads. During Christmas, Easter, and Thanksgiving, the shop is filled with customers.

St. Mark's Church-in-the-Bowery (Episcopal)

At the corner of Stuyvesant Street and 2nd Avenue
(church and cemetery)
212-674-6377

Built on the site of Peter Stuyvesant's private Dutch Reformed chapel, St. Mark's was completed in 1799, with the steeple added in 1828, and the cast-iron portico in 1854. Three different styles (Georgian, Greek Revival, and Federal) work well together to creating a welcome environment that looks like the rural church it once was. Stuyvesant Street was the pathway that led from the Bowery to the governor-general's farm to which he retired when the English captured the colony. From 1647 to 1664, Peter Stuyvesant was governor-general of the Dutch West India Company, which effectively owned the colony of New Netherlands.

After his death in 1672, he was buried under the small chapel, now the site of the much larger present church. His stone bust in the east yard near the portico, carved in 1915, should not be taken as an indication of his place of repose. The plaque affixed to the lower part of the church's schist basement wall indicates Stuyvesant's approximate burial site. Also interred in the west yard is Daniel D. Tompkins, governor of New York State (1807–1813) and vice-president of the United States during the administration of James Monroe (1817–1825). Tompkins bought most of the Stuyvesant estate from the former governor-general's heirs. St. Mark's Church-in-the-Bowery is a functioning Episcopal parish church, though it also serves as a vital community center. Here, in the early part of the twentieth century, Isadora Duncan danced, Carl Sandburg read, and Harry Houdini performed. It became the gravitational core for Beat poets and writers Allen Ginsberg, Lawrence Ferlinghetti, William Burroughs, and Ted Berrigan in the 1950s.

Note: Stuyvesant Street is Manhattan's only street that follows an east-west axis. The numbered east-west streets established by the 1811 grid plan were laid out to follow the geographic positioning of the island, which is closer to northeast-southwest.

Village East Cinema

189 2nd Avenue, at the corner of East 11th Street

Just another movie multiplex now, this neo-Moorish gem was built in 1926 as the Yiddish Art Theater, one of twenty Yiddish theaters once situated on 2nd Avenue. It became an avant-garde center in 1953 when it emerged as the Phoenix Theater. In 1990, it switched to featuring movies.

Restaurant Recommendations

B & H Dairy Restaurant (Kosher Deli)

127 2nd Avenue, between East 7th Street and St. Mark's Place
212-505-8065

This is the last of the 2nd Avenue Jewish Rialto delis. B & H is primarily a counter luncheonette, which has gained fame for its cheap prices and delicious egg creams, which are made with neither eggs nor cream, but with seltzer, chocolate syrup, and milk. Specials include thick Ukrainian style borscht (beet soup with other vegetables and no sour cream), split-pea soup, mushroom and barley soup, cheese or fruit blintzes (rolled crepes), pierogi (dumplings), and stuffed cabbage. The ubiquitous Eastern European dill is added to many dishes in this narrow, nonmeat restaurant.

Ukrainian East Village Restaurant

140 2nd Avenue, between St. Mark's Place and East 9th Streets
212-529-5024

Once you walk through the long, seedy hallway, you enter a cheerfully decorated bit of the old country, in this case Ukraine. Upstairs is the Ukrainian National Home, a retirement facility. The restaurant menu includes some Eastern European specialties like fluffy potato pancakes, large stuffed peppers, pierogi (dumplings), and Hungarian goulash (beef stew).

Otafuku (Japanese)

236 East 9th Street, just west of 2nd Avenue
212-353-8503

This minuscule food preparation place is 80 percent kitchen. It has serving counters on East 9th Street and along a narrow passage, which also manages to squeeze in three stools along a wall-shelf for eating. There are only two available choices and both are Japanese comfort food snacks: takoyaki (octopus balls), made by pouring a liquid paste of flour, finely chopped octopus, ginger, and scallions into round metal molds, and okonomiyaki (pancakes), made of egg batter, shredded cabbage, and meat or seafood. Both are unique and delicious, though takeout is the only way to go. Otafuku is on a block that is known as Little Japan.

Veselka Coffee Shop (Ukrainian)

144 2nd Avenue, at the corner of East 9th Street
212-228-9682

The slogan at Veselka is "Traditional Ukrainian Cooking in a Non-Traditional Setting." That accurately describes the hip restaurant with a loyal clientele of older immigrants as well as young people dressed in black. The traditional food is a broad array of hearty fare from Eastern Europe: tender veal goulash, vegetarian or meat-stuffed (beef and pork) cabbage, cheese blintzes, chicken cutlets, and Ukrainian meatballs (ground beef and pork, onion, mushroom, and egg). There are several vegetarian dishes based on kasha (groats), potatoes, cheese, and sour cream. Lunchtime finds many regulars ordering soups: Ukrainian borscht packed with beans, potatoes, and meat, split pea, lentil, mushroom and barley, chicken, vegetable, and cabbage.

John's Restaurant (Italian)

302 East 12th Street, just off 2nd Avenue
212-475-9531

Established in 1908, John's retains the simple rustic look of a village restaurant in Northern Italy. The food is a combination of spaghetti house standbys and fine roasted meats and cheese sauces from the north. The dark candlelit atmosphere adds to the romanticism. The restaurant is said to have been a favorite of Emma Goldman.

 Walk #4: Walking down 1st Avenue, start at East 5th Street.

9th Precinct Police Station (NYPD)

321 East 5th Street, between 1st and 2nd Avenues
212-477-7811

This stark six-story Greek Revival structure in the center of the block regularly received attention from aficionados of *NYPD Blue*, the television police show centered on the East Village. Only the facade of the building was shown on television, but many of the outside scenes were filmed in the neighborhood. Two large decorative light fixtures flank the entrance. Over the second-story window is a carved marble seal of the City of New York.

Village View Houses

Centered at East 5th Street Walkway, between 1st Avenue and Avenue A

Organized under the Mitchell-Lama Law, the seven large residential towers comprising Village View were built to provide affordable housing for middle-income New Yorkers and to tear down blighted blocks of tenements. This complex stretches from East 3rd to 6th Street between the two avenues. The Mitchell-Lama law, officially called the Limited-Profit Housing Companies Act, was cosponsored by Senator MacNeil Mitchell and Assemblyman Alfred Lama and enacted by the New York state legislature in 1955. Under the law, buildings could be built as landlord-owned rentals or limited-equity cooperatives. Mortgages were obtained with state guarantees in return for Department of Housing Preservation and Development (HPD) control over rental fees or maintenance payments, family composition, and income restrictions on entering. The goal was to coax middle-income New Yorkers to stay in the city when many were fleeing to the suburbs. By 1975, the program ceased to sponsor new buildings but in two decades, it had subsidized the construction of almost 140,000 units, including 15,500 in the enormous Co-op City development in the Bronx.

P.S. 122 Community Center (122CC)

150 1st Avenue at East 9th Street
212-477-5288

This four-story redbrick former public school is now a lively community center. It houses painting studios and performance spaces with dance and theater offerings.

Coyote Ugly (Bar)

153 1st Avenue, between East 9th and 10th Streets
212-477-4431

The movie *Coyote Ugly* ostensibly took place in this bar, but the real place looks nothing like the glitzy movie location. The inside is a no-frills dark, dingy, austere tavern. The blaring jukebox, dart games, and barmaids dancing on top of the bar late at night enliven this saloon. A lot of hard drinking goes on at Coyote Ugly, which tries very hard to live up to its name.

Theater for the New City

155 1st Avenue, between East 9th and 10th Streets
212-254-1109

Located in the former First Avenue Retail Market building where Mayor La Guardia banished neighborhood pushcarts in 1938, the Theater for the New City regularly produces Off-Off Broadway plays. In 2001, a large private residential tower was built over the city-owned property, protecting its Depression Era facade.

Russian & Turkish Baths

268 East 10th Street, between 1st Avenue and Avenue A
212-473-8806

Located in a brownstone on a residential block, and re-creating a ritual from an earlier time, this bath is unique in Manhattan, though new ones have opened in Queens. *Schvitzers* have patronized this establishment since it opened in 1892. There are still Eastern Europeans in the neighborhood, but now with five out of seven days coed (bathing suits, of course), the old-time Lower East Siders may not recognize it. Except for a few snacks and drinks, hot water and steam are the only commodities here. And then there's the Russian rub, a kind of beating with oak-leaf brooms and dousing with buckets of cold water after the steam room. This is heaven for the pores.

Russo & Son Groceries (Italian)

344 East 11th Street, just west of 1st Avenue
212-254-7452

This friendly hole-in-the-wall grocery is the place to come for reasonably priced Italian breads and a large selection of prepared pastas. Russo's squeezes in many Italian specialties: cheeses, hams, sausages, olive oils, capers, anchovies, dry pastas, and tomato sauces. It served the Italian community here beginning in 1909, but has adapted to its disappearance and does a zesty business.

Veniero's Pasticceria

342 East 11th Street, just west of 1st Avenue
212-674-7070

In this sleek, flashy pastry store there is table service as well as a counter takeout area. Brightly colored Italian butter cookies, cannolis, cream puffs, cheesecakes, and Napoleons bring customers from near and far. The favorite takeout item is a box of your choice of about twenty varieties of bite-size mini-pastries. The remodeled interior cloaks the 1894 founding date of Veniero's Pasticceria.

Restaurant Recommendations

La Palapa (Mexican)

77 St. Mark's Place, just west of 1st Avenue
212-777-2537

This creative Mexican bistro has a number of startlingly good dishes: cod with green pumpkin-seed sauce, barbecued lamb shanks, and chicken simmered with chiles and avocado leaves. The cellar once contained the office of *Novy Mir* (New World), a Russian émigré newspaper edited by Leon Trotsky and Nikolai Bukharin. (Trotsky was staying in the Bronx between January and March 1917.) Since the 1980s, the Mexican presence in New York City has grown appreciably, though not so much in the East Village. Mexican restaurants, however, have become commonplace.

National Café (Spanish Caribbean)

210 1st Avenue, between East 12th and 13th Streets
212-473-9354

Large flags of the Dominican Republic, Puerto Rico, and Cuba decorate the front window of the National Café. Diminutive but boisterous and friendly, National Café serves several meat and fish platters, green and yellow plantains, and nine different varieties of soup. The house specialty is the Cuban sandwich: ham, Swiss cheese, mortadella, mustard, and pickles pressed in something that resembles a waffle iron so that the sandwich's four sides are sealed.

First Houses (New York City Housing Authority)

*Along Avenue A between 2nd and 3rd Streets and around the corner on
3rd Street between 1st Avenue and Avenue A*

Often considered the most agreeable looking and best-designed public
housing project in the city, First Houses is noted for its small scale and
airy feeling. Each building is only four stories high with walkway spaces
and an open area in the rear. They were constructed in 1935 during the
Depression out of the shells of previously gutted tenements. First Houses
represents the resourcefulness of the La Guardia mayoral administration,
which quickly provided 122 modern apartments with central heating
costing six dollars per room each month. The low-rise building fit in with
the look of the neighborhood.

Most Holy Redeemer Church (Roman Catholic)

173 East 3rd Street, between Avenue A and Avenue B
212-673-4224

This was the tallest building in the neighborhood until the Village View
Houses were constructed. The eclectic limestone building, German
Rococo (which looks part Romanesque and part Baroque), was at first
home to a congregation of German Catholics organized in 1852 by
Redemptorist priests. (Eighty-five Redemptorists are buried in the church
crypt.) The present building dates from the 1870s. The inside has a
spacious nave with several Corinthian columns supporting a vaulted
ceiling. Vivid stained-glass windows allow light to flood the church. To the
right of the altar stands an ornate tomb, which is the reliquary for the
remains of St. Datian, a martyred Roman soldier so obscure as to be
missing from most hagiographies. A large crucifix and painted statues of
the Three Marys on Golgotha dominate the area behind the high altar.
Trompe l'oeil panels cover the front wall space and ceiling. Along the
sides, white marble bas-relief Stations of the Cross are set off by a blue
Wedgwood-like background. The pews are slightly elevated on four-inch

raised wooden platforms to insulate feet from cold floors in winter, as is commonly done in many churches in Germany and Poland.

Tompkins Square Park
Bounded by Avenues A and B, and 7th and 10th Streets

This park was initially an empty square used by Long Island farmers as a market. Daniel D. Tompkins, governor of New York State (1807–1813) and vice-president of the United States during the administration of James Monroe (1817–1825), owned the land. A major landowner and developer, Tompkins owned the land from 2nd Avenue to the East River. The park is named for him. As the square evolved into a park, it became a natural meeting place for New Americans. The encounters were not always friendly; ethnic and block turf wars were often played out in the park. Tompkins Square Park became the rallying point for the nineteenth-century labor movement. In January 1874, it was the site of the first labor demonstration in New York City, which was organized by the International Workingmen's Association (or First International), a group with headquarters in London that was set up by Karl Marx. The police attacked the workers and the Tompkins Square Riot ensued. (By the 1920s, Union Square usurped the role as the labor movement's rallying place.) In the 1960s, Tompkins Square Park became a center of radical activities: rallies against the war in Vietnam, marijuana smoke-ins, and concerts by the Fugs, Country Joe and the Fish, and the Grateful Dead. From 1988 until 1991, it was the scene of violent confrontations between police and squatters who had constructed shacks in the park. The struggle pitted the remnants of the hippie subculture and some of their neighborhood allies against the first wave of gentrification. Anti-gentrification graffiti was an upended martini glass with a slash through it and the inclusion of the ominous date 1933, the year Hitler assumed power in Germany. The NYPD and the Yuppies won. The squatters were removed, the park was closed and renovated, and by the time it reopened in 1993, the Yuppies were moving into the East Village, driving up rents, and opening Tuscan restaurants.

Temperance Fountain
West center section of Tompkins Square Park

Hebe at the Well, a zinc representation of the perpetually youthful daughter of Hera and Zeus, the cupbearer of the Greek gods, who provided them with nectar as well as ambrosia, stands on a three-tiered buffed granite canopy supported by four polished granite columns. Under the canopy is a water fountain, undoubtedly a service to the public, but also an advertisement for sobriety. To further drive home the point to the thirsty passerby who may miss the symbolism, the four entablatures carved in raised, upper case lettering call out: FAITH, HOPE, CHARITY, TEMPERANCE. Where did they get the slogan? St. Paul, in his letter to the Corinthians in the Christian Bible's New Testament, wrote:

> And now abideth faith, hope, charity, these three; but the greatest of these is charity. (1 Cor. 13:13 KJV)

It seems the temperance people sneaked in a fourth virtue. The placement of Hebe in Tompkins Square Park in 1888 was a calculated gauntlet thrown down by Henry Cogswell, a San Francisco dentist and temperance advocate, who commissioned and donated the statue. The park was the focal point of the northern segment of the Lower East Side, a working-class neighborhood of Germans, Russians, Poles, and Ukrainians that was filled with saloons. Each year, a week-long festival of public merrymaking, the Volksfest, was centered at this park. The residents ignored the sententious challenge and the statue still stands. But the area, known as the East Village since the 1960s, has one or two bars on every block.

General Slocum Ship Disaster Memorial
North center section of Tompkins Square Park

A modest stele of light granite, eight feet high with a bas-relief of two children looking wistfully into emptiness, and a lion's-head spigot and fountain, the monument memorializes the salient disaster for the area's German community, the burning and sinking of the paddle-wheel excursion vessel with 1,021 passengers aboard as it headed toward the Bronx for a picnic outing in 1904.

Dog Run (with bone carving)

East center section of Tompkins Square Park

The park has a well-used fenced-off dog run, which keeps canines out of the rest of the park and allows their owners time to socialize. A nine-foot-high tree stump carved by an anonymous folk sculptor into a vertical dog bone stands in the center. Cute.

St. Nicholas of Myra Church (Orthodox)

288 East 10th Street, at the corner of Avenue A
212-254-6685

The impressive 1883 redbrick Gothic Revival building was once an outreach chapel of St. Mark's Church-in-the-Bowery (Episcopal). It has a beautiful new iconostasis (icon screen) inside partially separating the sanctuary from the nave. The corner sign lists the official name as St. Nicholas Carpatho-Russian Greek Catholic Church. To the uninitiated, it appears to be Orthodox and Catholic, Carpatho-Russian and Greek all at the same time. In fact, that is true: Catholic in the sense of being universal, Greek in the shared Orthodox tradition brought to the Slavic lands from Greece, and Carpatho-Russian denoting the mountain people in eastern Slovakia, Ruthenia, southeastern Poland (Galicia), and far western Ukraine who are usually called Lemkos. Ecclesiastically, this church is affiliated with the Orthodox Church of America.

11th Street Bar

510 East 11th Street, just east of Avenue A
212-982-3929

A fine example of an East Village neighborhood bar stands 150 feet east of 1st Avenue. The bar manages to be a popular gathering place for numerous affinity groups who enjoy one another's company. It has dark wood furniture, exposed brick walls, tasteful music, subdued lighting, and an extended happy hour. The beer and cider menu is large, snacks include sandwiches and Tayto Crisps, televisions are turned on only for the occasional Liverpool football match or important American game. Most evenings, the spacious back room has scheduled bands. Sunday is traditional Irish seisún, and Monday is jazz night.

Restaurant Recommendations

Two Boots (a fusion restaurant teaching a geography lesson)

37 Avenue A, between East 2nd and 3rd Streets
212-505-2276

This is a culinary fusion restaurant based on the vaguely similar boot-like geography of Italy and Louisiana. Most of the dishes come in pure form, such as popular Italian dishes; others are creatively syncretic mixtures, such as Cajun-style pizza with barbecued shrimp and crayfish or New Orleans andouille (sausage). Two Boots is a particularly child-friendly establishment, which is something unique in the area.

 Walk #6: Going down Avenue B, start at East 6th Street.

Sixth Street & B Community Garden

Southwest corner of Avenue B and East 6th Street

The tall rickety forty-foot tower, the logo of this garden, was featured on the opening credits of *NYPD Blue*. It is a masterpiece of countercultural junk art. The jerry-built wood tower, part Sumerian ziggurat and part Christmas tree, was decorated with hanging bongo drums, teddy bears, dolls, flags, one camel, and several horses. The tower was dismantled in 2008. Throughout the garden is a maze of pleasant paths and seating for visitors. Sixth Street & B Community Garden is known for frequent concerts, workshops, and festivals.

Apartment House (originally Newsboys' and Bootblacks' Lodging House, or Tompkins Square Lodging House for Boys and Industrial School, Children's Aid Society)

127 Avenue B, at the corner of East 8th Street

One of many private, charity-operated shelters for children, it was run by the Protestant-dominated Children's Aid Society founded in 1887 by Charles Loring Brace. He eventually determined that an Emigration Plan would be a better way of handling the surfeit of orphans or runaways in

New York City and other large metropolitan areas. Orphan Trains sponsored by Brace and other groups, such as the Catholic-run Foundling Hospital, sent 250,000 children to Upstate New York and points far to the west to be taken in and sometimes adopted.

Apartment House (originally Christadora House)
143 Avenue B, at the corner of East 9th Street

Formerly a settlement house built in 1928, the Christadora originally contained a concert hall, which was part of the effort of reformers to uplift the culture of the poor. The building is still the tallest in the area and towers over the Tompkins Square Park. The large brick building is architecturally unexceptional except for a few touches of elegant neoclassical and art deco design.

 Walk #7: Walking down Avenue C, start at East 4th Street.

Modestly developed commercially, Avenue C has Chinese takeout storefronts, dry cleaners, car services, hair stylists, small bodegas (grocery stores), and candy stores accompanying large housing project buildings, and nondescript five- and six-story apartment buildings along its fourteen-block stretch. There is one interesting old church on East 4th Street and three community gardens of note.

San Isidoro y San Leandro Church (Western Orthodox Catholic Church of the Hispanic Mozarbic Rite)
345 East 4th Street, between Avenue C and Avenue D
212-673-0785

This 1895 row house was once a Russian Orthodox church. It is now a private chapel owned by a priest formerly affiliated with the Orthodox Church of America. The sign over the west door on the front reads MONASTERIO. Nonetheless, it is unaffiliated.

All People's Garden

315 East 4th Street, between Avenue C and Avenue D

Here, another neighborhood group took advantage of the removal of decrepit buildings and landscaped a humble community park. Under a fluttering Puerto Rican flag stands a casita, a little shack for off-hours gathering times, a common sight in Puerto Rico.

La Plaza Cultural Garden

Southwest corner of Avenue C and East 9th Street

This is a particularly large and uncluttered community garden with open spaces where dancing takes place and plays are performed. Steel half-barrels have been set up for holiday barbecues. The fence around the park is a design element of note. It is topped with scores of colorful metal pinwheels.

Ninth Street Community Garden and Park

Northeast corner of Avenue C and East 9th Street

This active community group keeps a welcome and large funky green spot open. They also sponsor art shows and movies during fair-weather months.

Restaurant Recommendations

Casa Adela (Puerto Rican)

66 Avenue C, between East 4th Street and 5th Street
212-473-1882

The powerful mixed aroma of pork, garlic, and adobo (Hispanic all-purpose seasoning) fill the air of Casa Adela, a tiny humble pregentrification restaurant serving large portions of Puerto Rican, Dominican, and Cuban foods. Pernil asado (roast pork) and barbecued chicken are full of flavor and come with mounds or rice and beans or richly flavored tostones (fried plantains). A real surprise and a treat is the tender octopus salad. The diners are all neighbors and there is a lot of talking from table to table.

Zum Schneider (German)

107 Avenue C, at the corner of East 7th Street

212-598-1098

This Bavarian restaurant is a reminder of Kleindeutschland days when the neighborhood sported many German eating and drinking establishments. Zum Schneider's is a very new restaurant, catering to a young crowd interested in socializing to the background of hip-hop music from the jukebox. Nonetheless, the table and bench seating and timbered walls evoke a Bavarian setting. The choices for dinner include the traditional three-sausage platter (weisswurst, bauernwurst, and wiener), pork chops, and roast chicken. Sweet cabbage, dumplings, and potatoes accompany almost all dishes. The smoky bar serves two dozen German beers, each in the appropriate style glass.

 Walk #8: Walk down Avenue D.

The entire east side of Avenue D from Houston Street to the Con Ed generating plant at East 13th Street is taken up by the well-maintained but very institutional edifices of the New York City Housing Authority grouped into two complexes: Lillian Wald Houses to the south and Jacob Riis Houses to the north. The area where the housing projects were built was previously occupied by several blocks of dreary tenements, warehouses, and commercial riverfront buildings. Lillian Wald was a whirlwind of social reform, and lived in New York City from 1889 until 1933. She founded the Henry Street Settlement House and successfully worked for reforms in health care, education, recreation, housing, and industrial safety. Jacob Riis was a social reformer who publicized problems with his photojournalism, especially *How the Other Half Lives* (1890). Both Wald and Riis were active in the Lower East Side. The west side of Avenue D is unexceptional, filled with vest-pocket-sized bodegas, a supermarket, several delis, and Chinese takeout restaurants.

BROOKLYN

BRIGHTON BEACH

Odessa by the Sea

Brighton Beach became a popular destination for New Yorkers soon after Coney Island achieved prominence as a recreational center. While Coney Island specialized in entertainment, Brighton Beach became home to resorts and family beach houses. The classy block-long Hotel Brighton opened in 1878, followed by a racetrack, music hall, and dance hall. In 1907, the Brighton Beach Baths opened, signaling an ethnic shift to Eastern European Jewish vacationers. The area was filled with summer cottages, most just three or four blocks from the ocean.

In the 1920s, residents winterized and enlarged the small beach houses. In addition, six-story apartment buildings were constructed, and the summer community became a year-round predominantly Jewish neighborhood. After World War II, the area went into a slow, steady decline. By 1970, many stores had closed, crime had soared, and the entire area had become a slum.

During the 1970s, Brighton Beach was reinvigorated when thousands of Soviet Jews (Refuseniks) came to New York City and settled in the area, attracted by its cheap rents, comparatively spacious old apartments, and proximity to the Atlantic Ocean. Their presence is announced by the shops, which cater to Russian tastes and styles and advertise wares in Cyrillic-lettered signs. In the 2000 census, Russians numbered 130,000 in New York City, officially the second largest immigrant group after Dominicans. They live in scattered neighborhoods in Brooklyn and Queens, but their best-known destination is Brighton Beach.

Little Odessa, so named because a large proportion of the Russian Jews came from Odessa, a Black Sea city in southern Ukraine, remains a nickname for Brighton Beach; but increasingly, new immigrants are arriving from Georgia, Kazakhstan, Tadzhikistan, and Uzbekistan.

Economic renewal for Coney Island and Brighton Beach has been spearheaded by the Russian immigration, artists moving into Coney Island in the 1980s, the recent construction of the Brooklyn Cyclones' stadium, and an upper-middle-class condominium complex called Oceana.

Walking Trip in Brighton Beach

Take the Q train to Brighton Beach Station. Walk east along Brighton Beach Avenue; or by car, take the Belt Parkway (Shore Parkway), and exit southward at Ocean Parkway. Or drive south through Brooklyn on Ocean Parkway to Brighton Beach Avenue.

Walk east along Brighton Beach Avenue under the El.

Mother Jones Apartment Building

3102–3116 Brighton 1st Place, just south of Brighton Beach Avenue

The name of this six-story brown brick apartment building is a testament to the socialist politics of many Eastern European Jews at the turn of the last century. The Irish-born labor leader, fiery orator, and political activist Mary Harris Jones (1830–1930), affectionately called Mother Jones, led a campaign against child labor and was an organizer for the coal mine and textile unions.

Classic Furs Galleria

221 Brighton Beach Avenue at Brighton 1st Road
718-332-5138

The streets of Brighton Beach are filled with fur-clad women (and some men) shopping and promenading during the winter months. Russian émigrés opt for furs because they are warm, last many years, and afford prestige to their owners. The status factor comes from Russia, where mink, ermine, sable, and chinchilla have long been associated with success. Lower on the ladder are coats and hats made from Persian lamb, fox, rabbit, and nutria. Classic Furs offers a broad selection of furs to an eager clientele.

Russian Books & Gifts Store

230 Brighton Beach Avenue, between Brighton 1st Road and Brighton 1st Place
718-891-6778

This store carries Russian novels, nonfiction books, and books for children, along with travel guides, study guides, newspapers, and a few greeting cards. It also sells children's clothing and Russian music and gifts.

M & I International Food

249 Brighton Beach Avenue, between Brighton 1st Place and Brighton 2nd Street
718-615-1011

This very large combination supermarket-delicatessen-bakery sells breads, smoked fish, caviar, pickles, sausage, and large selections of smoked meats, canned goods, and fruit juices and syrups. Deli specialties are shish kebabs, blintzes, potato pancakes, fried fish, and stuffed cabbage. There is also a large stock of Russian, Polish, and Czech beer.

Vintage

287 Brighton Beach Avenue, between Brighton 2nd Street and Brighton 3rd Street
718-769-6674

This Turkish sweetshop merchant offers dried fruits, candy, juices, syrups, and just about every product made with sugar. For good measure, Vintage also sells nuts and eight varieties of sunflower seeds. Homemade pomegranate, peach, and apricot juice is served from large vats.

Russian Favorite Gifts

292 Brighton Beach Avenue, between Brighton 2nd Street and Brighton 3rd Street
718-891-0719

Leather jackets are the main item at Russian Favorite Gifts, but the store also carries the usual Russian souvenirs: matryoshka dolls, enameled boxes, amber jewelry, and wooden spoons.

Sea Lane of Odessa Bakery

615 Brighton Beach Avenue, between Brighton 6th Street and Brighton 7th Street
718-934-9977

"Sweet" and "heavy" describe Russian desserts: strudel, cookies, cakes, sponge cake, buns, loaves of mandel bread (almond bread biscotti), and fruit-filled tarts. Breads are generally *bielo* (white), but they also make *chorny* (black) and braided challah.

 Turn right (south) on Coney Island Avenue one block and walk east on the Boardwalk.

Former Site of Brighton Beach Baths

Southeast corner of Coney Island Avenue and Brighton Beach Avenue at the Boardwalk

This was a sprawling lower-middle-class club, opened in 1907, which eschewed golf for urban specialties such as handball, table tennis, shuffleboard, basketball, volleyball, Ping-Pong, mah-jongg, and card games. Now, as Oceana, it is an immense 850-apartment condominium complex of several substantial buildings.

Boardwalk

The Boardwalk at Brighton Beach is the preeminent gathering place for immigrants from the former Soviet Union. Full-figured strollers and sunbathers go back and forth or just sit and take in the rays. There are three restaurants along the Boardwalk with outdoor eating areas. The broad sand beach is just down a flight of stairs.

 Turn left (north) on Brighton 15th Street one block, left again (west) on Brighton Beach Avenue.

Odessa Gastronom

1117 Brighton Beach Avenue, between Brighton 14th and
Brighton 13th Streets
718-332-3223

Gastronom means grocery store in Russian. Each Brighton Beach gastronom is more like a deli than a grocery store, but the name from the old country has stuck. Historically, Russian gastronoms had sparse shelves and post-1991 gastronoms were often foreign-owned and carried very expensive goods from Italy, the Netherlands, Germany, and Scandinavia. In this neighborhood, the prices are reasonable and the traditional foods are stacked everywhere and overflowing from the deli counters. Some Russian-style products, primarily the prepared foods, are made in the United States, but most goods are imported from Poland, Ukraine, Georgia, Romania, Bulgaria, with a few from Russia. The meat counter is laden with prepared meats: breaded and fried duck legs, roasted pork knuckles, and lamb kebabs. Sausages hang down from above. There is a large cheese counter where various types of pastries are stuffed with cheeses, mostly forms of farmer cheese. The fish section carries traditional Russian *farshirovannaya ryba* (gefilte fish or stuffed fish), not the elongated, sad little blobs swimming in gelatin found in American stores. True to its name, which means refilled fish, the fish meat is removed, mixed with egg white, spices, and a dash of sugar, then stuffed back into the skin of the carp or whitefish from which it came.

M & A Liquors & Wine

1109 Brighton Beach Avenue, between Brighton 14th and
Brighton 13th Streets
718-332-3502

Very polite bilingual clerks will help locate the appropriate bottle from their large selection of flavorful Georgian and Moldovian reds and whites; fruity wines from all over; dry (not very) Sovietskiy Champanskiy from Ukraine, Georgia, and Moldova; and every imaginable variety of vodka and brandy.

Golden Key (Zolotoy Kluchnik)

1067 Brighton Beach Avenue, at the corner of Brighton 12th Street
718-743-5841

This gastronom is so busy that it needs two cashier windows near the front door to sell goods stacked along the sidewalk. Russian cereals and Eastern European fruit juices and syrups are sold near the front. They have bottled kvass, a Russian near beer made of slightly fermented stale bread and raisins. The cheese counter offers smetana, delicious, fatty Russian sour cream. Sausages and prepared meats come in many varieties. The fish section has mostly dried and smoked fish, but regularly carries caviar and sturgeon as well.

Restaurant Recommendations

Russian cuisine is not the world's best developed, and most of the restaurants and cafés offer plates of desiccated smoked fish, tasteless caviar, and pickled vegetables to be washed down with vodka and cloyingly sweet wine. Many of the nightclubs set the tables before the guests arrive with plates and utensils as well as the first course of food, as is customary in Russia. Inexpensive American vodka, seltzer, and Coke come with the meal. The first course is fish and vegetables, usually cucumbers; then the large carbohydrate pot arrives filled with various forms of potatoes, followed in quick succession by various cheap cuts of roast meat and stuffed cabbage. Best bet is to eschew the Russian restaurants and go to the places specializing in food from other regions in the former Soviet Union.

Café Glechik (Russian and Ukrainian)

3159 Coney Island Avenue, half a block north of Brighton Beach Avenue
718-616-0494

This cozy restaurant, an exception to the above rule, succeeds because it does not attempt haute cuisine but serves simple peasant fare, most of it baked in crocks or deep dishes. *Glechik* is the Ukrainian word for crockery pot. The rabbit stew is served in a sweet cream sauce, the sweetened stuffed cabbage is covered with thick sour cream, the pork shoulder is robust and tangy, and the garlicky kulesh (dilled mushroom and barley soup) is full flavored and tender. Delicious pelemeni (dumplings) are available stuffed with potato, cabbage, meat, or farmer cheese. Soups include borscht and chicken soup. Café Glechik is decorated with peasant wood carvings, embroidered cloth, and braids of dried onions. There are no alcoholic beverages, but they offer kvass (fermented bread and raisin drink), compote (thick homemade fruit juice), seltzer, soft drinks, and tea.

Chio Pio (Uzbek)
3087 Brighton 4th Street, just south of Brighton Beach Avenue
718-615-9221

This inexpensive hole-in-the-wall has only five tables and an ad hoc decor that includes giant posters of Hawaii and copper plates showing medieval scenes from Western Europe. The food, though, is Central Asian. Several salads are available; all are large and tasty. Uzbekistan salad has shredded lettuce and carrots with cheeses, olives, and basturma (julienned meat). Lamb dishes are infused with green onions and dill—the delicious lamb samsa is a larger version of an Indian samosa with a good measure of cumin mixed in. Kebabs are plentiful and can be beef, chicken, lamb, and pork. Plov (rice pilaf with chickpeas, onion, cumin, and beef) is a specialty. Green tea comes in large teapots, while smaller teapots are used for pouring vodka into large-size shot glasses.

Volna Restaurant & Café
Boardwalk at 3145 Brighton 4th Street
718-332-0341

The view of the Atlantic Ocean is extraordinary from the outdoor tables set up at the edge of the Boardwalk. People-watching alone can keep you in your seat for a couple of stiff vodkas.

Nightclubs

Participating in the live-music nightclubs of Brighton Beach is an activity for those who want to experience gulianka: joyful dancing, singing, eating, drinking, and laughing. The *praznichno* (festive) atmosphere provides a peerless window into Russian émigré culture. You need to make reservations and pay in advance. The price covers the family-style food, drink, and merriment. Car services hover near the door at evening's end to get you home safely.

National
273 Brighton Beach Avenue
718-646-1225

Velvet Rope Lounge
273 Brighton Beach Avenue
347-554-8511

> **Detour:** Sheepshead Bay Dockside—continue eastward on Boardwalk, turn left (north) on Brighton 15th Street one block, turn right (east) one block to Corbin Place. Turn left (north) on Corbin Place, two blocks to Cass Place-Shore Boulevard in Manhattan Beach. Turn right (east) at Shore Boulevard for six short blocks, then turn left (north) and cross the footbridge over Sheepshead Bay. Turn right (east) on Emmons Avenue.

Piers 1–10
The docks in Sheepshead Bay are home to several party boats for half-day or full-day fishing trips on the Atlantic Ocean. Some of the lucky members of fishing parties who catch more than they want sell their fish, usually bluefish, striped bass, or porgies, to passersby from the docks. The area was named for sheepshead, a fish, now rare, that received the odd name because its teeth actually resemble those of a sheep.

Site of Lundy's Seafood Restaurant and Oyster Bar
1901 Emmons Avenue at Ocean Avenue

As Nathan's is in Coney Island, this was the famous eatery in Sheepshead Bay, a reminder of the days *When Brooklyn Was the World, 1920–1957*, as author Elliot Willensky put it. Since 1928, it was a valued destination in itself. But much has changed since a family feud closed the cavernous three-thousand-seat, pink terra-cotta Spanish Mission–style establishment in 1979. Formerly, there was no one to seat customers, and the waiters stood at the front entrance area in a cacophonous gaggle, loudly vying to get your business. If you agreed, one walked you over to his group of tables. Truncated into a much smaller and more subdued dining room for 730, it reopened as part of a mall in 1996. Lundy's magnificent oyster bar retained its vaulted ceiling and long wooden bar, which gave a romantic feeling of Old Brooklyn. Despite remodeling, Lundy's managed to keep a little of the Casablanca look in the dining room thanks to its high ceiling, very slowly revolving fans, stucco walls, palm plants, and shaded wall sconces. Failure to pay New York State taxes closed the restaurant in 2003.

Restaurant Recommendation

Randazzo's Clam Bar
2017 Emmons Avenue at East 21st Street
718-615-0010

Eating while enveloped in the ocean air seems entirely appropriate. This is a lively, informal restaurant with a broad offering of Italian comfort food with an accent on seafood, especially shellfish. Clam linguine is a favorite.

CONEY ISLAND

Popular Playground

Coney Island and Brighton Beach share an island and are beachfront communities, but they have developed in very different ways. Canarsie American Indians set up summer villages here to reap the gifts of the sea: hand-plucked oysters, clams, mussels, crabs, and lobsters. The Dutch called the sand spit at the southern end of Brooklyn Konijn Eisland (Rabbit Island) because of the immense rabbit population.

By 1830, there were already inns and resorts opening in the sea-swept area. Entertainment became a specialty of Coney Island and carousels, roller coasters, bars, brothels, gambling, and more innocent games of chance sprouted along the beachfront. Mixed bathing became popular on the beach. Eventually, this all merged into the peculiarly American phenomenon called the amusement park.

Railroads and trolleys, as always, facilitated development. After the Civil War, commuter railroad lines were built from Downtown Brooklyn to Coney Island. The Brighton, Culver, Sea Beach, and West End lines made it easier to spend a day (or week) at the beach. In the 1920s, the private railroad and subway company Brooklyn Manhattan Transit (BMT) bought out the railroads and integrated them into its new mass transportation system. (Later, the BMT, the Interboro Rapid Transit system, and the municipal Independent line were merged to form the Metropolitan Transit Authority, New York City's subway and bus system.)

By 1904, developers had erected three large amusement parks along Surf Avenue near the beach: Steeplechase Park, Luna Park, and Dreamland were three private and separate components of Coney Island with independent amusements sandwiched between them. The Steeplechase Race featured mechanical horses carrying customers around a track. Luna Park was a fairyland with a million incandescent bulbs outlining spires, minarets, and domes. The show *Its Trip to the Moon* featured an imaginary space ride. Dreamland promoted civic improvement, and its serene, spacious grounds mirrored the City Beautiful movement. A popular show at Dreamland was *Fighting Flames*, where a fake tenement fire was put out and women and children saved by an imitation fire department. It also featured replicas and murals of famous Western European tourist spots.

In 1910, small communities of year-round residents appeared, primarily Irish, Italians, and Jews. A decade later, both Coney Island and Brighton Beach developed sizable populations that stayed through the winter. The heyday of Coney Island was from 1900 until World War II. Afterward, general prosperity beckoned Brooklynites to Queens, Long Island, Staten Island, and New Jersey for recreation and often residency. From the record high attendance on July 4, 1947, when an estimated 2.5 million people packed Coney Island, the number of visitors dwindled as the electric age matured and the electronic age dawned, automobiles made transportation easy, and modern theme parks sprouted around the country. The Coney Island style of amusement park entertainment became outdated and hokey.

Eventually, the pervasive tackiness and seediness became part of the attraction. Surf Avenue, the main drag, was filled with tumbled-down buildings, street-level food and entertainment concessions, and rooming houses on the top floors. The movie *Went to Coney Island on a Mission from God* (1998), which portrays sad losers who inhabit the area and work at the concessions, gives an idea of the underside of the neighborhood. The three large amusement parks are gone, though much of their space is filled with new rides and amusements. Dreamland burned in 1911, Luna Park burned in 1944, and Steeplechase Park closed quietly in 1964. In the 1990s, a new Boardwalk was built with new comfort stations. Many of the old buildings in the entertainment area were demolished and new ones erected. Still, no one would ever confuse Coney Island with Disney World, Hershey Park, or a Six Flags venue.

Like comfort food, Coney Island has a timeless familiarity with its comfort games and comfort rides, the ocean, and the ageless Boardwalk. Whether in youth you visited it once or a hundred times, the cozy feeling always returns. Brooklyn is the most romantic borough, and Coney Island is a chief icon of Brooklyn romanticism.

Walking Trip Through Coney Island

Take the D, F, N, or Q train to Coney Island-Stillwell Avenue Station. By car, take the Belt Parkway (Shore Parkway) and exit southward at Coney Island Avenue. Or drive south through Brooklyn on Coney Island Avenue, Ocean Parkway, McDonald Avenue-Shell Road, or Stillwell Avenue to Surf Avenue.

Note: If you take the D train (West End Line), you pass through the immense Coney Island Subway Yard and over Coney Island Creek, which once (even before the Dutch colonial period) stretched the dozen blocks to connect with Sheepshead Bay, making Coney Island a real island.

Walk south toward the ocean from the corner of Stillwell Avenue and Surf Avenue (the center of Coney Island) to the Boardwalk. On the Boardwalk, first turn right (west) on the Boardwalk to West 21st Street, then reverse directions, walking east, and meander along the walkway until you reach the New York Aquarium at West 9th Street.

Boardwalk

Parallel with the beach about one hundred yards inland

The famous Boardwalk was built in 1923 by New York City and stretches four miles from Brighton Beach to Sea Gate. It is fifty feet wide, built just off the ground, and constructed of wooden planks placed in a zigzag pattern. Officially called the Riegelmann Boardwalk for Brooklyn borough president Edward Riegelmann, it was originally limited to Coney Island. In 1939, parks commissioner Robert Moses extended it through Brighton Beach. Along its north side range many commercial establishments, and toward the east are a few basketball, paddleball, and handball courts. Full sensory entertainment is provided in the summer by the rides and the shrieking laughter of their passengers, the food smells, the competing carnival music, the pitch of hawkers, and the beautiful Atlantic Ocean with a broad sand beach and a multitude of frolicking, tanning, and swimming New Yorkers. Above, small planes pull advertisements through the air. In the winter, an eerie sense of solitude pervades the nearly empty Boardwalk.

Food Concessions
Sprinkled everywhere along the Boardwalk and elsewhere

Food and drink are available from a host of boardwalk shops and kiosks where you can satiate yourself on any number of traditional beach specialties. Gird your stomach for the assault of grease and salt from fried clams, onion rings, Italian sausage, pizza, hamburgers, french fries, hot dogs, and corn on the cob, which rotate endlessly on warming machines. Dessert could be ice cream or dyed cotton candy. The treeless beach and entertainment area is hot. To wash down the oily snacks and assuage summertime thirst, a wide variety of sodas, both national brands and Brooklyn favorites, is available: Yoo-hoo Chocolate Drink, Manhattan Special Espresso Coffee Soda (produced on Manhattan Avenue in Greenpoint, Brooklyn), international brands like Coca-Cola, and Dr. Brown's Cel-Ray, Black Cherry, or Cream Soda. (The Havemeyer Sugar Refinery in Williamsburg, Brooklyn, was the largest refinery in the world at the turn of the last century. Brooklyn became home to numerous soft drink companies.)

Brooklyn Cyclones
Boardwalk Entrance at West 17th Street (main entrance at Surf Avenue, between West 16th and West 18th Streets)

The new $40 million Keyspan Park (2001) for one of the Class A farm teams of the New York Mets is a small, comfortable stadium with a capacity of eight thousand, intimate enough to see clearly from any location. With a keen eye on the past, the team's logo is a nostalgic Brooklyn Dodgers–like white B and an interlocked bright red C. The Baby Bums brought some semblance of the game back to Brooklyn forty-four years after Walter O'Malley took the Dodgers to Los Angeles. The ball field, first named for Keyspan, is now called MCU Park. It is a concoction of metal, glass, and tile, part 1960s and part postmodern. An angular fiberglass canopy covers some of the bleacher seats. The animated crowd is all Brooklyn. The fans dance in the aisles when "Saturday Night Fever" is played on the loudspeaker. Don't let the skyboxes fool you: this is local baseball. The outfield advertising boards tout Brooklyn patrons: L & B Spumoni Gardens, Midwood Appliances, Sal's Transmissions, and

Riviera—only One Wedding at a Time. The team, of course, is named for the roller coaster. Coney Island was always risqué, even sleazy, and the Cyclones are meant to sanitize the neighborhood, the way Manhattan's 42nd Street was cleaned up. That doesn't mean it will happen. Coney Island always appealed to the newest immigrants and to fans of nostalgia, and sanitization of the area is very low on their agenda.

Parachute Jump
Boardwalk at West 17th Street

Abandoned when Steeplechase Park closed in 1964, the Parachute's Eiffel-like tall frame hulk had always been a symbol of promise to Brooklynites that someday Coney Island would regain its old pizzazz. Waiting paid off, and the Parachute reopened in 2003.

Long Pier
At the Boardwalk and West 17th Street

The Long Pier is an extension of the Boardwalk, built one hundred yards out into the Atlantic Ocean. It affords a spectacular view of the coastline, accommodates photo opportunities, and provides a free, convenient place for fishermen to try their luck.

Kitchen 21 (formerly Childs Restaurant)
At the Boardwalk and West 21st Street, one block west of MCU Stadium where the Brooklyn Cyclones play baseball

The ornately decorated beige stucco building was constructed in 1923 to house a Childs restaurant. The architectural style may be called Spanish Colonial Revival, though its aesthetic elements reflect its beachfront setting. The fanciful terra-cotta reliefs and medallions colorfully invoke images of the sea: Neptune, mermaids, dolphins, seahorses, and ships. The baked clay is glazed with seven separate colors and is a spectacular example of the triumph of the local terra-cotta industry. The facade was declared a landmark in 2003. Childs, once the largest local restaurant chain, was founded in 1889. It was a pioneer in self-service and showed a fetish for cleanliness and the color white. The Childs floors were white ceramic, walls were white tile, counters and tables were white marble, and the staff wore starched white uniforms. The fare was comfort food and the prices ranged from low to moderate. The founders were supporters of the Temperance Movement and did not serve any alcoholic beverages. Smoking was forbidden and lingering was discouraged. Childs, which numbered fifty-three outlets at its height in the 1920s, experienced hard times after World War II and was bought by the Riese organization in 1961 and ceased to exist as an independent restaurant chain. In 2017, almost a half century later, Kitchen 21, a collection of five different eating and drinking venues, opened in the building. Choices at Kitchen 21 include the gastropub Parachute Bar, Test Kitchen, Community Clam Bar, The Café, and the rooftop bar Boardwalk and Vine.

New York Aquarium for Wildlife Conservation
610 Surf Avenue, between West 5th and West 9th Streets
718-265-3457

Despite its name, this public facility straddles the line between animal habitat and sideshow, but the kids love it! It is home to four hundred species of marine animals: fish, birds, and mammals. The most popular are the enormous whales, ponderous walruses, frightening sharks and electric eels, and the playful sea otters, dolphins, penguins, and seals. All feeding times are posted and watching animals gulp down fish provides great entertainment. In the Aquatheater, sea lions do tricks at feeding time.

Astroland Park
Between Surf Avenue and the Boardwalk, just south of the Aquarium

Astroland Park owns the largest rides and several of the games of chance and concessions at Coney Island (i.e., the Cyclone, Pirate Ship, Dante's Inferno, High Flyer, Astrotower, and Wonder Wheel). There is no separate admission charge.

The Cyclone (Roller Coaster)
At the east end of Surf Avenue, near the New York Aquarium

This 1927 wooden landmark, 1.6 miles of twisting tracks, is one of the few old-style roller-coaster survivors in the United States. Charles Lindbergh pronounced it "scarier than flying solo across the Atlantic." A ride on the Cyclone's old-fashioned wood-and-steel frame begins with a steep eighty-five-foot drop. Howls of joy and screams of fear can be heard from blocks away. Delight through predictable terror is the draw.

 Turn left (south) along Jones Walk.

Jones Walk

Main Concourse of Astroland

Here are arranged many traditional carnival entertainments: the high rocking Pirate Ship, the spooky ride called Dante's Inferno, the upside-down turning High Flyer, a tall round spire with a revolving viewing space known as the Astrotower, and the Wonder Wheel. The venerable slow-moving Wonder Wheel (Ferris Wheel) offers a magnificent view of the oceanfront. It has a more frightening internal track where swinging carriages rock and slide as the whole ensemble turns.

 Continue west from the center of Jones Walk along Bowery Street.

Bowery Street

Back Street of Coney Island

The Freak Show, Fun House, Skee-ball Lanes, Shooting Galleries, and various games of chance that line both sides of this lane are often used as backdrops for films. This is the quintessential Coney Island walkway. Play, earn points, and you could win a doll or stuffed animal.

Turn right (north) on Stillwell Avenue one block to Surf Avenue, then right (east) on Surf Avenue several long and short blocks until Ocean Parkway.

B & B Carousel

1045 Surf Avenue, between Jones Walk and West 12th Street

Brightly painted wooden horses with riders (often sitting with a parent) gently ease up and down a pole as they rotate on the platform. Familiar calliope music accompanies the riders as they go around and around. B & B Carousel is in pretty good shape for an original fixture at the park. To add a little bit of fun for older children, a brass ring sticking out from a wooden armature taunts riders. If you can pluck it, you get a free ride.

Return trip: Proceed north on Surf Avenue to Ocean Parkway (under the Elevated tracks). Only the D train stops at the Ocean Parkway Station above. Or, walk west to West 8th Street for the F or Q trains, or continue west to Stillwell Avenue for the F, Q, D, or N trains.

Coney Island Mermaid Parade

Artists finding cheap rents and large spaces in Coney Island have added some new effervescence to the old scene. Since 1982, humorously irreverent artist groups sponsor live sideshow performances, Sideshows by the Seashore, with outrageously politically incorrect acts, and an outlandish annual Mermaid Parade along Surf Avenue with marchers and revelers in various states of undress held the first Saturday after the Summer Solstice at 2:00 p.m.

Restaurant Recommendations

Nathan's Famous

Corner of Surf Avenue, at the corner of Stillwell Avenue
718-946-2202

Hot dogs are king at Nathan's! Presidential candidates come here to show affinity with one of Brooklyn's chief icons, a local fast-food stand that hasn't changed much since it opened in 1916. A hectic Independence Day noontime hot dog eating contest is held out in front and televised on all the local news programs. The bizarre gastronomic exercise began in 1915, and the record established by very skinny Japanese national 113-pound Takeru Kobayashi, who wolfed down fifty frankfurters in two minutes in

2001, stands. (He weighed 120 pounds following the contest.) Garish green and yellow signs cover the entire building hawking hot dogs, french fries, fried clams, and corn on the cob. Since the Brooklyn Cyclones and their fans joined the neighborhood, Nathan's greatly expanded its outdoor seating by knocking down the building to its west. The crowds keep coming for the kitsch, taste, and tradition.

Gargiulo's Restaurant (Italian)

2911 West 15th Street, between Mermaid Avenue and Surf Avenue
718-266-4891

This bustling restaurant dates from 1907 and has been popular ever since. The fare is hefty Neapolitan dishes: pastas, grilled meats, delicious veal dishes, and many tasty seafood choices. A 1990 remodeling removed the enormous colorful Styrofoam octopus from the ceiling, thus erasing a good deal of the old feeling. But Gargiulo's still exerts a pull, and people flock here for anniversaries, birthdays, and family get-togethers.

Carolina Restaurant (Italian)

1409 Mermaid Avenue, between Stillwell Avenue and West 15th Street
718-714-1294

This Neapolitan eatery dates from 1928. In its modern wedding-style dining room, it features the usual red sauce southern Italian specialties: spaghetti, lasagna, ravioli, and manicotti. The zesty puttanesca and mild tomato-cream sauces are memorable. It has a relaxed atmosphere with an active bar.

GREEN-WOOD CEMETERY

The Wisconsin ice sheet left a terminal glacial moraine like a curved spine along the interior of Brooklyn and Queens. When it receded ten thousand years ago, it deposited boulders, gravel, and soil in hilly deposits. During the English colonial period (1664–1783), the hilly area that Green-Wood Cemetery occupies was transformed into farmland. In 1776, American and British soldiers fought a skirmish during the Battle of Long Island here at Battle Hill, the highest elevation in Brooklyn. The commanding hills of Green-Wood make a fine site for a cemetery and provide a glimpse of Brooklyn's original geology.

There are two goals in strolling through this exceptionally beautiful cemetery: visiting the graves of famous people and appreciating the cemetery's layout and the gravestone architecture. Designed as a Romantic resting place, Green-Wood is a treasure trove of Romantic, Gothic Revival, and neoclassical designs situated on 478 acres, a commanding set of small hills overlooking all of Brooklyn and Lower Manhattan. The greatest hill, Battle Hill, is the highest elevation in Brooklyn: 220 feet above sea level. The peripheral skirmish occurred just before the main Battle of Long Island in the area now called Prospect Park and Park Slope. The cemetery was opened in 1840 and has remained a scene of local pride and national note. Well cared for by the owners, a nonprofit, non-sectarian cemetery association, Green-Wood is still a fashionable place to spend eternity.

Inside the gatehouse attached to the 1861 Gothic gate, office personnel will provide a map showing locations of some of the most famous burials among the more than five hundred thousand. They include preacher Henry Ward Beecher; Tammany Hall Democratic Party boss William M. Tweed; economist Henry George; inventors Peter Cooper, Samuel F. B. Morse, and Eberhard Faber; engravers Nathaniel Currier and James Ives; newspaper publisher Horace Greeley; family planning advocate Margaret Sanger; composer Leonard Bernstein; designer and businessman Louis Tiffany; architects Richard M. Upjohn and James Renwick Jr.; artist Jean-Michel Basquiat; and assassinated Mafia figures Albert Anastasia and Joey Gallo.

The first question often raised when entering Green-Wood is about motif. Why are there so many angels, draped palls, wreaths and garlands of fruit and flowers, palm fronds, leaves, lilies, ivy strands, urns, doves, women kneeling in prayer, and sleeping children in the arms of their mothers decorating monuments? The answer is about Americans accepting globalized artistic standards following independence. After an initial period of colonial American folk art (winged death's heads followed later by winged angel's heads), cemetery motifs changed abruptly around 1800 and a long period characterized by effusive, emotional symbols ensued. The dominant nineteenth-century memorial design was part of a broad artistic movement called Romanticism. The Romantic style has lasted in some instances to the present, though its period of dominance in the United States was the nineteenth century. Sometimes people use the indistinct term Victorian as a label, because Queen Victoria reigned in the United Kingdom for much of that century. Calling it the Rural-Cemetery Movement is a specific designation and historically accurate name, and it was often applied at the time. But using Romanticism as a term for cemetery and gravestone design ties it in with other forms of Romanticism and clarifies the movement.

Older portions of many cemeteries have countless examples of angels, which may best exemplify Romanticism in memorial art. There are resplendent angels, comforting angels, angels hovering over the dead or escorting them to heaven. There are angels who gesture (usually upward), who clutch crosses or wreaths to their chests, and those who sow flowers, petals, or leaves.

The word cemetery itself is a Romantic construct, which refers to the Greek noun *koimeterion* (sleeping chamber) and the verb *koiman* (to put to sleep). Prior to the early nineteenth-century cemetery movement, when park-like places were set aside for burials, the dead were buried in family plots on their farms or around village churches. As the United States industrialized, urban centers grew, and the tradition of burying the dead in rural plots or in churchyards needed updating. Cemeteries solved the space problem and became places where descendants, as well as strangers, could visit graves, admire tombstones, and meditate on death.

Romanticism was primarily an artistic and intellectual movement. It was a feisty response to political, economic, and social events of the period from about 1750 until at least 1860. The movement burst forth in the United States as well as in Europe, especially in England, France, and the German states. By the beginning of the nineteenth century, many Europeans and Americans were tiring of the artistic element of the Enlightenment, which stressed rationality, order, control, symmetry, and restraint in the arts. Neoclassicism, which artistically went hand in hand with the Enlightenment, used ancient Greek and Roman images as its models and stressed aesthetic rules and consistent standards. The cultural pendulum of taste swings back and forth, and as the popularity of Enlightenment and classical themes waned, the ebullient themes of the Romantic Reaction gained dominance.

In rapidly modernizing areas of Europe and the United States, the Romantic Reaction also targeted industrialization and urbanization, which were seen as ugly and unnatural. They felt the dehumanization caused by factory conditions and city life could be countered by expressing natural artistic emotions.

Romantics loved powerful emotions and intense feelings. They let their assertive egos show in art, literature, music, and architecture. They were unabashedly spiritual and loved nature, often portraying the enchanting or frightening aspects of the wilds as well as longing for the unusual and exotic.

In literature, Romantics abandoned formal poetry for direct, ordinary speech and often endowed simple subjects with lofty importance. Examples are *The Sorrows of Young Werther* by Goethe, *The Captain's Daughter* by Pushkin, the Leatherstocking Tales series by Cooper, *Leaves of Grass* by Whitman, and Poe's detective stories and frightening poem "The Raven." Wordsworth eschewed the noble rose for the wildflower simplicity of the daffodil in well-known verse. In a similar vein, Longfellow wrote a poem entitled "Seaweed."

Composers like Beethoven, Berlioz, Liszt, Chopin, Schubert, Tchaikovsky, and Paganini added enthusiasm and range in music, greatly enlarging orchestras by adding wind instruments and percussion as well as using more strings. Concert halls were built where music could be enjoyed as an end in itself, not just as a background for religious services and elegant dinner parties. The period of Romantic operas like those of Verdi and Wagner had begun.

In art, subjects were likely to be common people doing ordinary tasks or struggling with tempest-tossed seas or ensconced in remote or phantasmagorical locations. Either nature or political upheaval could be the setting. Delacroix painted the Greek War of Independence against the Ottoman Turks in *The Massacre at Chios*, and the French Revolution in *Liberty Leading the People*. The Romantics had moved as far away from Enlightenment and neoclassical restrained order as they could. All of life and all of life's emotions, including tragedy, were fit subjects for their attention.

Cemeteries, too, became places of intense feeling and models of nature. Like Vaux and Olmsted's countryside-emulating Central Park in New York City, which itself was patterned after Green-Wood, Romantic period cemeteries sought to reconstruct nature as well as to achieve spiritual heights by confronting intense emotions. The symmetrical pattern was out; curving roads, trees, flowers, and shrubbery were in. The winding roadways and profusion of trees and bushes are representations of the Romantic Movement. Monuments increased in size and became suffused with feelings. Death releases powerful emotions, and these were reflected by weeping willow trees, angels draping themselves over stones, lambs, dogs (for fidelity), and the Protestant use of the cross, often in the hands of an angel or made of branches or rough logs.

Most American cities had at least one Romantic style cemetery by the end of the last century. Today these cemeteries, such as Mount

Auburn, founded in 1831 in Cambridge, Massachusetts, Laurel Hill in Philadelphia, Graceland in Chicago, Lake View in Cleveland, and Green-Wood in Brooklyn are home to all manner of monuments exhibiting the emotional needs of the soul, as the Romantics put it. These were often patterned after the first Romantic cemetery, the famous Pére Lachaise in Paris, built in 1803. The grounds imitate nature with its beauty and uncertainty. David Bates Douglass, the landscape architect of Green-Wood, preserved hills, cliffs, and ponds, and built winding roads and footpaths to evoke a rural image. Countless anonymous artisans carved the monuments to fit the Romantic motif. The memorials show the full weight of sorrow as well as the joys of redemption and everlasting life. Romanticists held back nothing. They believed intense emotions like beauty, love, friendship, fear, and mourning could not be rationally defined; they had to be felt. The memorial designs captured those intense feelings in granite and marble. It represented a long period of Romantic philosophy and is reflected in Green-Wood perhaps better than anywhere else in the United States.

In 1823, new burials were banned in lower Manhattan, so people began looking across the rivers for cemetery sites. In 1838, Brooklyn businessman Henry Pierrepont, son of Hezekiah Pierrepont, who developed New York City's first suburb in Brooklyn Heights, was elected president of the joint-stock company that organized and built Green-Wood. His interest in the private, for-profit cemetery blended nicely with his Brooklyn real estate holdings and his ownership of the Union Ferry Company. Funeral parties from Manhattan needed to use a ferry to get to Green-Wood. Pierrepont's Union Ferry Company operated six separate routes between Manhattan and Brooklyn.

While officially nondenominational, Green-Wood primarily served Protestant families. Brooklyn was overwhelmingly Protestant until the twentieth century, and when people called it the City of Churches, they meant Protestant churches. The first Roman Catholic Church in Brooklyn, the original St. James, at the corner of Jay Street and Cathedral Place, was not constructed until 1822. (It became a cathedral in 1853, and was rebuilt in 1903.) Manhattan's first Catholic church, St. Peter's, on Barclay and Church Streets, dates only from 1786. The concept of consecrated burial ground does not exist in most Protestant denominations, as it does among Roman Catholics, Eastern Orthodox Christians, and Jews. Protestants may be buried anywhere the civil law allows, while other religions have special requirements. So being nonsectarian meant that while persons from other religions could be buried in Green-Wood, it remained primarily Protestant. Nonetheless, there are hundreds of stones with Catholic, Eastern Orthodox, Armenian Apostolic, Jewish, and Muslim insignias and decorations interspersed among the Protestant graves.

The careful observer will note, however, that while the dominant motif was Romantic, there are many examples of neoclassical monument design and newer, rather disappointing nondescript stones, which might charitably be called modern. The pleasure of an architectural walk is noting the styles, and this cemetery is a marvelous place for such a stroll. No matter which form was chosen to express grief and remember the dead, Green-Wood's memorials represent ostentation and financial bravado in an unparalleled display of nineteenth-century wealth and exceptional artistic style.

Walking Trip Through Green-Wood

 Take the R train to the 25th Street Station, walk uphill (east) on 25th Street for one long block to the main gate.

Green-Wood Cemetery

500 25th Street
Cemetery hours daily: 8:00 a.m. to 4:00 p.m.; Office hours daily:
9:00 a.m. to 3:00 p.m.
718-768-7300
Main Gate: 5th Avenue and 25th Street

Pausing at the main gate reveals a masterful example of all the enthusiasm of the Gothic Revival. This apotheosis of Romanticism has nothing of the controlled, rounded attributes of classical style. It has double portals, but most of the gate is soaring elaborate brownstone tracery with lacy buttresses and three main spires. The two outer bas-reliefs above the gates seen when entering Green-Wood portray the sad Death of Lazarus and the Entombment of Jesus, while the two inner panels seen when exiting the cemetery show the triumphant Raising of Lazarus and the Resurrection of Jesus. (Note the green parrots nesting at the top of the gate. Hawks, owls, and eagles also live in Green-Wood.)

A good understanding of the basic themes of the Romantic Movement's tombstone designs can be surveyed on a two-block walk. The rest of the cemetery is filled with interesting designs and graves of famous people. The initial two-block walk surveys the main design variables. From the inside of the gate, bear left along Battle Avenue to examine some outstanding memorials.

First Section
On the left side of Battle Avenue

The Smith stone is a tall light granite pinnacle with a woman standing on a pile of stones gazing at the large, slightly tilted log cross she is holding. The nearby Kingsland memorial is a short marble obelisk draped with a tasseled funeral pall. The Smith and Kingsland stones are two different types of the Romantic theme.

Second Section
On the right side of Battle Avenue

The stone memorializing J. W. Gerard portrays a kneeling angel on a pedestal staring sadly ahead with draped garb extended out to partly cover an urn, placed behind a modest, partly in-ground mausoleum.

Third Section
On the right side of Battle Avenue after crossing Bay-Side Avenue

Up a flight of six granite steps stand four small headstones in excellent condition, erected to memorialize children behind a set of three large Burr family stones. The stone for Albert Hubbell Wright (1875) features a forlorn, skyward-looking woman holding flowers, sitting on a tapered pile of ivy-covered rocks. The Hattie A. Burr (1860) headstone is an especially striking relief of two angels triumphantly escorting the child, with her hands folded in prayer, up to heaven. The monument to honor Henry A. Burr Jr. (1850) presents a winged angel carrying the infant up to heaven on a cushion of clouds. The Henry A. Burr (1882) stone shows a winged cherub with hand held to head in sadness. A few feet farther is the memorial for America Mora, a freestanding rough log cross on a jagged chiseled stone hillock. Three imposing stones in the bordered Spencer family memorial circle nearby present a striking assemblage. The Spencer family stone is a tall obelisk topped by an angel and flanked by urns. Mary (1843) has two weeping children bent over the knees of a downcast seated woman. Elizabeth (1863) shows a distraught woman slumped over and tightly clutching a tall, slightly angular cross.

Second Section

On the left side of Battle Avenue after crossing Bay-View Avenue

The Watkins memorial is a medium obelisk with an urn draped with a garland of flowers and a funeral pall. Two smooth headstones with bent-over palm fronds flank the obelisk.

Fourth Section

On the right side of Battle Avenue after crossing Highland Avenue

Perched on the crest of a small hill is the John Anderson Mausoleum (1864). A flight of eight steps leads to the stately neoclassical temple with four Ionic columns front and back. The statues of two bearded, robed men, almost certainly Christian saints, perhaps Matthew, Mark, Luke, or John, flank the doors at each end.

Third Section

On the left side of Battle Avenue after crossing the other end of curvilinear Bay-View Avenue

The eye-catching Vann Ness–Parsons corner memorial is a large pyramid with a sphinx, placed asymmetrically on the right, and two statues flanking the door: adult Jesus holding a lamb and Mary holding infant Jesus. On the metal crypt door is a crucifix superimposed over a circular zodiac of the planets. Symbols of Ancient Egypt, Christianity, and astrology are merged in this monument.

Wandering Through Green-Wood

The Romantic theme of the grounds will be obvious no matter where you amble. All the roads and paths are curvilinear, hugging the hills without even the hint of an imposed grid system. The names are naturalistic: Fern Avenue, Highland Avenue, Southwood Dale, Euonymus Path, Winterberry Oak Path. A wide variety of trees and bushes from around the world have been planted, giving much of Green-Wood the look of a hilly forest.

Brooklyn's highest point, 220 feet above sea level, is found on Battle Hill, which is reached by walking on Battle Avenue past the Vann Ness–Parsons pyramid, Fern Avenue, and the overlook above the south terminus of 7th Avenue, to the intersection of Border Avenue. The intersection of sections G and H, with crosswalks named Battle Path and Liberty Path, is the ridge called Battle Hill. The vantage point offers spectacular views in all directions, especially when the leaves have fallen from the trees. Battle Hill, farmland during the Revolutionary War, was the scene of a brief encounter on August 27, 1776, between elements from the left flank of the British invasion marching up Gowanus Road (approximately 4th Avenue) and an exploratory party of Americans from Maryland commanded by General William Alexander (Lord Stirling). The skirmish ended quickly with the Americans retreating in front of the much larger British force. The lots around the crest of Battle Hill were reserved for veterans of the American Revolution and the War of 1812.

The largest monument on Battle Hill is an elaborate Civil War Memorial. The Altar to Liberty, the Revolutionary War Memorial, is a few steps to the north. It is a statue of Minerva (Athena) next to a low Roman altar. The Goddess of War (as well as Wisdom) faces west and looks directly at *Liberty Enlightening the World* (the Statue of Liberty) on Liberty Island in the New York Harbor. Minerva wears a helmet and armor. Her breastplate is adorned with the snake-haired head of Medusa, a gift to her from Perseus for display. Minerva and Mercury (Hermes) had helped Perseus kill Medusa, a repulsive and terrifying Gorgon. (It was common to use Greek and Roman mythology as political metaphors in the Republic's first century when everyone was familiar with the stories.)

Along the western part of the cemetery, there are four small lakes, quaintly called waters—the largest two (Valley Water and Sylvan Water) not far from the main gate. To see them, bear right from the main gate along Landscape Avenue past the Gothic Revival chapel and right again along Lake Avenue. The ornate chapel has a soaring octagonal central dome flanked by four smaller octagonal domes. Glancing down on the waters from Vista Hill or Sylvan Cliff was designed to present a geography that would mentally transport the viewer to the countryside. Part of the Romantic charm is getting lost in the maze of Green-Wood. If you would rather not get lost, buy a map at the office in the base of the main gate.

WASHINGTON CEMETERY

Originally carved from farm fields in south central Brooklyn, Washington Cemetery is nestled between four residential neighborhoods: Flatbush, Borough Park, New Utrecht, and Bensonhurst. Washington Cemetery is a late-nineteenth- and early twentieth-century Jewish burial ground, which has used up most of its grave sites. From the elevated F train or car, it appears as a sea of mostly white marble and grey granite stones packed together without benefit of more than a handful of trees. Though contiguous, the cemetery is divided into five administrative sections by public streets.

Though only a fifth the size of Brooklyn's Green-Wood Cemetery, Washington Cemetery served the growing Brooklyn Jewish community and the large Lower East Side Jewish community from the time it opened in 1861 until the interwar years when several large suburban Jewish cemeteries opened in Long Island, Westchester, and New Jersey. New grave lots are not available except for immediate interment, which means one lot at a time, not as family plots. Some new single plots have been carved from unused space: narrowing roadways, filling in open areas along fences, and even using the yard around the cemetery office for burials. Washington Cemetery has become a forest of tombstones. Most of the new lots are purchased by the latest wave of Russian Jews who began arriving in the 1970s. There have been approximately 155,000 burials in Washington Cemetery.

Many of the older sections were purchased by landsmanshaften, Jewish mutual aid societies, which were organized around a common hometown, synagogue, political group, or trade association. Each landsmanshaft bought a section of lots, usually erected a gate, and sold graves to members. At one time, there were more than one thousand landsmanshaften in New York City. Few still exist, as the initial ties have grown too weak to sustain over three or four generations. Examples of landsmanshaften are the Free Sons of Israel, United Botoshaner American Brotherhood Association, Bialystoker Bricklayers' Association, Minsker Benevolent Association, Kiever Revolutionary Workmen's Circle, First Yezierzaner Sick Benevolent Association, Lodzer True Brotherhood Society, Polonnoye Independent Aid Society, and Independent Raudautz Bokowina Benevolent Association.

Landsmanshaften do not take up all the sections. Families and synagogues own many burial plots. Some have gates and fences. The symbolic use of portals carved on a stone or as a physical feature is the same. It refers to the Gates of Heaven (Shaarei HaShamayim).

Traditional Jewish symbols can be found on many stones in Washington Cemetery. At the top of most monuments and markers are the Hebrew letters *peh* and *nun* (p, n), which is an abbreviation for *poh nikbar* or *poh nitman* ("Here Is the Soul" or "Here Lies the Soul").

Five Hebrew letters *tet, nun, tzadi, bet,* and *heh* (t, n, tz, b, h) are often found at the bottom of an inscription. They form the intriguing abbreviation for "May His (or Her) Soul Be Bound Up in the Bond of Life."

Above the name on a stone, an engraved Star of David announces a man and candles proclaim a woman. Lions (usually a pair) framing the Decalogue (Tablets of the Ten Commandments) are found on some gravestones. Each tablet usually has five of the first ten letters of the Hebrew alphabet written vertically.

Many Jewish symbols common in Eastern Europe are not found in most American Jewish cemeteries. Here it is rare to find a carving of a Tree of Life, a chest for incense, a prayer house (indicating a caretaker, or *shamus*), a hand placing coins in a charity box (indicating philanthropy), or a crown (loosely meaning royalty and inferring scholarship or exalted lineage). Clusters of grapes or lemons, or the widespread use of border tracery made of flowers, leaves, or geometric designs are uncommon. The whimsical use of animals beside lions, so prevalent on Eastern European tombstones, is seldom seen in the United States. Bears, deer, peacocks, doves, and fish are part of Jewish cemetery folk design that did not cross the Atlantic.

Epitaphs are always interesting because they try to add a personal touch. Traditional English-language Jewish epitaphs include "Rest in Peace," "May His (or Her) Soul Rest in Peace," or "Gone but Not Forgotten." A very common addition used by Russian immigrants in English or Russian is "Forever in Our Hearts."

The deceased's father (almost always presented without a surname) is usually written in Hebrew, as in Yakov bar Reuven (Jacob son of Reuben), or Sarah bat Shmuel (Sarah daughter of Samuel). Relationships to the deceased are also indicated; relatives who erected the memorial are frequently included. "Beloved Mother, Wife, and Sister," or "Beloved Father, Grandfather, and Great Grandfather" can be found.

Cemetery customs brought over by contemporary Russian Jews mirror those of Christians and nonbelievers in the republics of the former Soviet Union. There are four noticeable differences between the new stones for Russian Jews and the older stones for Jews from all over Eastern Europe, including Russia. While earlier tombstone inscriptions were written in German and English or Hebrew and English, the new immigrants use Russian and English. Plastic and live flowers, not usually part of traditional Jewish burial customs, are placed on the graves and around the stones. Large laser-point likenesses of the deceased are etched on the front of most stones. The older parts of the cemetery reveal only a few examples of photographs on small porcelain enamel ovals attached to monuments. Some of the new stones for Russian Jews boast lively and individualistic epitaphs, such as "One of the Nicest Human Beings," "So Much of You Is Left with Us and So Much of Us Has Left with You," "I Cry Because You Are Not There and I Cannot Say the Word Mama to Anyone," "The Pain of Loss Will Not Be Fulfilled Because to Us You Are Irreplaceable," and "We Love You, Remember You, and Are Grieving."

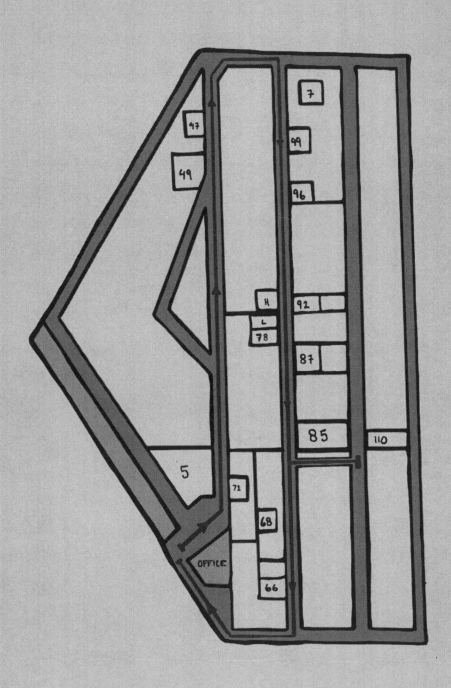

Washington Cemetery

718-377-8690

Some new single plots have been carved from unused space: narrowing roadways, filling in open areas along fences, using the yard around the cemetery office for burials.

- J. & M. Lefkowitz
- Sol Kalish
- C. & B. Reubens
- Samuel Kuller
- Semen Shargorodskiy
- Julie Schlesinger
- Congregation C.A.A.L.
- Weathered Gate
- W. & F. Henne
- Landauer Family Plot
- King David Society
- Society Wisdom of Man
- Schancapp Mausoleum
- Cong. Ohel Scholem
- United W. B. Association

 Take the IND F subway train to the Bay Parkway Station. Proceed down the stairway from the elevated station to the main office at 5400 Bay Parkway at the corner of McDonald Avenue.

The office staff is helpful and will distribute a free map of the grounds, which clearly marks all roads and sections, and labels grave sites of celebrities. Hours: 8:00 a.m. to 4:00 p.m. Sunday through Friday. Closed Saturday. There are public restrooms in the office.

Inside the cemetery, follow Jasmine Avenue, which is marked and located behind the left (east) side of the office building.

Jeremiah Lefkowitz (died 1913) and Miriam Lefkowitz (died 1909)

Left side of Jasmine Avenue, third row back in Range 5 on the left

The urn covered by a funeral pall on top of the stone is a nondenominational Romantic era motif found in many Protestant, Catholic, and Jewish cemeteries in the United States. The Old English script is also a Romantic notion.

Sol Kalish (died 1912)

Left side of Jasmine Avenue, second row back in Range 5

The tall tree stump prematurely chopped is a Romantic image.

Charles Reubens (died 1916) and Beatrice Reubens (died 1913)

Right side of Jasmine Avenue, second and third stones in on a paved walkway in Section 71

Here are two tall Romantic style stones, each made of grey granite—one an urn covered by a pall, the other a cut-off round column.

Samuel Kuller (died 1941)

To the left of the gate, inside a fenced section on left side of Jasmine Avenue, along the roadway in Section 49

A prominent violin and bow sandblasted on the top of the stone informs us that Samuel Kuller was a musician. His name is also written in Hebrew: Shmuel Bar Eliahu Yosef (Samuel son of Eliahu Yosef). Samuel Kuller was buried in the Chevra Ahaw Sholom Anshe Krinker section, which is so packed with graves that the gate will not fully open. The burial society uses the English transliteration of its Hebrew name: "Love of Peace Burial Society of the People of Krinker."

Semen Shargorodskiy (died 2001)

Left side of Jasmine Avenue, along the roadway in Section 47

The etching shows a Soviet Red Army officer and is inscribed in English: "Beloved Father And Grandfather, A Doctor And A War Hero, Forever In Our Hearts." His name is written in English and in Hebrew: Shepsil Bar (Son of) Leib.

At the end of Jasmine Avenue, turn right on Hyacinth Avenue along a row of mausoleums; turn right on Aster Avenue.

Julia Schlesinger (died 1886)

Corner of Aster Avenue and Hyacinth Avenue in Range 7

This prominent statue on top of a stone shows a young maiden, slightly downcast, spreading flowers. It is a common image aimed to evoke feelings of sadness, a goal in Romantic memorial art.

Congregation Chai Adam Anshei Lomza (Hebrew transliterated to English: Congregation Life of Adam People of Lomza)

Left side of Aster Avenue, first, second, fourth, and fifth stones on left side past the gate in Section 99

These stones show variations in the use of the menorah (candelabra) as a symbol for Jewish women. Freda Marks has five candles, Dora Stern has seven, and Fannie Weingart and Rachel Abkowitz each have three. Two candles, to represent Sabbath candles, can also be used.

Unreadable Weathered Gate

Left side of Aster Avenue in Section 96

In this section, descendants from the family of Cohens (kohanim, or priests) and Levites (assistant priests) display their clan symbols. Through the gate, the third stone on the left in the second row, Bela Lowy, and the thirteenth stone, Bernard (Yitzkach) Fligel, have pitchers, which are the symbol of the Levites. On the right, the first stone, Marcus Gold, and the fourth stone, Samuel Gold, each show a pair of hands, the symbol of the temple priests in Jerusalem. One can be a Cohen or a Levite without carrying the surname Cohen of Levy. Lowy, however, is a modification of Levy, and Cohn, Kohn, Kone, Kahn, and Kagan are all variations of Cohen.

William Henne (died 1903) and Fanny Henne (died 1935)
Right side of Aster Avenue in K-L-M-N Range, across from Section 92

This stone marks the graves of a couple from Württemberg and Bavaria. It is written entirely in German, testifying to the degree of assimilation and identification once felt by many German Jews toward Germany.

Landauer Family Plot
Right side of Aster Avenue in Section 78, across from Section 90

The front left granite monument is topped with a small marble statue of an angel and marks the grave of Irene Landauer, who died in 1908 at age ten. An angel is a Romantic image rare in Jewish cemeteries.

King David Society
Right side of Aster Avenue in Section 78

The third stone through the gate on the left-hand side memorializes Isaac Strauss (died 1912). A patriotic seal with stars and stripes adorns the top. The inscription reads: "A Veteran of the Civil War, He Fought to Save the Union."

Society (of the) Wisdom of Man
Left side of Aster Avenue in Section 87

Two lions, symbolizing strength, dignity, and royalty, top the marble gate of this landsmanshaft section. Judging by the name, this may have been a landsmanshaft of freethinkers (nonreligious people).

Schancapp Mausoleum
Left side of Aster Avenue, behind Sections 84 and 85 in Section 110, between Lotus Avenue and Evergreen Avenue

Off to the west in the next section rises the enormous Schancapp Mausoleum, not inscribed except for the family name. The design of the imposing grey granite sepulcher is mainly neoclassical with a few Baroque elements on top. The pediment has a bas-relief angel blowing an elongated trumpet.

 Return to Aster Avenue and continue south.

Congregation Ohel Scholem
Right side of Aster Avenue in Section 68

Two important symbols adorn front-row stones in this synagogue section. On the right, inscribed completely in Hebrew, is the monument of Shimon Yitzkach Bar (Son of) Yehuda Tsvi Finkelstein (The five books engraved on top mark him as a scholar.) On the left, written in English, is a stone for Elias Kaplan Cohen decorated with hands of the Cohens (kohanim) making the traditional priestly blessing.

United Wilner Benevolent Association
Right side of Aster Avenue in Section 66

This landsmanshaft is for people from Vilna (or Vilnius), now Lithuania. The granite gate has a marble arch showing clasped hands of brotherhood under an urn covered by a funeral pall. The inscription on the arch is written in Yiddish and English, United Wilner Benevolent Association, and the list of officers of the landsmanshaft on the gateposts is written in Yiddish.

Walking in to the United Wilner Benevolent Association plot, there are several examples. The second row on the right is the stone for Harris Mintzer (died 1935). The Hebrew inscription reads "Hersh Bar Shimon," and in English, "Beloved Husband and Father." On the left in the seventh row is a stone for Rebecca Z. Cassell (died 1907), which adds a line in Hebrew: "Rivkah Zlata Bat Reb Avraham" (Rebecca Goldy Daughter of Rabbi Abraham).

 At the end of Aster Avenue, turn right on Sage Avenue to return to the office and main gate.

Restaurants Near Washington Cemetery

There are no nearby eateries in the immediate vicinity of Washington Cemetery. If you want to eat before returning, you can take the B6 bus southbound at the bus stop across Bay Parkway from the cemetery office. Take the bus to the Bay Parkway Station of the N train at 66th Street or the Bay Parkway Station of the N train at 86th Street. Around each subway station, there are clusters of restaurants and coffee shops.

WILLIAMSBURG

Five Separate Communities in One Neighborhood

F irst settled by Dutch and English farmers with their African slaves, Williamsburg grew very slowly, but finally became politically independent from the Town of Bushwick in 1810. It was named for its surveyor, Colonel Jonathan Williams. Produce from Brooklyn farmers crossed the East River for sale in Manhattan, and Manhattan hunters and hikers boated to Williamsburg to take advantage of the nearby rustic countryside that remained largely rural until the mid-nineteenth century.

After the failure of the 1848 Revolution in the German states, the area became part of the broad band of German settlement that stretched from Williamsburg through Bushwick, Ridgewood, and Maspeth, Queens. It was in Williamsburg that several German-style breweries, including the Rheingold Brewery, were established. Hamlets and villages grew into each other, and by the latter nineteenth century, Williamsburg had become urban. It was incorporated as a city in 1851, and then folded into New York City as part of the Consolidation of 1898.

In 1848 Charles Pfizer, a German immigrant, began manufacturing chemicals in a plant on Bartlett Street. Havemeyer and Elder, a sugar refinery eventually bought by Domino, was established near the corner of South 4th Street and 1st Avenue. Pottery manufacturers produced drainpipes, cookware, plumbing supplies, and flowerpots. Porcelain and glassware manufacturers, iron foundries, spice mills, printing companies, ink manufacturers, woodworking shops, distilleries, breweries, an oil refinery, and America's largest glue factory (owned by Peter Cooper) huddled near the increasingly environmentally degraded river. The shoreline, which had consisted of sandy bluffs over the East River, was rapidly developed, and the early bucolic look was completely transformed by factories, mills, and warehouses. A handsome business district with several large, impressive banks built as temples of commerce developed at the intersection of Broadway and Roebling Street.

The opening of the Williamsburg Bridge in 1903 led to the rapid transformation of the neighborhood. Dubbed *The Jews' Highway* by some New York City newspapers, it carried thousands of Jewish, as well as Italian and Slavic immigrants, from the Lower East Side to more spacious apartments in Williamsburg. Immigrants pouring in from the Lower East Side settled separately: Jews opting for the south side, Italians for the east side, and Russians, Lithuanians, and Poles settling in the north side up through Greenpoint. In New York City, no single ethnic group is ever completely dominant, so Irish, Germans, and others lived sprinkled amid the larger and more recent ethnic concentrations. Williamsburg was the setting for *A Tree Grows in Brooklyn*, by Betty Smith. It portrayed a gritty Williamsburg from 1902 to 1919 with its competing and colluding ethnic enclaves. The tree in the title was the tenacious Ailanthus, euphemistically called the Tree of Heaven. No matter where its seed fell, it made a tree, which struggled to reach the sky. It grew in boarded-up lots and out of neglected rubbish heaps, and it was the only tree that grew out of the cracks in cement. It grew lushly, but only in the tenement districts.

The bridge and the BMT subway line, both aimed at the heart of the old business district, cluttered and destroyed the aesthetic unity of the central plaza of Williamsburg at Broadway and Roebling Street. Stores and offices left and new business areas developed, catering to local ethnic communities to the north, south, and east. In the two decades before World War II, Williamsburg had been decentralized. It became a single neighborhood in name only. The balkanized area was transformed into five very separate neighborhoods, and the old downtown, a core of elegant, aging bank buildings that were stranded and strangled amid a jumble of bridge entrances, elevated train tracks, and bus lots, became an isolated ghost town.

The Hasidic neighborhood in the south, the Italian area to the northeast, the Slavic section to the north now cohabited with throngs of young East Village hipsters, and a still robust but shrinking Puerto Rican presence sandwiched in between the Orthodox Jews and the hipsters (between Grand Street and Broadway) all share Williamsburg. The Puerto Rican area is being encroached upon rapidly by both north and south, as hipsters and Hasidim seek expansion into those blocks.

North side Williamsburg is the best-preserved example of a late-nineteenth-century New York City industrial neighborhood. Most of the factories and warehouses are still operational. Because the area has been enlivened by thousands of newcomers with new stores, restaurants, and bars, it is also a particularly pleasant and welcoming place to visit. The entrepreneurial activity of the artists and their entourage resurrected a sluggish neighborhood and turned it into an interesting residential–commercial–industrial mix. In general, the factories predominate in the northwest section of Williamsburg.

Between north side and south side, the eerily empty old downtown center stands both as a monument to exuberant, triumphalist architecture and a local spirit of boosterism, but also as a reminder of how modern amenities (bridge and subway) often disrupted the patterns of everyday life in the old neighborhoods.

Architecturally, the housing throughout Williamsburg is a mixture of two- and three-story wooden row houses, almost all having had their original facades covered with one or more layers of asphalt shingles or aluminum siding, and more substantial brick row houses, with a few apartment buildings on the avenues. Bedford Avenue is the main shopping street on the north side of Williamsburg and for six blocks is completely commercial with new cafes and bars coexisting with older Polish restaurants, *cukiernas* (bakeries), and *kwiaciarnias* (florists).

Italian east side Williamsburg is primarily a residential community with a very small shopping district along Metropolitan Avenue. Largely Roman Catholic, it possesses an active parish, Our Lady of Mount Carmel on North 8th and Havemeyer Streets, and sponsors the yearly festival in July honoring both St. Paulinus of Nola (Campania) and Our Lady of Mount Carmel. Interestingly, in the first three decades of the twentieth century, there was also a lively Italian Protestant presence in east side Williamsburg. The Italian Baptist Church was located on Devoe Street, an Italian Baptist seminary at Jackson Street (demolished by the Brooklyn Queens Expressway), and a summertime tent meeting at the corner of Ten Eyck Street and Union Avenue. No Italian Protestant congregation has survived.

The Hasidic groups came to south side Williamsburg after World War II. They were remnant communities from Eastern Europe who had escaped the Nazis. The Hasidic sects settled among other Orthodox Jews who had lived there for half a century. The Hasidim thrived and now dominate the neighborhood. Rabbi Israel Ben Eliezer (1698–1700) of

Okopy in the Carpathian Mountains of Podolia (Western Ukraine) had sparked their movement. Known as the Besht, from the acronym *B-Sh-T*, meaning Baal Shem Tov, or "Master of the Good Name," and believed to be a wonder-worker, he emphasized love of God, Israel, and Torah, and infused his teachings and study with joyful singing and dancing. The word *hasid* means pious in Hebrew. Chief followers and interpreters of the Besht were called tsaddiks (righteous men). Each established a court around his synagogue, school, and house. Subsequent leadership of the developing tradition, usually one per town or shtetl (village), was passed to his oldest male descendant, who was given the title *rebbe*. Communal decisions and religious interpretations are made for each sect by the rebbe, the dynastic leader. Because the Hasidic tradition in Europe was centered in Poland, Ukraine, Belarus, Lithuania, Romania, Hungary, and Slovakia, it was effectively destroyed in the Holocaust. Brooklyn is now the center of Hasidic life, and south side Williamsburg is one of the three large Hasidic neighborhoods in the borough.

Living space is a crucial problem for all communities in Williamsburg. The Satmar Hasidim, for example, with twenty-five thousand followers in Williamsburg, established a satellite town of thirteen thousand residents called Kiryas Joel in suburban Orange County, forty-five miles north of New York City, to relieve some of the pressure of a booming population. According to the 2000 US Census, 8.6 percent of the people in south side Williamsburg are under the age of one. Hasidic and Puerto Rican leaders fight bitterly over apartment allocations in public housing projects in the north part of the neighborhood. It is, of course, more complicated because, along with Puerto Ricans, there are other Hispanic groups (Dominicans, Mexicans, Guatemalans, Salvadorans) and the Hasidim are divided into several dynastic sects.

Cultural icons mark each neighborhood in Williamsburg. The five domes of the Russian Orthodox Cathedral in north side Williamsburg; front-yard statues of Jesus, St. Mary, St. Dominic, St. Francis, St. Lucy, and others in east Williamsburg; Hebrew and Yiddish writing (using the same alphabet) in south side Williamsburg. It can also be marked by what is missing. You may notice the absence of dogs in south side. By cultural disinclination more than religious prohibition, Hasidic Jews rarely keep dogs. A walk through Williamsburg will counter the notion that New York City is becoming increasingly homogenized.

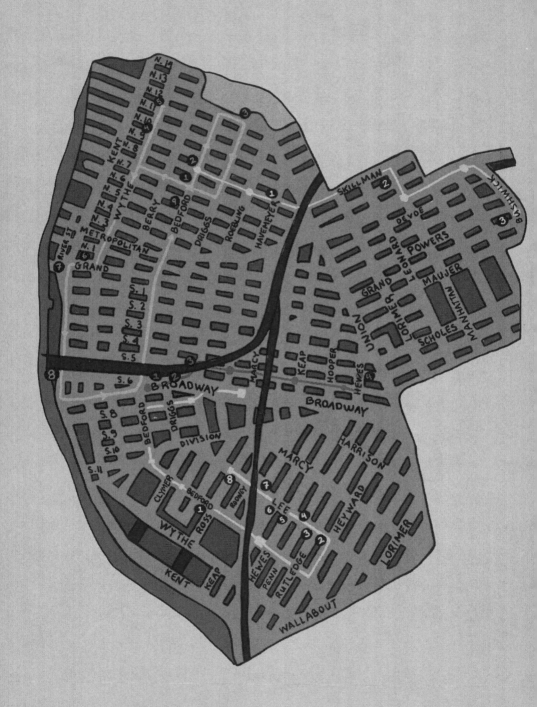

Williamsburg

▲ North Side: Hip Artist Community

1. Salvation Army Thrift Store
2. Café Beit
3. Transfiguration Church
4. Rosenwach Wooden Water Tank Factory
5. Brooklyn Brewery
6. Private House
7. Grand Ferry Park (Domino Park)
8. Apartment Complex (Formerly Domino Sugar Refining Company)
9. Spoonbill & Sugartown

⬣ East Side: Italian Neighborhood

1. Our Lady of Mount Carmel Church and Shrine
2. Manhattan Special Bottling Company
3. Williamsburg Houses, NYCHA

■ South Side: Hasidic Community

1. Congregation Yetev Lev D'Satmar
2. Oitzer Judaica
3. Sander's Kosher Bakery Shop
4. Waldman's Dry Goods

5. Felty Hats
6. Early Morning Housekeeper Shape-up
7. Lee Avenue Sforim (Satmar bookstore)
8. Williamsburg Silver Center

● Three Temples of Commerce: Center of Old Downtown Williamsburg

1. Williamsburg Art and Historical Center (originally Kings County Savings Bank, 1868)
2. Weyline Events Space (formerly HSBC, originally Williamsburgh Savings Bank, 1875)
3. Holy Trinity Cathedral of Ukrainian Autocephalic Orthodox Church in Exile (originally Williamsburg Trust Company, 1906)
4. Continental Army Plaza

Walking Tour 1
North Side Williamsburg: Hip Artist Community Amid Old Factories

 Proceed in a loop around the north side, starting on Bedford Avenue from L subway train at Bedford Avenue and North 7th Street, just one stop from Manhattan.

Salvation Army Thrift Store
180 Bedford Avenue, at the corner of North 7th Street
718-388-9249

The Salvation Army shop is an old-time emporium specializing in used clothing, but also offering books, furniture, decorative knickknacks, and kitchen implements. This is the place to find a preowned fondue set, lava lamp, convection oven, or Crock-Pot. Nonprofit thrift shops are increasingly rare, since most used clothing stores today are operated as for-profit enterprises and previously owned garments have acquired enough panache to be called vintage clothing.

Café Beit
158 Bedford Avenue, near North 8th Street
917-909-1430

Café Beit is a friendly place to gather, chat with neighbors, and people-watch. Coffee, tea, hot chocolate, and cold drinks are on the menu with soups and sandwiches and quiche. They also have a selection of wine, beer, and cider.

Walk north on Bedford Avenue five short blocks to North 12th Street; at North 12th Street turn right (east) one block to Drigggs Avenue.

Transfiguration Church (Russian Orthodox)

One block detour right (east) at 228 North 12th Street, at the corner of
Driggs Avenue at the edge of McCarren Park
718-387-1064

At the edge of McCarren Park is a strikingly magnificent church with a large central copper onion dome flanked by four smaller domes turned green by time, which dominate the skyline and provide the Eastern European top to this tall 1927 neoclassical structure that can be seen for miles, notably from the Brooklyn-Queens Expressway. Formerly a Russian Orthodox Church, since 1970, it has been an affiliate of the autocephalous (self-governing) Orthodox Church in America. Four large triple pillars support the central dome in the large interior. Icons and candle stands are on every wall. The three-tiered iconostasis (icon screen) at the front has three richly decorative doors and separates the sanctuary from the nave. In keeping with traditional Orthodox canon law, there are no pews or instrumental music. Worshippers stand or kneel amid scores of icons and the smells of liberal doses of incense.

Proceed south on Driggs Avenue five short blocks to North 7th Street, then turn right (west) on North 7th Street toward Manhattan past Bedford Avenue and Berry Street. Turn right (north) on Wythe Avenue for five short blocks along the formerly industrial segment of the walk.

Rosenwach Wooden Water Tank Factory

Wythe Avenue, between 9th and 10th Streets

While not open to the public, this venerable company is notable as the producer of most water tanks that perch on top of so many New York City buildings. Rosenwach has been in business since 1896. Across the street from Rosenwach, along 9th Street, is a particularly well-preserved string of modest two-story row houses built for workers.

Brooklyn Brewery

Corner of Wythe Avenue and North 11th Street
718-486-7422

In 1879, Brooklyn had forty-three breweries, making it a big business in the borough. By the 1960s, there were only three breweries left; Piels closed its plant in 1963, and Schaefer and Rheingold left in 1976, leaving Brooklyn without a local beer. The Brooklyn Brewery redeemed the borough and Williamsburg when it was established in a set of empty factory buildings and warehouses in 1988. Brooklyn Lager and Brooklyn Brown Ale have gained widespread acceptance and are available throughout the United States. Tours of the brewery and samples of beer are available Saturdays from 12:00 p.m. until 5:00 p.m. Tap Room is open to the public at the corner of Wythe Avenue and North 11th Street. Tours begin at the Malt Room: 118 North 11th Street, between Wythe Avenue and Berry Street

> At North 11th Street, reverse directions and walk south on Wythe Avenue for eleven short blocks to Grand Street. Turn right (west) on Grand Street one block to Kent Avenue along the East River.

Private House (originally North Side Bank, 1889)

33–35 Grand Street, between Wythe Avenue and Kent Avenue

This one-story bank was instrumental in financing many Williamsburg factories and businesses, and its bold design of Romanesque stature but metallic tracery on top is a surprising sight in the heart of the industrial district. It stands alone among large factories, but its rough stone front darkened by years of soot and four imposing archways give it gravity.

Grand Ferry Park (Domino Park)

At the western foot of Grand Street, 300 Kent Avenue
212-484-2700

A small park now marks the former site of the Williamsburg to Manhattan ferry (from Grand Street to Grand Street), which ran from 1802 until 1918, when the new bridge rendered it unprofitable. This is one of the only places where you can actually approach the shoreline of the East River, stand on the rocks, and touch the water. The park has a bit of grass, some benches, and a reconstructed round seventy-foot smokestack from the old Pfizer factory as an industrial monument. The park also affords a view of the tall but graceless Williamsburg Bridge, which was tremendously significant to Williamsburg when it opened in 1903. It offered an escape for Jewish and Italian immigrants from the crowded Lower East Side to the comparative openness of Williamsburg. It also gave more commercial possibilities to both areas, though it destroyed Williamsburg's downtown district by intruding into its center. There is a pedestrian walkway, which offers unique views of both shores of the East River. Sustenance is available from the Tacocina Food Stand (Mexican).

 Walk south on Kent Avenue six blocks to Broadway (proceeding under the Williamsburg Bridge)

Apartment Complex (formerly Domino Sugar Refining Company, originally Havemeyer and Elder Sugar Refining Company, 1890)

325 Kent Avenue, between South 5th Street and South 2nd Street along the East River

South on Kent Avenue stands a new apartment complex built on what the neighborhood people once called the sugarhouse. This sugar processing plant was once a big employer, one very important to the economy of the area. It was the largest sugar refinery in the United States and the reason so many soft drink companies were located in Brooklyn. The owners chose an industrial version of Romanesque Revival architecture to highlight their large factory complex, which has mixed in an interesting way with modern architecture of the apartments.

 Turn left (east) on Broadway three blocks; then left (north) on Bedford Avenue eleven blocks to return to North 7th Street Subway Station.

Spoonbill & Sugartown, Booksellers

218 Bedford Avenue, near North 6th Street
718-387-7322

New and used books are sold in this large, pleasant space. In a nod to neighborhood tastes, there is a large art component to the stock, as well as a broad selection of architecture and design books, prints, and old postcards.

Tour 1 Restaurant Recommendations

Veracruz (Mexican)
195 Bedford Avenue, near North 7th Street
718-599-7914

This is an upscale neighborhood pioneer, catering to both the young artist crowd and old-time neighborhood people. There is a friendly, informal atmosphere in the long, brightly painted, though dimly lit dining room. Veracruz offers food popular in central Mexico, not Tex-Mex. Margaritas, of course, are a welcome American addition to the bar menu. The specialty and trademark appetizer is elote a la Mexicana, grilled corn on the cob topped with a delightful and unlikely mixture of mayonnaise, queso Cotija (aged white cheese), and chili powder. Veracruz has a shady garden in the back.

Miss Williamsburg Diner (New American)
206 Kent Avenue at North 3rd Street
718-963-0802

The aroma of sizzling burgers and herbes de Provence waft through the air in this small, out-of-the-way eatery. The small menu has some high-quality American, French, and Italian specialties. The ricotta and spinach ravioli in a sage butter sauce is deliciously creamy, and the sliced pork loin sprinkled with rosemary and sage served with crispy new potatoes and braised artichoke leaves is a culinary triumph.

Walking Tour 2
East Side Williamsburg: Italian Community

 Walk north from Bedford Avenue Station (L train) on Bedford Avenue for one block; turn right (east) on North 8th Street three blocks to Havemeyer Street.

Our Lady of Mount Carmel Church and Shrine (Roman Catholic)

275 North 8th Street at Havemeyer Street
718-384-0223

A three-block detour east on North 8th Street to the intersection with Havemeyer Street (the corner signs show secondary street names: Padre Pio Way and Christopher Columbus Way) takes you to a squat three-story orange brick church completely lacking in pulchritude. For eleven days in early July, the parishioners, many with ancestral ties to the town of Nola, in Campania, Italy, celebrate a double feast honoring Our Lady of Mount Carmel and St. Paulinus (354–431 AD), the town's bishop, with an exuberant street fair. Since 1887, 120 men carry an eighty-five-foot high, 4.5-ton giglio in a daily procession through the streets surrounding the church. *Giglio*, which means lily, is a highly decorated cylindrical tower. The giglio is gently *danced* through the streets while Italian folk music is played and onlookers quaff soft drinks and beer and eat zeppole, calzones, and sausages. Since 1966, the giglio frame, which has colorfully painted papier-mâché scenes in the saint's life, has been made of aluminum to reduce the weight.

> Proceed east on North 8th Street under the elevated Brooklyn-Queens Expressway where North 8th Street becomes Skillman Street. Continue east on Skillman Street three blocks to Manhattan Avenue.

Manhattan Special Bottling Company

342 Manhattan Avenue, between Skillman Street and Conselyea Street
718-388-4144

Founded in 1895 by Dr. Theresa Cimino, this tidy, small plant produces the quaint bottles of Manhattan Special extra sweet soda, a blend of espresso, cane sugar, and seltzer found in independent corner grocery stores throughout the city. The proximity of the Havemeyer Sugar Refinery was a boon to various Brooklyn soda companies. Manhattan Special soda quickly became a favorite in Brooklyn Italian neighborhoods.

Turn right (south) on Manhattan Avenue two blocks to Metropolitan Avenue; turn left (east) on Metropolitan Avenue three blocks to Bushwick Avenue; turn right (south) four blocks to Grand Street Subway Station (L train).

Williamsburg Houses, New York City Housing Authority

One short block past Grand Street from Maujer Street to Scholes Street and from Bushwick Avenue to Leonard Street

Built during the Great Depression (1937), the Williamsburg Houses are considered by many architects to be the best-designed public housing ever built in New York City. Four-story muted art deco buildings are built around courtyard spaces. Apartments are reached directly from the outside without long institutional common corridors.

Tour 2 Restaurant Recommendations

Bamonte's Restaurant (Italian)

32 Withers Street, just off Lorimer Street near Mount Carmel Church in the shadow of the Brooklyn-Queens Expressway
718-384-8831

This neighborhood restaurant with a borough-wide reputation is located in the small Italian enclave of east Williamsburg. A large parking lot testifies to the popularity of this establishment; people drive in from throughout Brooklyn and from the surrounding areas of Greater New York. Waiters don tuxedoes, the walls sport dark coral paint, and gilded chandeliers hang from the ceiling. Most of the diners come dolled up. Seafood, fifteen varieties of pasta, steaks, lamb, veal, and chicken fill an expansive menu.

Frost (Italian)

193 Frost Street, at the corner of Humboldt Street, five blocks west of Metropolitan Avenue
718-389-3347

The building looks like a concrete and brick fortification, and the inside is decorated like a slightly upscale, generic all-American diner. But Frost is a slice of relaxed ethnic Williamsburg hidden away from the main streets and known mostly to locals. The cuisine is standard Southern Italian fare: spaghetti, lasagna, ravioli, stuffed ziti, and gnocchi, with many veal, seafood, and chicken dishes. Beyond the hearty plates of pasta, this is a marvelous place to people-watch.

Walking Tour 3
South Side Williamsburg: Hasidic Community

Walk west (toward Manhattan) on South 8th Street four blocks to Bedford Avenue from Marcy Avenue Station (J, M, or Z trains), or a long walk south on Bedford Avenue from L subway at Bedford Avenue Station; turn left (south-southeast) on Bedford Avenue seven blocks to Ross Street.

Congregation Yetev Lev D'Satmar (Cheerful Heart of Satmar, the Satmar Hasidic Grand Synagogue)
530 Bedford Avenue at Ross Street and 13 Hooper Street

This is the main synagogue and home of the rebbe, Rebbe Menachem Mendl Teitelbaum, dynastic leader of the Hasidic sect, which began in Satu Mare, Hungary, in the eighteenth century. The remnants of the Satmar community moved to Williamsburg in 1946 after the Holocaust and have thrived. Today, the twenty-five thousand Satmars form the largest Hasidic group in New York City. Rebbe Moses Teitelbaum led the group from Europe. Under the previous rebbe, Joel Teitelbaum, they vehemently opposed Zionism and the State of Israel, making the argument that the Jewish people could be gathered in the Holy Land only after the coming of the *mosiach* (messiah). They also opposed the inclusion of women in the Israeli military and performing autopsies on the dead. Their stand has softened somewhat in the past decades. The new Satmar grand synagogue, constructed of steel, concrete masonry, and stucco, is the largest in the world, displacing Temple Emanu-El in Manhattan.

Turn left (northeast) on Heyward Street one long block, then turn left (northwest) on Lee Avenue eight short blocks, passing over the Brooklyn-Queens Expressway to Wilson Street.

Oitzer Judaica

191 Lee Avenue, between Heyward Street and Rutledge Street
718-218-7100

In this small religious articles shop, books, games, mezuzahs, yarmulkes, calendars, prayer cards, and a limited selection of silver items can be found. Primarily a bookshop, Oitzer's carries basic volumes for study and will take orders for difficult-to-locate books.

Sander's Kosher Bakery Shop

159 Lee Avenue, at the corner of Penn Street
718-387-7411

In this friendly corner shop, bakers turn out a limited selection of breads, buns, rolls, honey cakes, cookies, rugelach (cinnamon and raisin pastry twists), and challah (twisted white or egg bread for Sabbath or holidays). Nothing is labeled, but the staff will be glad to assist by answering questions.

Waldman's Dry Goods

156 Lee Avenue, at the corner of Penn Street
718-522-2003

Various items of basic Hasidic women's clothing are available here. The selection is primarily dresses, blouses, aprons, and hats. Hasidic women may wear upscale outfits from stylish stores as long as the cuts are modest. Waldman's is primarily for everyday outfits. (Married women, following the Hasidic custom, shave their heads and wear either a babushka or, much more likely, a wig, called a sheitel.)

Feltly Hats

185 Hewes Street, at the corner of Lee Avenue
718-782-0700

The distinctive hats worn by Satmar Hasidim may be purchased in this second-floor shop. Feltly Hats is the exclusive American distributor for Italian hatmakers Barbisio and Cellini. Each Hasidic sect uses a separate style of black hat, which is whatever is chosen by the rebbe of that community. For example, the Satmar wear a moderately brimmed high hat with a flat top; the Bobov, a wide-brimmed hat with a low rounded crown; the Lubavitch, an oversized fedora, almost as large as a Stetson, with a creased crown; and the Stolin wear a round hat with a two-inch crown and a sombrero-style upturned brim. The Spinka, Ger, Pupa, Belz, Skwere, Munkacz, Vizhnitz, Sopron, Klausenberg, Pressburg, Debrecen, Bratslav, and two hundred other groups each don a slightly different style of black hat. Hasidim wear their hats over the yarmulke (skullcap). On Sabbath and on holidays, an optional large broad-brimmed fur-edged hat, the shtreimel, is worn by many men in most Hasidic traditions.

Other distinctive aspects of Hasidic men's appearance are their untrimmed beards and payos (sidelocks). In some sects, the sidelocks are clipped at marriage to one-half inch, but most retain them, though married men wrap them around their ears while unmarried men curl them and allow the curls to dangle on the sides of their faces.

Male Hasids always wear a tallit katan (small striped shawl). Married men wear a full talis during prayer. The tallit katan (abbreviated form of the talis) with tzitzit (knotted, dangling fringes or strings) is worn like a poncho by Hasidic boys and men. Most sects wear it under their white shirts, though some wear it over their shirts. In either case, the tzitzit, braided into four sections and knotted to make the number 613, hang outside the coat as a constant reminder of the goal to observe the 613 biblical commandments.

Even the cut of the ubiquitous black coats distinguishes Hasidic groups. They range from the Lubavitch, who wear a standard modern suit jacket, to the Satmar, and others, who favor long frock coats. Trousers are also black, though Stolin men wear black or white leggings that show to just below their knees.

Lee Avenue and Hooper Street
Early Morning Housekeeper Shape-up

Early mornings at the corner of Lee and Hooper finds Polish immigrant women standing and bargaining with Hasidic women who have come to the shape-up to find a cleaning lady for the day. Friday morning is the busiest time as the Hasidim prepare for Sabbath. Vigorous and acrimonious debates about money, hours, and the nature of work take place between the buyers and sellers of labor.

Lee Avenue Sforim (Satmar Bookstore)

114 Lee Avenue, between Hooper Street and Williamsburg Street
718-782-7782

Because secular books are forbidden, the theme of all books, tapes, and games is the Jewish religion from the perspective of the Satmar community. The shop also sells rebbe cards, which, like baseball cards, feature a photo of a venerable rabbinic leader on the front and biographical information on the back.

Williamsburg Silver Center

67 Lee Avenue, between Rodney Street and Ross Street
718-387-0832

Special silver containers for ethrog, a ritual fruit used at Rosh Hashanah, are on the shelves with menorahs, Sabbath candles, dinner table candelabra, mezuzahs, goblets, cutlery, and serving plates. The brightly lit store with crowded shelves also repairs silver articles.

Turn right (northeast) one block on Wilson Street; continue ahead on Marcy Avenue two blocks to the Marcy Avenue elevated subway station for J, M, or Z trains.

Tour 3 Restaurant Recommendations

Itzu's

45 Lee Avenue, between Ross Street and Wilson Street
718-384-8631

Itzu's is a small, kosher dairy restaurant specializing in cheese and potato blintzes (crepes), and potato latkes (pancakes) with sour cream or applesauce. The division between meat and dairy restaurants is part of kashrut (dietary laws), and comes from a Talmudic interpretation of the biblical injunction in Exodus 23:19: "Thou shalt not seethe a kid in its mother's milk" (KJV). Kashrut rules regulate the amount of time that must pass between ingesting milk or dairy products and meat (two hours), and between meat and milk or dairy products (six hours). Foods that are neither meat nor dairy can be eaten with either category and are called pareve.

Lee Avenue Kosher Pizza

108 Lee Avenue, between Rodney Street and Ross Street
718-387-4736

Lee Avenue Kosher Pizza is a kosher dairy pizzeria and serves nothing made with meat. The cheese contains no rennet, the inner lining of the fourth stomach of a calf or lamb, which is an animal product. (Rennet as a dried extract is used to curdle milk in cheese making.) Pizzas have familiar vegetable toppings, such as onion, pepper, mushroom, broccoli, and spinach, along with rennet-free cheese.

Gottlieb's Restaurant

352 Roebling Street, between South 9ᵗʰ Street and Division Avenue
718-384-9037

Gottlieb's is a kosher meat restaurant, offering corned beef and pastrami sandwiches, chopped liver, matzoh ball soup, split-pea soup, kishka (thick sausage-shaped lengths of groats held together with chicken fat), and kasha varnishkes (groats with bow-tie noodles). It has some multicultural entrées as well: chicken cacciatore, chicken chow mein, and Hungarian goulash.

Autumn Holiday Visits (September–October):

If you visit Williamsburg south side between the High Holy Days of Rosh Hashanah and Yom Kippur (actually the day before each holiday), you may see the outdoor kapparot ritual, when the father of a family swings a chicken three times over the heads of his family symbolically expiating sins by transferring them to the fowl: roosters for males and a hens for females. (*Kapparot* means expiation.)

During the Festival of Booths (Succoth, or Sukkot), a week after Yom Kippur, each family constructs a booth or tent-like structure (sukkah). They must be open to the sky with branches or bamboo loosely covering the top. Evocative of the harvest, the sukkah tradition comes from a biblical commandment in Leviticus 23:42–43, which reads, "Ye shall dwell in booths seven days; all that are Israelites born shall dwell in booths: That your generations may know that I made the children of Israel to dwell in booths, when I brought them out of the land of Egypt: I am the LORD your

God" (KJV). During Succoth, each family buys ritual produce imported from Israel: ethrog (a citron, or lemon-like fruit) and lulav (a slender palm frond). Sukkahs dot the neighborhood, appearing on porches, balconies, fire escapes, front and backyards, driveways, open spaces on grounds of Hasidic-occupied public housing, sidewalks, and even in the streets behind specially erected police department barricades. Newer housing is constructed with staggered balconies, since each sukkah must be open directly to the sky. Owners of older buildings have often added steel or wood platforms for the sukkah. Construction materials include wood panels, lumber, pressed wood chips, canvas, and plastic.

Simcha Torah (Joy of the Torah), eight days after Succoth, finds the Hasidim celebrating the start of a new cycle of reading portions of the Five Books of Moses. The Torah scrolls, replete with crowns and coverings, are removed from the Ark at the front of the synagogue, taken outdoors, and danced ecstatically in the street. Two other Brooklyn neighborhoods, Borough Park (Bubov Hasidim) and Crown Heights (Lubavitch Hasidim), are places to see dancing with the Torah, sukkahs, and kapparot.

Walking Tour 4
Three Temples of Commerce: Center of Old Downtown Williamsburg When It Was an Ethnically United Neighborhood

To visit the Center of Old Downtown Williamsburg, take the J, M, or Z trains to the Marcy Avenue elevated subway station. The sites are all at the Brooklyn foot of the Williamsburg Bridge.

Williamsburg Art and Historical Center (originally Kings County Savings Bank, 1868)
135 Broadway at Bedford Avenue
718-486-7372

This four-story Second Empire wonder has slender columns, random Keith Haring–style designs on the stonework, and a carved beehive over the front door. Presently, it is an art center, often holding public exhibitions.

Weylin Events Space (formerly HSBC, originally Williamsburgh Savings Bank, 1875)

175 Broadway at Driggs Avenue

The looming eclectic, marble masterpiece in superb condition has neo-classical and Renaissance elements with a Victorian cupola on the dome. It was still owned by the same banking corporation (retaining the *h* in its name) until 1999, which must be some kind of a banking business record.

Holy Trinity Cathedral of Ukrainian Autocephalic Orthodox Church in Exile (originally Williamsburg Trust Company, 1906)

185 South 5th Street at Hewes Street
718-388-4723

This beautiful building is now headquarters for a splinter Eastern Orthodox Christian group, which broke from the Moscow Patriarchate. The only significant change in the building's exterior has been the addition of a three-barred Orthodox cross on the dome.

Continental Army Plaza

Across the street from Holy Trinity Cathedral, South 4th Street at Hewes Street

This is a small nondescript square with a triumphal equestrian statue of General George Washington in commemoration of the hard winter at Valley Forge. Regrettably, the general now faces ingloriously onto one of the exit ramps of the Williamsburg Bridge.

Tour 4 Restaurant Recommendation

Peter Luger's Steak House (established in 1876)

178 Broadway, between Bedford Avenue and Driggs Avenue
718-387-7400

Despite the location, this is not a kosher restaurant. In fact it is considered by many to be Brooklyn's premier steak house. Sturdy tables with bentwood chairs, a decorative tin ceiling, dark wood-paneled walls, and a sawdust-covered floor give Peter Luger's a traditional manly Old New

York steak house look. Through most of its long history, it has been owned and managed by just two men. Peter Luger operated the restaurant until 1941; it went broke in 1950 as industries and offices moved out and Hasidim (who can't eat there) moved in; and it was bought on the bankruptcy auction block by sole bidder Sol Forman, who operated it until his death at age ninety-eight in 2001. Ten tons of steak pass under the kitchen broilers each week. The beef, lamb, and pork are mouth-watering, and there are always seafood and chicken entrées for the less carnivorous. Lunchtime hamburgers are a bargain for a juicy and flavorful patty of chopped beef dressed with a thick slice of raw onion.

GREENPOINT

From Farming Communities to Center of Heavy Industry to Residential Neighborhood

The Dutch presence in Greenpoint, the northwestern corner of Brooklyn, dates from 1630. The fertile sandy soil, meandering streams, several springs, and proximity to Manhattan attracted pioneer farmers. After several bloody skirmishes with Native Americans, Dutch, English, and Scandinavian settlers established hamlets along the East River and Newtown Creek. Waterways rather than roads were the chief avenues of travel and transportation.

The area was originally called Green Point, but evolved into Greenpoint in the nineteenth century. Greenpoint has shorelines on both the East River and the Newtown Creek, which made it convenient for ferry landings to transport farm products to markets in New Amsterdam. Docking facilities grew as farms increased and manufacturing began to take hold.

After the opening of the Erie Canal in 1825, East River commerce increased exponentially. Greenpoint's heyday of shipping and shipbuilding was the mid-nineteenth century. It became a significant center of heavy industry in the two decades before the Civil War. During the war, it was the birthplace of the Union's ironclad vessel, the *Monitor*, which launched on January 30, 1862. It gained naval distinction by engaging the South's reoutfitted ironclad, the *Virginia* (formerly the North's *Merrimack*), in an epic battle on March 9, 1862, in the watery expanse of Hampton Roads, between Hampton and Norfolk, Virginia. They fought to a draw. Neither could defeat the other, but together they signaled the end of wooden warships. (Late in 1862, the *Monitor* sank in a storm off Cape Hatteras, North Carolina. In 2002, divers lifted the remains of the vessel.) The Sneeden and Rowland Shipyard, where the *Monitor* was built from components crafted by the Hecla Iron Works, also produced huge cast-iron pipes to carry drinking water from Westchester County reservoirs to Manhattan.

Greenpoint was the home of the five black arts: printing, pottery, gas, glass and porcelain, and iron. The name "five black arts" came from the black smoke and soot that poured out of their factory chimneys. Each of the industries needed extremely hot furnaces, so coal yards dotted the landscape.

Charles Pratt founded the Astral Oil Works for high-quality kerosene refining in 1867. It was one of scores of refineries set up near the waterfront of Williamsburg, Greenpoint, and Long Island City. Crude oil was shipped to Greenpoint, refined, and then sent out to communities throughout the East Coast. In 1875, Charles Pratt's Astral Oil Works merged with John D. Rockefeller's Standard Oil Company.

Greenpoint became a beehive of production. Beside the five black arts, it was once the home of the Schaefer Brewery, Kirsch Beverages, and the Eberhard Faber Pencil Company, corporations still extant, but doing business elsewhere. Distilleries, chemical plants, glue factories, and paint manufacturers also thrived in Greenpoint. The heavy industries began leaving in the 1920s, seeking cheaper labor and more room to expand. In the years after World War II, Greenpoint further deindustrialized as the light industries also left, frequently because of high labor costs and transportation bottlenecks. By the 1960s, shipping had been eclipsed by trucking, and what little ship traffic remained in Brooklyn gravitated to newer docks in Red Hook and Sunset Park. By 1980, Greenpoint had become a residential community without an industrial base.

Industry's gain was a great loss for Newtown Creek, the body of water separating the northern part of Brooklyn from Queens. The waterway, which was used in colonial times to transport agricultural products on small barges from riverside farms in Brooklyn and Queens to Manhattan, became the repository for sludge and acids from the new industries in Greenpoint (as well as Williamsburg and Long Island City). Constantly dredged and widened, the channel now resembles a fetid canal rather than a creek. Fortunately, by 1980 the Sanitation Department stopped discharging raw sewage into the waterway. Today, Greenpoint sits on top of a massive sludge repository from years of poor stewardship by the industries ridding themselves of waste by pouring effluent into the ground or nearby waterways.

Row houses were built between the 1850s and 1890s in most parts of the neighborhood, and traces of rural life ceased to exist. Greenpoint's housing stock is variegated. There are some very impressive brownstone and brick townhouses, especially in the area between the docks and Manhattan Avenue. Much of the housing, however, was built for workers and consisted of small, simple wood frame buildings or featureless brick apartment houses. Extensive exterior remodeling, much of it lacking in any historical sense, must have resulted in fat commissions for salesmen of siding products. Homes refaced in the 1940s and 1950s carry a layer of asphalt shingles, and those protected from the elements in the past half century are covered in aluminum siding. For extra measure, most houses have installed aluminum door and window awnings. The churches in Greenpoint are much more impressive architecturally than the houses.

Following American independence, Greenpoint began adding German and Irish immigrants to its Dutch, English, and Scandinavian population base. Poles and Italians began settling in Greenpoint at the end of the nineteenth century as they accepted jobs in the area's industrial facilities. In North Greenpoint, the Italian presence has withered as immigration from Italy dried up in the 1950s. Mexicans have replaced most Italians in the north part of the neighborhood, with some enclaves of Chinese, Pakistani, Dominican, Ecuadorian, and Colombian immigrants. Polish immigration skyrocketed after the collapse of the Soviet Union's Eastern European satellite system, and new Polish immigrants have been added to the previous wave that came to South Greenpoint prior to the Great Depression and World War II. Its Polish ethnic composition rejuvenated, Greenpoint has a distinctly Polish flavor: many pharmacies are called *apteka*, flower shops are *kwiaciarnia*, bookshops are *ksiegarnia*, restaurants are *restauracja*, butcher shops are *masarnia*, bakeries are *cukierna*, and many advertisements are written in Polish, whether for imported Okocim beer or Sok fruit juices.

Two well-known bridges crossing the Newtown Creek, both in Greenpoint, are named for American Revolutionary War heroes from Poland who aided General George Washington: Casimir Pulaski (Pulaski Bridge at McGuinness Boulevard) and Tadeusz Kosciuszko (Kosciuszko Bridge at the Brooklyn-Queens Expressway).

While the five black arts yielded jobs and profits and contributed enormously to the neighborhood's development, they also seriously degraded the water table and land below Greenpoint factories by irresponsibly dumping waste products in their yards, where they seeped into the ground. The main environmental problem facing Greenpoint is that the neighborhood rests on a base of polluted sludge, a combination of Brooklyn's natural sand and pollutants wantonly discarded by the five black arts in the nineteenth century. The lake of oily sand is estimated to range from six to fifty feet underground. Since 1995, several pumps have been extracting industrial sludge from the sandy soil. In 2001, it was estimated that 10 million tons of sludge remain to be pumped out of the ground under Greenpoint. The existence of the industrial residue may pose a long-term health risk.

Walking Trip in Greenpoint

 Take the G train (BMT Brooklyn-Queens Crosstown line) to Nassau Avenue Station at Manhattan Avenue.

Or take the L train (BMT Canarsie line) to Bedford Avenue Station (at North 7th Street) in Williamsburg; walk northeast on Bedford Avenue through McCarren Park to Nassau Avenue and Manhattan Avenue. The B61 bus runs northward from Williamsburg through Greenpoint to Queens along Bedford Avenue and Manhattan Avenue.

Walk six short blocks east from the corner of Bedford and Nassau Avenues to Humboldt Street.

Steve's Meat Market

104 Nassau Avenue, between Leonard and Eckford Streets
718-383-1780

A butcher shop with a reputation for superior meats, Steve's sells seven varieties of kielbasa, a smoked sausage, that is 95 percent pork and 5 percent beef, each variety infused with garlic. Some of the choices are krajana (thickly ground, chunky meat), siekana (flecked with coarsely ground black pepper), jalowcowa (with crushed juniper berries), wiejska (village-style with paprika), and skinny kabanosy. Steve's Meat Market also sells bacon slabs, hams, pork chops, and cheeses. All the signs are in Polish, but if pointing won't do, the butchers will use some English to help you out.

 Turn right (south) one long block on Humboldt Street.

St. Stanislaus Kostka Church (Roman Catholic)
607 Humboldt Street at Driggs Avenue
718-388-0170

Enormous with its asymmetrical octagonal towers visible from afar, St. Stanislaus Kostka Church, built in 1890, dominates the east end of Greenpoint. The substantial stone edifice contrasts sharply with the small frame houses surrounding it, a testament to the importance of Roman Catholicism here. The icon of the Mother of God of Czestochowa (from the Jasna Gora Monastery in Czestochowa, Poland) is the focus of much attention from worshippers. Outside, the intersection has two additional names: Pope John Paul II Plaza and Lech Walesa Place. (Lech Walesa was the spokesman of the strike at the Lenin Shipyard in Gdansk and leader of the Solidarity Movement throughout Poland, which helped topple the Communist regime. He later served as Poland's president.)

 Turn right (west) on Driggs Avenue for five blocks, then right (north) on Manhattan Avenue eight blocks to India Street.

Greenpoint Fish & Lobster
174 Nassau Avenue, at the corner of Eckford Street

Catering to a neighborhood appetite for freshwater fish is not so easy in New York, but this lively fish store manages to have large carp, perch, and Polish eels in stock, along with cold water ocean fish, especially cod and mackerel, as well as lobster and shrimp.

Sidewalk Clock

In front of 733 Manhattan Avenue, between Norman and
Meserole Avenues

Protected by landmark designation, this is one of only a handful of sidewalk clocks left in New York, which once advertised watchmaker shops and jewelry stores throughout the city. It represents a time when common people rarely had the money to have their own timepieces.

Green Point Savings Bank

807 Manhattan Avenue, at the corner of Calyer Street

The light granite neoclassical structure built in 1908 with a large dome was an impressive temple of commerce for the neighborhood at the intersection that was once its business hub. The layered slate fish-scale shingles distinguish it from other domed buildings in the city. Green Point Savings Bank, incorporated in 1869, was the leading bank in the neighborhood in the nineteenth century. The building is presently a Capital One Bank.

Markowa Apteka Pharmacy

831 Manhattan Avenue, between Calyer and Noble Streets
718-389-0389

This full-service pharmacy carries grooming paraphernalia, creams, lotions, soaps and cosmetics, and toothpaste from Poland, as well as American and European vitamins. This is where the neighborhood women seek difficult-to-locate cosmetics better known in Poland than in the United States. Advice is freely given about beauty enhancement.

St. Anthony of Padua and St. Alphonsus Church (Roman Catholic)

862 Manhattan Avenue at Milton Street
718-383-3339

German Catholics formed St. Anthony's congregation in 1856, though Irish immigrants soon became the majority. St. Alphonsus Church (on Manhattan Avenue) merged with it a century later, and the united congregation kept both names. The church is a strikingly bright, two-toned house of worship constructed in 1875, which towers over the surroundings in both height and architectural features. The style is a type of French Gothic articulated by white limestone zipper-like quoins at the corners. The basic construction material is red brick. The church sports a tall central spire at its front embedded with clocks. Located at a slight bend in Manhattan Avenue and situated to face west on Milton Street, the church is a noted neighborhood landmark. The interior space is bright and airy, with slender columns and eight large stained-glass windows on each side. The windows tell the story of the life of Jesus, beginning at the left with the marriage of Anna and Joachim, Mary's parents, and ending on the right with the Descent of the Holy Spirit. Most statues are white marble except for painted statues of St. Theresa and St. Francis at the rear of the church. Presently, the congregation serves a mixed community with masses in English, Polish, and Spanish.

Old Poland Bakery

926 Manhattan Avenue, between Greenpoint Avenue and Kent Street
718-349-7900

This bakery produces traditional Polish white and black breads, rurki (cream-filled rolls), cheese babka (coffee cake), markowiec (poppy-seed cake), apple cakes, jelly donuts, and prune, apricot, and cherry pastries.

St. Elias Byzantine Greek Rite Church (Roman Catholic)

145 Kent Street, just west of Manhattan Avenue

Built in 1869 as the Dutch Reform Church of Green Point, the building is a combination of brownstone, limestone, and brick with interesting red and grey striped arch stones in the front, and an octagonal belfry. Next to it is an octagonal Sunday school. Inside, much of the church still reflects simple Protestant tastes: large airy barnlike space with stained-glass windows adorned only with geometric designs. The front has been substantially modified with two side altars, four icon stands (Jesus, Mary, Nicholas, and Elias), and an overpowering white, gold, and blue Baroque baldachino (stone canopy) over the altar. Everything is in view because there is no iconostasis (icon screen), as there would be in an Eastern Orthodox Christian Church. Above and behind the altar is a painting of

St. Elias (Prophet Elijah) in the wilderness being fed by birds. Services in the Byzantine Greek Rite Church are very similar to the Western Church (Roman Catholic), with some noticeable differences: liberal use of incense, crossing from right to left, priests facing the altar instead of the congregation, and the Eucharist as mixed wine and bread accepted from a spoon in Orthodox fashion. This Uniate church served a small, mostly Slovakian and Ruthenian community in Greenpoint. Greek Rite churches are known as Uniate churches in Eastern Europe, the product of a 1596 agreement at the Council of Brest-Litovsk when six out of eight Orthodox bishops present accepted a compromise union with the Roman Catholic Church in which they recognized the ecclesiastical supremacy of Rome but kept their Greek (Byzantine) rituals. They have a separate hierarchy, an exarchate, up to the level of bishop. This was done when western Ukraine and Slovakia were part of Jagiellonian dynasty Poland, so it is seen as a political as well as religious decision. The church building is presently closed and up for sale. The nearest Byzantine Greek Rite Church is St. Mary's at 15th Street and 2nd Avenue in Manhattan (212-677-0516).

 Turn left (west) on India Street one long block to Franklin Street; walk south on Franklin Street five short blocks to Noble Street.

The Astral Apartments
184 Franklin Street, between India Street and Java Street

This massive six-story apartment complex was built in 1886 for the workers in Pratt's kerosene refinery. Patterned brickwork and rough brownstone and brick arches decorate the building. The low doorway arches give the ground floor a cave-like appearance. Despite the dark, medieval look, the Astral Apartments were carefully designed to maximize internal light and space and were heralded at the time as a great reform in workers' housing.

Eberhard Faber Pencil Company
Corner of Franklin Street at Greenpoint Avenue

Eberhard Faber, a German pencil company, opened in 1872 and closed in 1956. The former factory that manufactured the well-known pencil brand is decorated with a series of eye-catching large yellow #2 pencils standing on end on all sides along its top floor. The space is now home to several light manufacturers and artisan shops.

Polish Home Service Agency (originally Mechanics and Traders Bank)

144 Franklin Street, at the corner of Greenpoint Avenue
718-389-6117

This beautiful and gracefully slim 1895 bank building, constructed to resemble a Florentine villa, has particularly large windows and a substantial cornice. It is made of all the coveted building materials of the day: brownstone, red brick, and intricate terra-cotta.

 Turn left (east) on Noble Street one block to Manhattan Avenue.

Congregation Ahavas Israel of Greenpoint (Jewish)

108 Noble Street, between Franklin Street and Manhattan Avenue
718-383-8475

A metal Star of David rests on the gable of the two-story beige brick building with large windows rounded at the top. A congregation of German Jews organized the Orthodox synagogue in 1893 and built the narrow structure in 1904 next to an older Reform synagogue, built as a Congregational Church in 1871. The two Jewish congregations merged, though the older structure, covered in brick-faced perma-stone, is unused except for the basement. The interior of Ahavas Israel (Love of Israel), up a set of steep stairs, is long and remarkably narrow, illuminated by front and rear windows and by three circular skylights with red, white, and blue stained glass in a pie-wedge pattern. The sconces along the walls are highlighted by delightfully whimsical folk designs. There are primitive folk-style menorahs and Stars of David decoratively painted on the plaster walls. The Ark is made of hand-carved wood with a pair of magnificent lions guarding the two tablets featuring the Ten Commandments. The women's balcony wraps around three sides of the interior. Greenpoint never had a large Jewish population, and this congregation is the only synagogue in the neighborhood. (Saturday services are held at 9:00 a.m.)

Turn left (west) on Manhattan Avenue two blocks to the G subway station at Greenpoint Avenue.

Or once at Manhattan Avenue, turn right (south) on Manhattan Avenue for five blocks, then right (south) on Bedford Avenue through McCarren Park and Northside Williamsburg to L train at Bedford Avenue Station at North 7th Street.

Exit Greenpoint south on Bedford Street through McCarren Park.

Rev. Jerzy Popieluszko Triangle

North corner of McCarren Park at Bedford Street and Nassau Avenue

This patriotic monument was erected in honor of Polish anti-Communist, pro-Solidarity priest Fr. Jerzy Popieluszko, who was murdered by the authorities in 1984. The rough granite stone, cut in the shape of Poland, is topped by the head of the popular young Roman Catholic priest from Warsaw. Neighborhood women voluntarily tend the garden, which is just north of the large pink and beige Brooklyn High School of Automotive Trades and at the end of the line of mature London plane trees shading Bedford Street.

McCarren Park

At the south end of Greenpoint, forming the dividing line between Greenpoint and Williamsburg

A welcome patch of green between two neighborhoods with sparse park space, thirty-six-acre McCarren Park was completed in 1910 and named for state senator Patrick McCarren, who sponsored the legislation to build the Williamsburg Bridge, which connected Brooklyn's Williamsburg-Greenpoint-Bushwick sections with Manhattan's Lower East Side in 1903. Truncated into four parts by area streets, each segment serves a different use: tennis courts, softball diamonds, soccer field, and playground. London plane trees fill the bordering areas and provide shade for picnickers. The city's largest swimming pool, three times the dimensions of an Olympic pool, was opened in 1936 by Mayor Fiorello La Guardia and parks commissioner Robert Moses in the eastern section of McCarren Park. It can hold 6,800 swimmers.

Restaurant Recommendations

Krolewskie Jadlo (Polish)

694 Manhattan Avenue, between Norman and Meserole Avenues
718-383-8993

This intimate and welcoming Polish restaurant is a cheerful place for lunch or dinner. The half-timbered interior with heavy dark wooden picnic booths has a studied rustic look. The staff is friendly and tries to be helpful answering questions about the food. The menu is broad but predictable: stuffed cabbage, golonka (pig knuckle with a thick layer of crispy fat), Hungarian potato pancakes (stuffed with goulash meat), pierogi, bigos (hunter's stew), various chicken, pork, and fish dishes, mostly deep fried cutlets. The soup selection usually includes barszcz (strained Polish-style beet borscht), Lithuanian borscht (with hard-boiled egg), zurek (fermented, slightly sour soup with bits of sausage, a hard-boiled egg, and a potato dumpling), refreshingly light pickle soup, pea soup, and chicken soup. Large helpings are guaranteed and always accompanied by mashed potatoes with gravy, one scoop of sweet sauerkraut, and one scoop of a vegetable, such as sweetened carrots, turnips, or peas. There is a full bar at the front of the restaurant.

Polish and Slavic Credit Union (Polish)

177 Kent Street, between Manhattan Avenue and McGuinness Boulevard
718-349-1033

This quiet modern cafeteria caters to an older crowd who come for a good bargain. Hearty black or white bread, soup of the day like barszcz or warm cucumber soup, and one of several familiar entrées are the daily fare: meat loaf, roast chicken, veal cutlets, stuffed cabbage, pierogi, golonka, and mashed potatoes sprinkled with dill. The Polish and Slavic Credit Union, organized in 1903 in Williamsburg, subsidizes the meals. It is also the main banking institution involved in financing house purchases in Greenpoint. The church building (formerly St. Alphonsus Roman Catholic Church) between the bank and the restaurant, part of the three-building complex, is the Polish and Slavic Credit Union Cultural Center.

Rzeszowska Restaurant (Polish)

931 Manhattan Avenue, between Kent Street and Java Street
718-349-7501

Decidedly elegant among its proletarian competitors, Rzeszowska is decorated in a monochromatic scheme with tables set farther apart amid a profusion of plastic flowers and Christmas lights. Prices are set a bit higher than the other Polish restaurants. Outside, the awning reads *Polskie Obiady* (Polish meals) and a large sign advertising Zywiec, a popular Polish beer, dominates the front. The menu is basically the same as everywhere else, though the specials sometimes rise above the level of folk cuisine. One way to try everything is to order the house sample platter, featuring bigos, kielbasa, blintzes, sauerkraut, and four varieties of pierogi. The restaurant's signature dish is the Rzeszow cutlet, a fried pork cutlet in the style of the city of Rzeszow, served with a layer of mushrooms and processed American cheese over the meat, a garnish of beets, pickles, onions, and beans, and accompanied by boiled potatoes liberally sprinkled with dill. Meals may be accompanied by sweet Polish wine, or imported beer: Zywiec, Hevelius Kaper, Piast, Krakus, Okocim, or Zubr.

CROWN HEIGHTS & WEEKSVILLE

Crown Heights History

Crown Heights, along both sides of Eastern Parkway, is the area north of Lefferts Gardens and south of Bedford-Stuyvesant. It is a residential community built on colonial farmland. None of the colonial-era buildings exist, though four nineteenth-century houses, once part of Weeksville, a village of free blacks, survive in the northeastern part of the area.

The center of Crown Heights is built upon a glacial moraine, the southernmost extension of the Wisconsin ice sheet. On the crest of the moraine, colonists built an east–west thoroughfare along an American Indian path. Today, Eastern Parkway is situated on the older road.

Farmland predominated in the area until the mid-nineteenth century. Farmers took advantage of the nearby urban market in southern Manhattan, which paid comparatively high prices for fresh vegetables, dairy products, and livestock. The roads from north central Brooklyn to the towns of Williamsburg and Brooklyn (now the northern end of Brooklyn Heights where it meets DUMBO) were filled with farm wagons on their way to East River ferries.

Population in the area increased markedly with the 1825 opening of the Erie Canal, and clusters of wood frame houses were built in Crown Heights. The northern section developed first due to its proximity to Bushwick and Williamsburg. East of the center of Crown Heights was Weeksville, the free black community. European immigrants, mostly Roman Catholics from Ireland and Germany, moved into the large surrounding area in the years between the Civil War and World War I.

By 1900, the southern part of Crown Heights began filling with substantial three-story single-family and attached two-family houses. Apartment buildings were constructed during the boom years of the 1920s. Between World War I and II, southern Crown Heights became a middle-class Jewish area.

Ebbets Field, home of the Brooklyn Dodgers from 1913 until 1957, was located at Bedford Avenue and Sullivan Place, now the site of an apartment complex named for Jackie Robinson. The Dodgers were originally the Brooklyn Trolley-Dodgers, an allusion to the borough's reputation for being reticulated with a maze of trolley lines.

The centerpiece of Crown Heights is the grand boulevard, Eastern Parkway, which was designed in 1866 by Frederick Law Olmsted and Calvert Vaux, architects of Central Park, Prospect Park, and Ocean Parkway. It was reputed to be the first six-lane roadway in the United States. Four lanes comprise the artery's center, flanked by wide tree-lined medians with promenades and horse paths. Service lanes run along the edges. The effect is an elegant parkway only somewhat diminished by the transition from horse carriages to automobiles over the past fourteen decades.

Eastern Parkway was designed to be a noncommercial, park-like passage. Business districts sprouted up along the north–south avenues: Bedford, Franklin, Nostrand, Brooklyn, Kingston, Utica, and Schenectady. An impressive cluster of significant cultural institutions stood at the west end of Eastern Parkway. The Brooklyn Museum, the Brooklyn Botanic Gardens, the main branch of the Brooklyn Public Library, Prospect Park, and Medgar Evers College compose the core of Brooklyn's cultural center. Other institutions are scattered around the borough, but the concentration near the western end of Eastern Parkway gives gravity to the location.

Following World War II, large numbers of Brooklynites left for the suburbs in Long Island and New Jersey. Crown Heights whites were replaced by Caribbean blacks, mostly from Jamaica, Haiti, Trinidad, Guyana, Barbados, the east coast of Panama, and the smaller islands of the Caribbean. Between 1940 and 1950, the black population in Brooklyn soared from 108,000 to 208,000. About half the black population of Brooklyn is of Caribbean ancestry. By 2002, a half million West Indians lived in the borough. Many settled in Crown Heights and the areas both north and south. The entire north central core of Brooklyn, including

Crown Heights, is sometimes referred to as Bedford-Stuyvesant. Caribbean immigrants also reside in East Flatbush.

Hasidim began arriving in Crown Heights during the war years. *"America iz nit anderesh"* (in English: "America is no different"), proclaimed Rebbe Yosef Yitzchak Schneersohn in 1940, as he authorized settlement in the changing neighborhood where secular Jews and Irish were leaving and blacks from the Caribbean and the American South were arriving. The Lubavitch Hasidic community newly arrived from Eastern Europe was a remnant of the Holocaust and numbered only in the hundreds. His Yiddish statement became an article of faith; the Lubavitch community was determined to sink roots and stay in Crown Heights.

Rabbi Israel ben Eliezer (1698–1760) of Okopy in the Carpathian Mountains of Podolia (alternatively in Western Ukraine or Eastern Romania) initiated the Hasidic Movement. He is known as the Besht from the acronym B-Sh-T, meaning Baal Shem Tov or Master of the Good Name. Miraculous cures and feats were attributed to the mystical kabbalist. The Besht emphasized love of God, Israel, and Torah, and imbued his teachings and study with blissful singing and dancing. The term *hasid* means pious in Hebrew.

To the Hasidim, pious fervor in prayer was as important as Talmudic learning. Inspired laymen replaced cantors in Hasidic synagogues. Storytelling and parables were used to make theological points, and hundreds of wondrous legends grew around the movement's leaders. Opponents of the Hasidim, called Misnagdim (literally opponents), viewed them as excessively emotional and populist, blasphemous, and sacrilegious, and reacted against some of their changes in Jewish worship.

The kabbalah (received tradition, or gnostic knowledge) dates from medieval Europe. It is a collection of hidden meanings based on esoteric interpretations of Hebrew scriptures, many deduced from the gematria of words, the numerical value of the Hebrew letters, which are also numbers. Kabbalah, reserved for advanced scholars by the Misnagdim, was introduced to everyday life and discourse by the Hasidim.

The followers of Hasidut vigorously opposed Haskala (the Enlightenment) and the secularization of education in eighteenth-century Europe. Their method of Hasidic study, pilpul, is meant to infuse scholarship with energy and intellectual challenges. Two students take sides in an argument from the Talmud and, in a role-playing exercise, argue all the possibilities of each issue. The excitement of pilpul was meant to steal the thunder from the Enlightenment.

Two centuries before the establishment of the State of Israel, Hasidic leaders opposed secular Zionism on several grounds: most Zionists rejected exile (*galut*) and a messiah-led return to Israel, and Zionists embraced the Enlightenment and rejected Jewish orthodoxy.

Local proselytizers of the Besht's school of thought are called tsaddiks (righteous men). Each tsaddik establishes a court with a synagogue, school, and residence. Succeeding leadership of the Hasidic tradition, generally one per town or shtetl (village), is passed down through his male descendants, each of whom assume the title rebbe. The rebbe makes communal decisions and interprets the Torah and commentaries. Since the Hasidism in Europe was centered in Eastern Europe, it was mostly destroyed in the Holocaust. Today, Brooklyn is the worldwide center of Hasidic life, and Crown Heights is one of the three large Hasidic neighborhoods in the borough. There are about two hundred large and small Hasidic groups in Brooklyn.

Israel Ha-Besht was succeeded in leadership by Dov Ber, the Great Maggid (preacher) of Mezeritch. Schneur Zalman of Liadi (1745–1813) was the founder of Chabad Lubavitch and the first of seven Lubavitcher rebbes. The three consonants of the acronym *Chabad* stand for wisdom, understanding, and knowledge. Each of the seven Lubavitch rebbes is also known by a familiar name: Schneur Zalman (Alter Rebbe) was succeeded by Dovber Schneuri (Mitteler Rebbe), then Menachem Mendel Schneerson (Tzemach Tzedek), Shmuel Schneerson (Rebbe Maharash), Sholom Dovber Schneerson (Rebbe Rashab), Yosef Yitzchak Schneersohn (Frierdiker Rebbe), and Menachem Mendel Schneerson (The Rebbe). The village of Lubavitch lies near Vitebsk, Belarus, close to Smolensk, Russia.

Menahem Mendel Schneerson assumed leadership on the death of his father-in-law, Yosef Yitzchak Schneersohn—referred to by Lubavitchers as the Frierdiker Rebbe (previous rebbe)—in 1950 and internationalized Chabad Lubavitch through Agudas Chasidei Chabad-Lubavitch, the movement's representative body. They used modern means (sound trucks, radio, fax machines, cable television, and ultimately computers and cell phones) to aggressively proselytize among Jews. The point was not to convert Jews wholly to embrace the Lubavitch perspective, but to persuade Jews to be incrementally more observant (i.e., to affix mezuzahs to doorposts, wear yarmulkes, light Sabbath candles, keep the Sabbath, celebrate holidays, put on tefillin, attend synagogue regularly, join study groups, and keep kosher homes). Lubavitchers are active in New York City and Israel as street missionaries. They proselytize on college campuses and operate a large system of Jewish day schools. Two thousand young rabbis volunteer as unpaid shluchim (missionaries) around the globe, frequently serving synagogues without resident clergy. Lubavitch rabbis currently lead the main synagogues in St. Petersburg, Russia, and Minsk, Belarus. Lubavitchers proselytize among Jews, which is in striking contrast to other Hasidic groups, which insulate themselves from non-Hasidic Jews as well as other ultra-Orthodox Jews. Lubavitchers claim two hundred thousand followers.

In Crown Heights, portraits of the seventh Lubavitcher rebbe, Menachem Mendel Schneerson (1902–1994), are omnipresent. While alive, he was believed by many of his followers to be the *mosiach* (messiah) who would soon reveal himself to the Jewish people. While never proclaiming himself messiah, Schneerson frequently claimed redemption was at hand, saying our generation is the final generation of *galut* (exile) and the first generation of the *geulah* (redemption).

During the last few years of his life, a large English banner stretched across the front of the Grand Synagogue read: *We Want Mosiach Now!* Inside, a Hebrew banner along the southern wall remains:

Yechi Adoneinu Moreinu V'Rabbenu Melech HaMosiach L'Olom Vo'ed! (Long Live Our Master, Our Teacher, Our Rebbe, King Messiah Forever and Ever!)

Schneerson's death in 1994 severely altered the notion of singular dynastic leadership and the proposition that he was the messiah. He is buried next to his father-in-law in Montefiore Cemetery in St. Albans, Queens. The group's leaders have not chosen a successor to the childless rebbe, and may never do so. At first Lubavitchers were in denial that the rebbe had died and would not return. Many still speak of him in the present tense. The explanation for his death most often heard is that

Schneerson, like Moses, who temporarily left the Jewish people to go to Midan and later to Mount Sinai, will ultimately return, as Moses did.

The Lubavitchers occupy only one part of Crown Heights. The area surrounding the Hasidic enclave and the neighborhoods around Crown Heights together constitute the largest black community in New York City. West Indians predominate among blacks in north central Brooklyn.

The West Indian Day Parade, the largest ethnic parade in the city, is a kind of Carnival held not at Mardi Gras, because of the cold weather, but at Labor Day in September. It moved from Harlem to Crown Heights in 1960. The parade symbolizes the enormous impact of Caribbean immigration to Brooklyn and the city. The parade, the signature public event of Caribbean Islanders, moves along Eastern Parkway and lasts several hours with as many as two million people participating and observing. The theme is West Indian cultural identity, and each national group's participants march with dazzling costumes to live music and perform vibrant dance steps while receiving thunderous applause. Onlookers eat a selection from hundreds of amateur vendors selling curried goat, jerk chicken, roti, coconut bread, and Jamaican beef patties.

The tense relations between the Lubavitch and the West Indian communities erupted in 1991 as the last car in the Lubavitcher Rebbe's entourage ran a red light and killed a black child. The driver, who subsequently fled to Israel, ran the red light to keep up with the caravan heading to Montefiore Cemetery in Queens to pray at the grave of the previous rebbe. A riot ensued and a visiting Australian Hasid was knifed. He died several hours later at Kings County Hospital. Racial divisions were polarized by the event. Since then, there has been peace and calm in the neighborhood as the two groups keep an uneasy truce.

Weeksville History

Weeksville is a remnant community of a free black settlement in central Brooklyn's agricultural lands where former slaves gravitated to farm and carry on mechanical trades. The community developed in 1838 after James Weeks, a New York stevedore born in Virginia, purchased land for a farm from the estate of the Lefferts family who owned vast acreage in central Brooklyn. In 1827, slavery was abolished in New York State, though the law did not go into full effect until 1841. Sensing better days ahead, many free blacks were looking to buy land and establish their own community. Perhaps some were also encouraged by the desire to comply with the $250 property requirement imposed on black men as a prerequisite for voting. Slavery had been a major institution in colonial Brooklyn. Dutch farmers, in particular, used African slaves to tend their vegetable, grain, livestock, and dairy farms.

The Weeksville community developed churches, a cemetery, a school, an orphanage, and an old age home. While no trace of the cemetery has been found, other institutions thrive. The Bethel Tabernacle African Methodist Episcopal Church, organized in 1847, and the Berean Missionary Baptist Church, started in 1851, remain active congregations, though not in their original buildings. Colored School #2 was formed in 1847. The Brooklyn Howard Colored Orphan Asylum was founded in 1866 and named for Freedmen's Bureau leader, General Oliver O. Howard. The Zion Home for the Colored Aged was established in 1869 to provide for the impoverished elderly.

By 1890, Brooklyn's black population had reached ten thousand. But the immense European migration from Germany, Ireland, and Italy greatly outpaced black settlement. By the 1920s, farmland had disappeared, and row houses and apartment buildings lined the streets. Roman Catholic churches and Jewish synagogues became far more numerous than either black or white Protestant churches. Weeksville ceased to exist as a separate community and was gradually forgotten by most people.

In the 1940s and 1950s, the area changed again. Caribbean and American blacks moved into north central Brooklyn. By 2000, Brooklyn's black population reached five hundred thousand, two-thirds in Bedford-Stuyvesant. Not much of Weeksville physically survived all the building projects and ethnic changes.

Only three modest houses from Weeksville along the last remnant of Hunterfly Road, a rural north–south artery built to connect seventeenth-century settlements in Bushwick and Canarsie, remain. Hunterfly Road itself was displaced by later street grids except for two short sections: the one-block stretch that remained as an unmarked alley with the three houses, and Hunterfly Place, a short one-block street four blocks northwest. Hunterfly Place, like the rest of this portion of Bedford-Stuyvesant, lacks any original buildings from Weeksville.

Walking Trip in Crown Heights

 Take the IRT #3 train to Kingston Avenue Station. Cross Eastern Parkway's service road to the south.

Lubavitch Hasidim Grand Synagogue

770 Eastern Parkway, at the corner of Kingston Avenue
718-774-4000

The unassuming, four-story redbrick apartment building with the ground floor and basement scooped out to make a large synagogue is the Lubavitch World Headquarters. The shabby look of the building's exterior is matched on the inside, which is a large, stark room covered with brown paneling. The disregard for pulchritude underscores the Lubavitch commitment to intense religiosity. Men are seen exuberantly davening (swaying) while reciting prayers and gesticulating in intense religious debate during pilpul study. The large unadorned space serves a dual purpose. During the day, tables and chairs are set up for men to assume sides arguing in pilpul fashion on various questions raised in the Talmud. The furniture is then removed for services when the faithful crowd into the synagogue for group prayers. Everyone stands, and periodically the assemblage breaks out in robust niggunim (wordless melodies with filler syllables, and energetic dancing one behind the next in circular snaking patterns [hakafa]). There are twenty-five other Lubavitch synagogues in Brooklyn, but holidays and special events draw thousands to 770 Eastern Parkway. One event that fills the synagogue is the periodic farbrengen (get-together), when men gather for several hours at the final days of the Three Festivals: Pesach (Passover), Shavuot (celebration of the conclusion of the grain harvest and the revelation of the Torah at Mount Sinai), and Succoth (Festival of Booths). The faithful come to listen to the rebbe or other community leaders expound on religious issues. The women's balcony, along the northern wall, has thick yellow plastic over the glass to cut the possibility that men will be distracted. Few women attend services, though the enclosed balcony serves as a place where women can go to read prayers or study.

Rebbe's House

770 Eastern Parkway, next to the synagogue, one hundred feet west of Kingston Avenue

The three-story brown brick building is a well-known, frequently photographed symbol of the Chabad Lubavitch movement. Beneath its three gables, the large house contains a study room, meeting rooms, the museum of the history of the Lubavitch sect, the rebbe's apartment (upstairs), and his study. The rebbe's book-lined study, untouched since his death, is left intact with its door open. Above the front entrance of 770 is an inscription placed there in 1940 by the previous rebbe on his arrival in Brooklyn: *Ohel Yossef Yitzchock, Lubavitch, Beis Agudas Chasidei Chabad* (Tent of Joseph Isaac, Lubavitch, House of the Chabad Hasidic Association). The Lubavitch built an exact replica of 770 Eastern Parkway in Kafar Chabad, Israel. Mystical Jewish tradition holds that when the messiah comes, all Jews will fly on clouds to Israel. The look-alike house awaits the messiah. (None of the Lubavitcher rebbes ever visited Israel.) The third floor of the museum is interesting, though few of the exhibits are labeled in English. It is arranged around the Baal Shem Tov, the Maggid of Mezeritch, and the seven Lubavitcher rebbes. Handwriting samples of the rebbes, the passport of the previous rebbe, and the ma'amorim (encyclicals) of the rebbes are displayed in glass cases. A model of the Temple in Jerusalem is also exhibited. Next to the rebbe's house is a miniature artificial river, a mechanically powered contraption twenty-feet long and built of cemented fieldstones, to simulate moving water so landlocked Crown Heights Hasidim can symbolically cast their sins into a river at Rosh Hashanah in a ceremony called tashlich. Most Lubavitchers fulfill this obligation by driving to the East River or the Atlantic Ocean during the Days of Awe, between Rosh Hashanah and Yom Kippur. Those who cannot make the trip may cast their bread in this water.

 Walk back to the corner of Eastern Parkway and Kingston Avenue; proceed south on Kingston Avenue.

Lubavitch Library

305 Kingston Avenue, between Eastern Parkway and Union Street

Down a flight of steps is the Lubavitch community library and reading room, where men, women, boys, and girls mingle to take out books or read them at any of several round tables. Most Hasidim own the key Talmudic commentaries and various devotional books in their personal libraries, so the community library is rarely crowded.

Hasofer, Inc.

1442 Union Street (2nd floor), at the corner of Kingston Avenue
718-221-2222

Six sofrim (scribes) and technicians work in this lively production and repair shop. The scribes, males only, write Torahs (scroll of the Five Books of Moses), ketubahs (marriage contracts), and inscriptions for mezuzahs (small containers placed on doorjambs) and tefillin (phylacteries, or leather boxes on straps worn around the arm and head during certain prayers). Producing a Torah is a yearlong undertaking and is normally done on contract from a synagogue. The scribe uses sixty rectangular segments of animal hide (usually cow, but sometimes goat or sheep) for the scroll. The separate sheets of hide parchment are later sewn together with cow sinew. Ink must be made from a boiled mixture of acid from gall nuts, gum Arabic, and copper vitriol. The writing quill comes from a kosher goose or turkey, carefully cut by the scribe. As the scribe copies each letter, he needs to say the letter aloud to help assure accuracy. If the Torah is even one letter off, the scroll is not kosher and cannot be used. People bring old mezuzahs and tefillin so the scribes can open them and check the accuracy of the inscriptions. If there is an error, or if the writing is deteriorating, new inscriptions are written and resealed in their containers.

Eber's Liquors & Wine

314 Kingston Avenue, between Union and President Streets
718-604-8700

This is a shop of surprises. Eber's stocks an enormous variety of kosher wines from Israel, California, France, Italy, Argentina, Chile, Australia, and South Africa. It also offers a large selection of other liquors, including single malt scotch, bourbon, rye, gin, and vodka with brand names such as J&B, Johnnie Walker, Stolichnaya, Absolut, Jim Beam, and Crown Royal. Any edible product can be sold as kosher. Wine can be kosher, though grapes are pareve, or neutral (neither milk nor meat), and obviously do not need slaughtering. Imported wines from Israel, France, Italy, and elsewhere can be certified kosher. That has long been the case with local wines, such as Mogen David, Kedem, and Schapiro's. The kosher certification establishes that the vineyard does not have a Christian religious shrine, the grapevines were not blessed by a Christian priest, and nothing nonkosher touched the wine during processing.

Raskin's Fish Market

320 Kingston Avenue, between Union and President Streets
718-756-9521

This small fish shop offers a variety of finfish: salmon, flounder, tuna, sole, halibut, and sea bass. The fish are sold whole, though the countermen will clean, scale, and fillet the fish on request. Raskin's carries only seafood deemed kosher. Certain sea creatures are prohibited in the Bible:

> These shall ye eat of all that are in the waters: whatsoever hath fins and scales in the waters, in the seas, and in the rivers, them shall ye eat. And all that have not fins and scales in the seas, and in the rivers, of all that move in the waters, and of any living thing which is in the waters, they shall be an abomination unto you. (Lev. 11:9–10 KJV)

The prohibition includes eels, catfish, crayfish, squid, octopus, lobsters, shrimp, mussels, oysters, and clams.

Judaica World Gift Shop

329 Kingston Avenue, between Union and President Streets
718-604-1020

This combination gift and bookshop is abundantly stocked with biblical commentaries, devotional literature, videos, yarmulkes, candelabras, mezuzahs, goblets, and Passover serving plates. Most of the key chains, photos, refrigerator magnets, wall clocks, wallet cards, and posters feature the likeness of Rebbe Schneerson.

Crown Heights House of Glatt

385 Kingston Avenue, at the corner of Crown Street
718-467-9411

This glatt-kosher butcher shop carries a full line of kosher meats and a modest variety of deli products (potato pancakes, beef dumplings, stuffed cabbage, potato pudding). *Glatt* means extremely or extra, which is how the Hasidim describe their oversight of kosher food. Crown Heights Kosher, symbolized by a small HK inside a larger C and topped with a crown, is the emblem of the Lubavitch rabbinical authority overseeing kosher food. In the ritual slaughtering process (shekhitah), the Jewish shohet (slaughterer) slits the throat of the animal with a horizontal cut across the windpipe and gullet and carefully drains out the blood. The chalaph (knife) must be sharp and free of notches, dents, or cracks. If the knife is not sharp, it will cause drassa (pressing of the knife against the skin of the neck), which renders the process unkosher. This method of slaughtering delivers what is considered a painless death as required by Judaism. No blood is allowed, because it is prohibited in several passages in Leviticus and Deuteronomy:

> Moreover ye shall eat no manner of blood, whether it be of fowl or of beast, in any of your dwellings. Whatsoever soul it be that eateth any manner of blood, even that soul shall be cut off from his people. (Lev. 7:26–27 KJV)

> Only be sure that thou eat not the blood: for the blood is the life; and thou mayest not eat the life with the flesh. Thou shalt not eat it; thou shalt pour it upon the earth as water. (Deut. 12:23–24 KJV)

After the jugular vein of an animal is severed, most of the blood runs out. Much of the rest is extracted by soaking the meat for a half hour in warm water (but not more than 120 degrees) and sprinkling it with medium grain salt (kosher salt). There are other prohibitions. Fat that is not intermingled with flesh (*kheleb*) and forms a separate layer is forbidden, though fat that is intermingled with flesh (*shuman*) is allowed. The hindquarters of an animal (behind the twelfth rib) are prohibited to eat. Any adhesions between the lungs and the thoracic walls or discoloration of the lungs, liver, and spleen disqualify the animal for certification as kosher.

Kosher Foods

Kosher laws were initially practiced piecemeal, since no central Jewish authority (like the Vatican) exists. Hasidic Jews felt prevailing kosher standards were too low in the United States and came up with their own certification: *glatt kosher*, which means extremely kosher. Because there are more than two hundred Hasidic groups in New York, leading Hasidic rabbis often certified products using differing standards. The Kosher Meat Riots of 1902, 1910, 1929, and 1937 were sparked by consumer claims of price gouging and lax food-processing standards. State laws regulating products deemed kosher were passed fragmentarily beginning in 1882. Eventually the state government stepped in forcefully, and the New York Department of Agriculture and Markets was established to enforce the law so that food represented as kosher really was kosher. In 2000, a federal judge in Brooklyn ruled the laws unconstitutional because they violate the First Amendment, separation of church and state, by involving the government in religious practices. Judge Nina Gershon ruled:

> The entanglements involved here between religion and the state are not only excessive in themselves, but they have the unconstitutional effect of endorsing and advancing religion.[8]

Kosher boards still exist, but they are private and no longer under state authority. Since all boards are presently Hasidic, all kosher food products and eating establishments are also glatt kosher. By the 1950s, half the Jewish population was living in many scattered communities in the United States, and large companies began accepting kosher oversight by rabbis to certify some of their products as kosher. Oversight meant that a rabbi would periodically visit the food-processing plant to certify that the foods were being prepared in accordance with kosher rules. The mark indicating kosher found on many foods is a circle (standing for the letter *O*) surrounding the letter *U*, verifying approval by the Union of Orthodox Hebrew Congregations. (The symbol is called the *O-U*.) A letter *K* also signifies kosher. Some food companies have always produced traditionally Jewish foods, such as Manischewitz, Rokeach, Mother's, Wolff's, Gold's,

---

[8] Robert McFadden and Joseph Fried. "Judge Voids Law Certifying Kosher Food." *The New York Times*, August 4, 2000.

and Goodman's. Others are mainstream corporations that choose to have some of their product lines certified as kosher to be acceptable to Jewish customers who wish to keep a kosher kitchen. Common examples certified by *O-U* are Nestlé, Quaker Oats Company, McCormick & Company, General Mills, Mueller's, Ronzoni, Heinz, Wish-Bone, and Bumble Bee. Companies that use *K* are Post Cereals, Red Cheek, Kellogg's, Wesson, Sun-Maid, Red Pack, Hunt's, Del Monte, and Orville Redenbacher's. Not all the products of these large corporations are kosher. Heinz can have their ketchup certified as kosher, but not their pork gravy, because kosher laws prohibit pork products.

Shabbas Siren

Northwest corner of Kingston Avenue and Montgomery Street

The Sabbath Siren sounds twice before official sundown each Friday. The cluster of twelve horns arranged in a circle on a pole four stories high sounds fifteen minutes before candle lighting time, and then again one minute before the Sabbath. Observant Jews still on the street rush to a synagogue or home for the beginning of the Jewish Day of Rest.

Mitzvah Tanks

Parked along the street

Winnebago campers can be seen parked along Kingston Avenue. These are the portable headquarters for young men who proselytize on street corners, especially during Jewish holidays. The shluchim (missionaries) politely inquire of passersby if they are Jewish. If the answer is no, the person is wished a good day. If yes, they attempt to persuade the subject to acts of devotion. To a Jewish woman, they will give a small menorah (ritual candelabra) on Hannukah, or hamantaschen (triangular fruit-filled pastries) on Purim. They try to persuade Jewish men to step into the mitzvah tank and recite a prayer, especially kaddish for the dead. The shluchim provide prayer aids: yarmulke, tallit, and tefillin. The word *mitzvah* means *good deed*. The Rebbe called the vehicles tanks in the war against assimilation.

Visiting the Rebbe's Grave in Queens

718-528-1700

Montefiore Cemetery, where the last Lubavitcher Rebbe is buried, is located in St. Albans, Queens, in the southeastern part of the borough near the intersection of the Cross Island Parkway and the Southern (Belt) Parkway. The main entrance is on Springfield Boulevard, between 130th Avenue and 121st Avenue–Francis Lewis Boulevard. Menachem Mendel Schneerson is buried in section 94 in the northeast part of Montefiore on Abraham Avenue (a cemetery road) next to Yosef Yitzchak Schneersohn. (Though distant cousins, the last two rebbes sometimes transliterated their common surname differently.) They are interred below ground in a ten-foot-high, twenty-foot-square granite ohel (roofless mausolum; literally a tent in Hebrew), where followers come to pray, recite psalms, and leave heaps of written notes scattered over the two rebbes' graves. Four shelves of memorial candles burn along one wall of the tomb. Pilgrims remove their shoes and stand in their white socks at the site. In a nearby house on Francis Lewis Boulevard, the rebbe's followers pray, sing, study, watch videos of his life, and maintain a twenty-four-hour video camera trained on his grave. Requests and wishes sent by fax and email from around the world are received in the house and deposited in the ohel. In the house, called the Ohel Chabad Lubavitcher Center, two sinks are maintained for washing hands, a Jewish tradition after visiting a cemetery. Coffee and cookies are available for those who have fasted before praying at the grave site. Several homes on the block are owned by the Lubavitchers to accommodate overnight guests, and one has been turned into a mikvah (ritual bathhouse). Maps are available for free at the Montefiore Cemetery office. Yarmulkas (skullcaps) are sold for 25 cents each.

 At Montgomery Street, reverse directions and walk north on Kingston Avenue four long blocks back to Eastern Parkway.

Walking Trip in Weeksville

Proceed east (to the right from the Kingston Avenue walk) on Eastern Parkway four long blocks to Utica Avenue. Turn left (north) on Utica Avenue seven short blocks to Bergen Street. Turn right (east) on Bergen Street one and a half blocks to Weeksville Houses on Hunterfly Road. (An alternative to the long walk would be to take the IRT #1 train from Kingston Avenue Station one stop east to the Crown Heights-Utica Avenue Station, then transfer to the northbound B46 bus for a seven-block ride.)

Weeksville Houses

1698–1708 Bergen Street

718-623-0600

(By appointment only with the Society for the Preservation of Weeksville and Bedford-Stuyvesant History)

The confusing addresses on the east–west Bergen Street are used because Hunterfly Road is no longer an official city street. The three houses are located on the former Hunterfly Road, which runs north–south in the middle of the block, parallel to the streets on either side, Rochester and Buffalo Avenues. Unofficial Hunterfly Road (with no vehicles allowed) is entered from Bergen Street.

Three unadorned wood cottages built for workmen between approximately 1840 and 1870 line a narrow lane that was once a rural road running between Bushwick and Canarsie. Hunterfly Road's name may be an Anglicization of the Dutch term Aander Vly (Swampy Place). The houses are the only buildings left from this sprawling nineteenth-century community of free blacks. The village was named for James Weeks, an early homeowner. The one- and two-story clapboard houses were restored in the 1990s and now constitute a preserved local historic monument.

Weeksville Houses are a work in progress, and historical researchers and community fundraisers are busy supporting the endeavor. Professors and graduate students from the Pratt Institute and the City University of New York worked on the early research. Support galvanized in 1968, and the Society for the Preservation of Weeksville and Bedford-Stuyvesant History was formed in 1971.

The preservation society has gathered a trove of household artifacts, lanterns, and furniture to use in setting up displays of late-nineteenth- and early twentieth-century African American life in Brooklyn. Lectures and tours can be arranged for school groups or adults. Each house is outfitted for a different period: one for the 1840s, two for 1900, and one for the 1930s. The buildings and yard have undergone dramatic reconfiguration. Meanwhile, a profusion of flowers thrives around the houses: daisies, black-eyed susans, bachelor buttons, and hollyhocks, which provides a hint of once-rural Brooklyn.

Reverse directions one-half block on Bergen Street; turn right (north) on Rochester Avenue three short blocks to Atlantic Avenue. Turn left (west) one-half block on Atlantic Avenue; turn right (north) one short block on modern Hunterfly Place. Turn right (east) one-half block on Herkimer Street; turn left (north) one short block on Rochester Avenue to Fulton Street; turn left one block to Utica Avenue. Return via the IND A or C trains at the Utica Avenue Station. Or, alternatively, return to Eastern Parkway and take the IRT #3 or #4 train at Utica Avenue.

THE BRONX

BELMONT

A Historically Italian Neighborhood

The little neighborhood now called Belmont was once part of the large estate called Fordham Manor, a series of wilderness holdings put together by John Archer just after 1664. It included the entire West Bronx, all land now in the Bronx between the Bronx and Hudson Rivers, and north of the Harlem River and Spuyten Duyvil Creek. At first Archer only leased land to tenants, but began selling property for estates in 1678. Eventually, several large landowners, such as the Philipse, Van Cortlandt, Valentine, and Lorillard families, and the Dutch Reformed Church gained control of much of Fordham Manor. They, too, began subdividing their estates. The Dutch Reformed Church owned the land where Belmont is situated and first leased, then ultimately sold, property for family farms. Initial buyers were Dutch and English farmers.

Irish and Germans settled the area in the 1890s, the Irish to work as laborers and domestics to prosperous farmers and country house owners, and the Germans to operate small garden farms. The nearby Edgar Allan Poe Cottage was originally a bunkhouse for farm laborers on the Valentine estate.

The Italians came to the area as mass transit rail lines were built. In fact, some became acquainted with the area while working on construction jobs for the elevated rail lines. Most early residents of Little Italy in the Bronx came from the southern provinces of Sicily, Calabria, and Campania. Priests organized a mission church in 1906, which eventually became Our Lady of Mount Carmel Parish. A great deal of neighborhood life has revolved around organizations and festivals at the church.

Belmont residents enjoyed soccer, bocce (Italian lawn bowling) in the park, and excursions to nearby amenities: Van Cortlandt Park, Orchard Beach, the Bronx Zoo, and the Bronx Botanical Garden. Men went to cafés or joined social clubs organized by hometown compatriots, where dialect could be spoken, cards played, soccer teams followed by radio and later television, and politics debated. Women shopped, cooked, and cared for large families. Young people went up on the roofs for privacy, to fly kites, and called it *tar beach* when they sunbathed. Until the 1960s, Belmont rooftops supported numerous pigeon lofts, an amusement generally favored by older men. The streets were filled with children playing stickball and hanging out. As residents became Americanized and fewer Italians sought to immigrate to America, Belmont lost some of its immigrant enclave charm, though the shopping and restaurant scene remains much the same.

Even with its numbers thinning, Belmont is arguably the most cohesive Italian community remaining in New York. The romantic feel of Belmont is inviting to filmmakers who choose it over Manhattan's Little Italy for its authentic look. This is an outdoor neighborhood, the sidewalks filled with local residents shopping and strolling, not just tourists and restaurant-goers. Italian flags and provincial banners fly from buildings, and Catholic statues and small shrines are found in almost every store. Italian can still be heard on the streets. It was the neighborhood of Dion DiMucci's Dion and the Belmonts, the 1950s rock 'n' roll group that gave us "Runaround Sue" and "The Wanderer." Belmont was the opening setting of E. L. Doctorow's novel, *Billy Bathgate*. (In the 1991 film *Billy Bathgate*, directed by Robert Benton, an early scene includes this dialogue: "Where ya from, kid?" "The Bronx. Bathgate Avenue.") *A Bronx Tale*, both the 1989 play and the 1993 film, are set in Belmont. Belmont is still such a prototypical turn-of-the-last-century Italian American neighborhood that scenes from *The Godfather* and *Mean Streets*, purporting to show Manhattan's Little Italy, were filmed in Belmont. Oddly, *Billy Bathgate*, which has references to Belmont, was not.

After World War II, Belmont's shopkeepers did not follow some of their customers to the suburbs. More Italians moved in through the 1950s, and the area thrived. Unlike Manhattan's Little Italy, which shrunk to a collection of red-sauce restaurants in a neighborhood populated by Chinese immigrants, Belmont kept a residential population that buys the food carried in the shops. Visitors are usually suburbanite Italian Americans returning to stock up on provisions. Even if the same products can be purchased at new one-stop emporiums in Westchester, Nassau, or

New Jersey, the old-fashioned experience of going store to store remains appealing.

With a somewhat undiminished Italian population, and lacking brownstones and picturesque row houses, old-time Belmont has seemed gentrification-proof. The housing is mostly tenements and newer apartment buildings, few of which are interesting architecturally. Nonetheless, it becomes slightly less Italian each year as increasing numbers of immigrants from Albania and Albanian regions of former Yugoslavia settle here. Two blocks north of Our Lady of Mount Carmel, the Musa Mosque has opened at 189th Street and Belmont Avenue. A small number of Mexican and Puerto Rican families also live in the section, and Mount Carmel now offers masses in three languages: English, Italian, and Spanish.

A walking trip through Belmont, an authentic Italian neighborhood, is mostly about cooking provisions and traditional Italian American family dinners. Architecture is not outstanding, but it is familiar as an icon of New York during the Great European Migration at the turn of the last century. The corner of Arthur Avenue and East 187th Street is the neighborhood's center. The area is almost tourist-free, which reflects its distance from Manhattan and may also stem from the lingering reputation of the Bronx, especially the South Bronx, when it was in steep decline—a misfortune amplified by Tom Wolfe's novel (and subsequent film) *Bonfire of the Vanities*, and the movie *Fort Apache: The Bronx*. (Visitors should note that most shops are closed on Sundays.)

Walking Trip to Arthur Avenue/Belmont

To Arthur Avenue: Take the Metro North commuter line from Grand Central Station to Fordham Station at East Fordham Road (at Webster Avenue); or take the B or D (BMT) subway trains to Fordham Road Station at East Fordham Road (at the Grand Concourse); or take the IRT #4 subway train to Fordham Road Station at East Fordham Road (at Jerome Avenue). Walk east along East Fordham Road to Arthur Avenue, or take the eastbound Bx 12 bus.

Walk south on Arthur Avenue from East Fordham Road.

Marie's Roasted Coffee & Gifts

2388 Arthur Avenue, between East 186th and 187th Streets
718-295-0514

This variety mart sells delicious dark-roasted coffee beans (whole or ground), coffee grinders, Italian cassettes and CDs, decorative pasta platters, flags, soccer shirts, T-shirts, and machines for making spaghetti, cavatelli, cappuccino, or espresso. There are chandeliers for sale, as well as decorative statues, paintings, and porcelain versions of Leonardo da Vinci's *Last Supper*. Like the other stores in Belmont, Marie's provides Italian Americans and others with an array of Italian supplies.

Belmont Italian American Playhouse

2385 Arthur Avenue, between East 186th and 187th Streets
718-364-4700

The upstairs facility is both an acting school for adults and children and a small theater. The Playhouse sponsors periodic cultural and historical walking tours of Belmont.

Teitel Brothers

2372 Arthur Avenue, at the corner of East 186th Street
718-733-9408

This small corner store, founded in 1915, is so packed with people and goods it is hard to squeeze in through the crowd. They have one entire wall stacked with various types of dried pastas, big selections of cheeses and meats, figs, dates, nuts, dried chickpeas, polenta, and Arborio rice for risotto. Outside the front door, gallon containers of Italian olive oil, including unfiltered varieties such as the green-tinted Don Luigi brand from Sicily, are stacked, each with its competitive price written in large numerals. Except for the shop's name and the Star of David embedded in the tile floor of the entrance, it would seem the owners were Italian rather than Jewish. It demonstrates the closeness of many of the older ethnic groups in New York City whose people had many symbiotic relations with one another.

Belmont Branch—Enrico Fermi Cultural Center, New York Public Library

Around the corner at 610 East 186th Street and Hughes Avenue
718-933-6410

This roomy and inviting public library branch houses a special Italian-language collection of books, periodicals, and videos, named for the Nobel Prize–winning physicist. It sponsors readings and travelogues focusing on Italian heritage. It recently added Albanian and Spanish collections.

Biancardi's

2350 Arthur Avenue, between East 186th Street and Crescent Avenue
718-733-4058

The front window will stop you cold. Hanging down from meat hooks are furry rabbits and fuzzy lambs. A small pink pig lies underneath. This meat market is the place to come for whole lamb, goat, pig, or rabbit. From the ceiling behind the counter hang rows of hams, spiced bacon slabs, and soppressata sausage (filled with cut, not ground, meat). The long counter offers a large variety of more commonly bought products, especially veal, calf's liver, oxtail, and pork tenderloin. Fourteen butchers are employed by Biancardi's to fill the mountain of daily retail and wholesale orders.

Arthur Avenue Retail Market

2344 Arthur Avenue, between East 186th Street and Crescent Avenue

The streets once bustled with pushcarts until legendary mayor Fiorello La Guardia banned all outdoor pushcarts in 1938 and drove them into city-owned covered malls, an action enormously pleasing to rent-paying shopkeepers. The Arthur Avenue Retail Market, a cavernous Depression Era *civic moderne* structure, was put up in 1940. It has preserved some of the older street atmosphere, though the stalls are much larger than pushcarts and fully modernized with electricity and running water.

Peter's Meat Market
Arthur Avenue Retail Market

The meat cases are packed with neighborhood favorites and a phalanx of butchers ready to fill your order. Offerings include chicken and veal cutlets, calf's liver, plain and stuffed pork chops, flank steak pinwheels (beef rolled around layers of mozzarella and prosciutto), fresh rabbits, quail, and seven kinds of homemade sausage. Veal is the specialty and veal cutlets appear to be the store's most popular item.

Mike's Deli
Arthur Avenue Retail Market

Dried chickpeas, beans, and chiles; bins of olives and salted capers; a variety of cheeses and salamis; and deli specialties like pickled artichoke hearts and peppers are available at Mike's Deli along with authentic pannini (pressed sandwiches).

Boiano Food
Arthur Avenue Retail Market

This sprawling fruit and vegetable emporium occupies the Arthur Avenue Retail Market's center. All items can be found in large quantities, but there is an accent on specialties of Italian cooking: *finocchio* (fennel), *carciofi* (artichokes), *melanzane* (eggplants), *uva* (grapes), *limone* (lemons), *peperoni* (bell peppers), *pomodori* (tomatoes), and *aglio* (garlic).

Mount Carmel Gourmet Food
Arthur Avenue Retail Market

This store offers a selection of reasonably priced staples: *baccala* (dried cod), salted sardines, Italian sodas and coffee, nuts, dried mushrooms and spices, pastas, and packaged gnocchi (potato dumplings).

Frank Randazzo's Sons Fish Market
2327 Arthur Avenue, between East 186th Street and Crescent Avenue

718-367-4139

This is a busy fish market offering fish and shellfish of all varieties. Notable is the selection of calamari (squid), sepia (cuttlefish), polipi (octopus), scungilli (conch), and baccala (dried cod). There are several thicknesses of baccala; Randazzo's even keeps some dried cod soaking in water so it can be cooked that day. They also carry shellfish (lobsters, crabs, crayfish, shrimp, mussels, clams, scallops) as well as bluefish, striped bass, porgies, fluke, flounder, blackfish, weakfish (sea trout), tuna, swordfish, and red snapper.

 Reverse directions and return north to East 187th Street. Turn right (east) and walk four blocks to Beaumont Avenue.

DeLillo Pastries

606 East 187th Street, between Arthur and Hughes Avenues
718-367-8198

The counters are brimming with mini pastries: cannoli (cream-filled pastry tubes), sfogliatelle (sweet ricotta cheese turnovers), napoleons, and éclairs. There is also gelato and spumoni and an ice-cream parlor venue in which to enjoy it.

Tino's Salumeria

609 East 187th Street, between Arthur and Hughes Avenues
718-733-9879

This narrow market is a salumeria, specializing in Italian meats and sausages. It also has many traditional cheeses: hard varieties like asiago, parmigiano reggiano, pecorino, and soft types such as gorgonzola and stracchino. Arborio rice (for risotto), pine nuts, sardines, anchovies, capers, olives, olive oil, pancetta, and other hams are also offered.

Borgatti's Ravioli & Egg Noodle Company

632 East 187th Street, between Hughes and Belmont Avenues
718-367-3799

Just behind the counter, the family produces its own manicotti and ravioli. The sheets of egg-yellow pasta are rolled out by one machine and then sliced to order by another, depending on desired thickness. The pasta is dusted with polenta (fine cornmeal) and wrapped in white paper. Borgatti's also has a broad selection of dried imported pastas from Italy.

Our Lady of Mount Carmel Church (Roman Catholic)
627 East 187th Street, at the corner of Belmont Avenue
718-295-3770

This bulky 1917 church is more beautiful and richly ornamented on the inside than out. The main altar and front side altars to St. Mary and St. Joseph are excellent examples of elaborate interior design often found in southern Italian churches. Several statues of Italian favorites are here: St. Catherine of Siena, St. Rocco, St. Jude, St. Dominic, St. Anthony of Padua, Mary Queen of Heaven, and St. Lucy with her eyeballs on a plate. A statue of St. Mary Virgin of Montevergine draws much attention from the faithful. Marble Corinthian columns line the aisles, and four large white marble genuflecting angels hold holy water fonts where the pews begin at the back. Vibrant polychrome Stations of the Cross have been placed below the unexceptional stained-glass windows. The building's pink brick facade has combined elements of neo-Gothic and Romanesque architecture. The second week of June is the feast of St. Anthony of Padua, when East 187th Street is closed off as a street fair. On the first Sunday after July 16, the neighborhood celebrates the feast of Our Lady of Mount Carmel with an Old World street procession through the area.

Terranova Bakery
691 East 187th Street, between Cambreleng and Beaumont Avenues
718-367-1237

The delicious rustic breads, breadsticks, and rolls in all sizes and shapes displayed in the front window have been pulled from the vintage coal-fired oven in the back room. Specialties include prosciutto bread and olive bread. A few condiments are available, but Terranova is all about fresh, hearty breads.

 Reverse directions to return to the intersection of East 187th Street and Arthur Avenue.

Sites off Fordham Road near Belmont

Fordham University (Rose Hill Campus)

441 East Fordham Road, between Webster Avenue and Crotona Avenue
718-562-3225

New York City's premier Roman Catholic University is located on East Fordham Road between Webster and Crotona Avenues. Archbishop John Hughes, New York's most colorful and powerful Roman Catholic bishop, founded the institution as St. John's College in 1841. The Society of Jesus (Jesuits) has staffed the college since 1846. The name was changed to Fordham University in 1907, in reference to Fordham Manor, the large tract of land that once included all of the West Bronx. The university became coeducational in 1964 and has been operated by a lay board of directors since 1969. Presently, the university enrolls fourteen thousand graduate and undergraduate students. The statue of Archbishop Hughes, the Jesuit Cemetery, and the University Church (Our Lady Mediatrix of All Graces) are worthwhile campus destinations. The church was completed in 1845; its stained-glass windows were gifts from King Louis-Philippe of France.

Entry to the fenced university compound is permitted only to card-holding students, faculty, staff, and visitors with permission. Call 718-817-3901 to make an appointment. The main pedestrian entrance is at Bathgate Avenue and East Fordham Road, and the vehicle entrance is on Southern Boulevard across from the New York Botanical Garden.

At the back of the campus, very near the glass conservatories of the New York Botanical Garden, Fordham erected a 260-foot-tall radio tower for their commercial-free public radio station, WFUV-FM, in 1994. Fordham University claims the site is needed for a strong signal, and the New York Botanical Garden sees it as an obtrusive visual element.

1950s Culinary Note: Just south of Fordham University at 550 East Fordham Road, the northern border of Belmont, stands one of the city's few remaining White Castle eateries, famous for their tiny inexpensive hamburgers.

Edgar Allan Poe Cottage

In Poe Park, Grand Concourse at Kingsbridge Road
718-881-8900

The small cottage was leased to Edgar Allan Poe for one hundred dollars a year from 1846 until his death at forty in 1849. He moved there because he thought the country air in what was then the southern part of rural Westchester County would strengthen his wife, Virginia, who was ailing from tuberculosis. The relocation did not cure her, and she died the next year. Poe expired while visiting Baltimore two years later. While living in the cottage, the family was so poor that Poe's mother-in-law, who was living with them, picked dandelion stems in the orchard and foraged in nearby meadows for food. Inside is a comfortable living room and the minuscule bedroom where Virginia died. Two more bedrooms, a little more than six feet high, are up a flight of stairs. The house is furnished with period pieces, though only three items actually belonged to the author. Poe wrote "The Cask of Amontillado" and the poem "Annabel Lee" while living here. The one-and-a-half-story wood house was built in 1812 as a bunkhouse for farm laborers on the Valentine estate. It was saved from destruction by the Shakespeare Society in 1890, and is now owned by the Bronx County Historical Society. The house was moved from the other side of Kingsbridge Road in 1913. Hours: Saturdays 10:00 a.m. to 4:00 p.m.; Sundays 1:00 p.m. to 4:00 p.m.; closed weekdays.

Restaurant Recommendations

Dominick's (Italian)

2335 Arthur Avenue, between East 184th and 186th Streets
718-733-2807

Not exactly a secret, Dominick's is very busy. There are no menus, no checks, no credit cards—just large portions of hearty Italian fare in this small, noisy restaurant packed with adoring patrons. The waiter will announce what is available and give recommendations. Specialties include insalata di mare (seafood antipasto), osso bucco (veal shank), fettuccine puttanesca (tomato sauce with capers, anchovies, and olives), calamari and shrimp in a piquant marinara sauce, and pork chops in hot vinegar-pepper sauce. The ambiance is reminiscent of a church supper. Customers sit at long communal tables with brown vinyl table coverings. The walls are paneled with knotty pine, and the decorations include American flags and a poster of Marlon Brando from *The Godfather.*

Pizzeria Margherita

673 East 187th Street, between Cambreleng and Beaumont Avenues
718-295-2902

Margherita-style pizza was named for Margherita, queen of Italy, the wife of King Umberto I (1878–1900). The simple peasant dish was elevated in national consciousness when the queen decided to try the plain pie with mozzarella, tomatoes, and basil, making the red, white, and green colors of the Italian flag. Pizzeria Margherita, however, serves several varieties of pizza. It also makes rice balls: deep-fried balls of rice stuffed with a sauce that includes tiny pieces of meat and peas. Potted palm trees and walls painted with a scene of Neptune cavorting with the Nereids decorate the walls of this cozy neighborhood gathering spot. It combines elements of a pizzeria, cafe, and saloon. Unlike most New York pizzerias, this one has a liquor license and an active bar at the front.

Roberto's (Italian)

603 Crescent Avenue, between Arthur and Hughes Avenues
718-733-9503

Often called the best restaurant in the Bronx, Roberto's attracts diners from throughout the city and suburbs, and is a favorite of Fordham faculty. The kitchen serves ample portions of superb food in two large and quiet dining rooms. Some of the specialties are grilled octopus, veal scallopini, guanciale with penne and peas, osso bucco, and whole fish. Besides beef, pork, and chicken, they offer a selection of lamb, rabbit, and goat dishes. There is a full bar with a wide selection of wines. Roberto's is closed on Sundays.

CITY ISLAND

City Island is a long finger of land located in the East River before it blends into Long Island Sound. City Island is located between the Bronx mainland and Hart Island, home of potter's field. The only terrestrial access to the one-and-three-quarter-mile sliver is over City Island Bridge. City Island Avenue, the main street, runs the length of the island on a north–south axis and is crossed by two dozen short streets in a fishbone spine pattern.

At the northeast corner is a boardwalk-causeway to High Island, a three-acre, rocky speck of land that has at various times been a place of quarantine for yellow fever victims and an artist colony of twenty bungalows. Now closed to the public, High Island anchors a tall WCBS-AM and WFAN radio transmitting tower with fifty thousand watts of broadcasting power. Only one bungalow is left and serves as the caretaker's residence.

Local Lenape American Indians called the island Minnewits, and the British dubbed it Minneford Island, when they settled it in 1685. It received its present name from developer Benjamin Palmer in 1761. He had hoped the village would grow into a city and thought of it as an actual rival to New York City at the southern tip of Manhattan Island. (NYC only had about eight thousand people in 1761.)

As expected, the island residents earned income from oystering, clamming, and fishing nearby waters. A saltworks was established in 1830 to make salt by evaporating seawater. Shipbuilding companies lined the long coast, and a profitable niche was developed: yacht construction. The last shipyard closed in 1982, but sail makers, dry docks, and motor assembly and repair shops still exist.

As the commercial fishing and ship industry declined, the island became more of a summer resort with modest bungalows and apartments for rent. For anglers, there are sport fishing, boat rental, marine supply, and motor repair shops. Numerous seafood restaurants and antique, souvenir, and craft shops cater to day-trippers.

New Englanders migrating southward as well as immigrants from England, Germany, Ireland, and Norway populated City Island. Today's resident population is still overwhelmingly white, though visitors come from many ethnic and racial backgrounds.

Traditionally, most islanders lived in single-family wood houses. Multiunit condominiums are beginning to threaten the small-town nature of City Island and are regularly lamented in the local newspaper.

Despite the bridge and the condominiums, City Island's community of five thousand has some elements of insularity, especially in winter. Residents share the same telephone exchange (885), *The Island Current* chronicles all things that matter to City Islanders and really reads like a small-town newspaper, and natives (*clam diggers*) remain proud of their claim to have a distinct accent.

Walking Trip in City Island

 Take the #6 IRT subway to Pelham Bay Park Station; transfer to the Bx29 bus.

Or by car, go over the City Island Bridge from the Hutchinson River Parkway or the Pelham Bay Parkway.

Begin at the north end of City Island Avenue and Bridge Street, just behind the first bus stop. Walk one block northeast on the curved Bridge Street.

Zigzag left (north) on Minnieford Avenue, then east on Terrace Street to the gate leading to the closed High Island Boardwalk-Causeway. Walk south on King Avenue two blocks.

Victorian House

688 King Avenue, between Terrace and Sutherland Streets

This elaborate nineteenth-century frame Victorian house has a long slender-columned portico and colorful shingle patterns on the sharply pitched roof.

Turn right (west) on Kilroe Street one block; left (south) on Minnieford Avenue four blocks to Ditmars Street; left (east) on Ditmars Street two blocks to King Avenue; right (south) on King Avenue three blocks to Fordham Street.

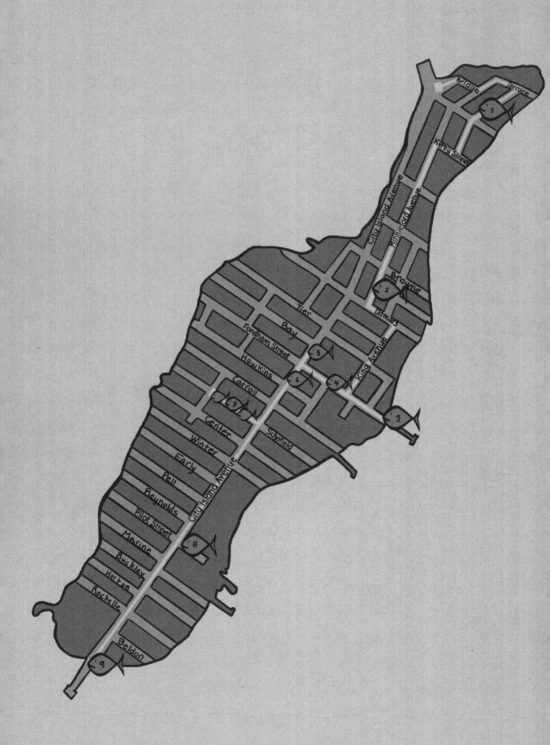

City Island

During World War II, City Island had seventeen shipyards. Today it has six yacht clubs.

1. Victorian House
2. Pelham Cemetery
3. Fordham Street Pier
4. City Island Nautical Museum
5. New York Public Library
6. Apartment House
7. Schofield Houses
8. Grace Church
9. Belden Point

Pelham Cemetery
King Avenue, between Ditmars and Bay Streets

The town cemetery is not filled with grand monuments, though some of the designs are noteworthy. There are several marble obelisks and a few well-preserved prefabricated cast-iron tombstones. Older sections have stones bearing English, Irish, and German surnames; newer stones carry a variety of names, though Italian predominates.

 Walk left (east) on Fordham Street to Fordham Street Pier.

Fordham Street Pier
Fordham Street at Fordham Place

The pier at the foot of Fordham Street from City Island to the forty-five-acre potter's field on Hart Island is closed to the public. The forbidding sign reads, DEPARTMENT OF CORRECTIONS: NO TRESPASSING. About 2,700 unclaimed bodies each year make the one-way trip to interment in tarpaper-lined pine boxes placed in long communal trenches by convicts from Rikers Island prison. The trenches, dug by a backhoe, are stacked three high, two across. About half of Hart Island dead are infants or still-borns, placed in tiny coffins, stacked five high and twenty across in separate trenches. There is a third trench where organs and limbs from hospital operations, wrapped in black plastic bags, are buried. The public cemetery for paupers, all in unmarked graves, was opened in 1869 and holds the remains of at least one million people. Before 1869, Hart Island had been a military training camp, a prison camp for captured Confederates during the Civil War, an insane asylum, and a workhouse for the poor. The closed, city-owned facility has several unused buildings on it. The island is administered by the New York City Department of Corrections.

 Walk west on Fordham Street four blocks to City Island Avenue.

City Island Nautical Museum

190 Fordham Street, between Minnieford and King Avenues
718-885-0008

The museum occupies an 1898 schoolhouse and is packed with model ships, nautical equipment, and photos of maritime pursuits, especially the shipyards where seven America's Cup–winning yachts were built. During World War II, City Island had seventeen shipyards. Today it has six yacht clubs. Hours are limited to Sundays and by appointment. (An extension at the back of the building houses a condominium complex.)

City Island Branch, New York Public Library

320 City Island Avenue, between Fordham and Bay Streets
718-885-1703

In addition to its regular collection, the new brick building (with two portholes, a yardarm, and a rounded ship's prow entrance) houses material on seafaring industries and local history.

 Walk south on City Island Avenue three blocks to Schofield Street.

Apartment House

284 City Island Avenue, between Fordham and Hawkins Streets

This 1898 narrow five-story wood apartment house with orange brick trim sports a gambrel roof and numerous full-size windows. Rare for a small island settlement, the apartment building was a precursor of condominiums a century later.

 Turn right (west) on Schofield Street to William Avenue.

Schofield Street Houses
Between City Island and William Avenues

Number 65 is a two-story regal Greek Revival with an addition built on its east end. The gingerbreading on the verandah is tasteful and not overpowering. Its neighbor, number 84–86, is a single-story house with an immense mansard roof. It may be called ostentation on a budget.

 Turn back east on Schofield Street to City Island Avenue; turn right (south) on City Island Avenue eleven short blocks to Belden Point.

Grace Church (Episcopal)
104 City Island Avenue, at the corner of Pilot Street

Built in 1861, the Gothic Revival wood structure is elegant in its simplicity. The steep gable matches the tall belfry, and good care has preserved the shingled facing.

Belden Point
Southern tip of the island at the end of City Island Avenue

The former pier has rotted away to a few posts, and Tony's Pier Restaurant and Johnny's Reef Restaurant have asphalted their land for outdoor picnic tables right up to the water's edge. There is a narrow walkway along the shore on the east side of City Island Avenue accessible from the parking lot of Johnny's. It offers an unhindered view of Long Island Sound and northeastern Queens.

 Return trip: via Bx29 bus at City Island Avenue and Rochelle Street (one block from southern tip) to Pelham Bay Park Station for #6 IRT subway.

Restaurant Recommendation

Lobster Box

34 City Island Avenue at Belden Street
718-885-1952

Since 1946, this crowded and popular seafood restaurant on a hill at the island's southern tip has excelled at providing two things: lobster and the view overlooking Long Island Sound. Periodically advertised on radio and television, it may be the best-known location on the island. Diners may choose among a menu loaded with seafood appetizers and entrées featuring crab, shrimp, finfish, steak, some Italian pasta dishes, and the house signature dish: the one-and-one-half-pound lobster.

QUEENS

CALVARY CEMETERY

Woodside

In 1846, Archbishop John Hughes purchased the eighty-acre Alsop farm on the north bank of Newtown Creek in Blissville, Queens, to use as a cemetery for the city's rapidly growing Roman Catholic community. Space in the small walled churchyard of the old St. Patrick's Cathedral, at Mott and Spring Streets in Manhattan, was almost gone, and the cathedral's crypts were too expensive for most to afford. Some Catholics were sending their deceased relatives to Protestant cemeteries or to the potter's field. Hughes wanted to provide enough ground consecrated by the Catholic Church for all burials. Since then, Calvary Cemetery has gown to hold three million remains, larger than any other cemetery in the United States in number of interments.

The archbishop purchased the Alsop farm for eighteen thousand dollars through the Trustees of St. Patrick's Cathedral. It was named for the hill (Calvary or Golgotha) where Jesus was crucified outside the walls of Jerusalem. From 1867 until 1900, various adjacent farmlands were purchased for inclusion in Calvary. The cemetery's boundaries now encompass 250 acres.

In terms of topography, some cemeteries in New York City give a good idea of the original lay of the land, since relatively little landscaping, except for roads and paths, was done in many of them. While most of the city has been flattened to facilitate development, Calvary Cemetery has several small hills and valleys. There are few trees in the cemetery, except for a cluster around the chapel.

The large Roman Catholic necropolis surrounds the Alsops' small Protestant family cemetery. A provision of the deed provided that the family graveyard remain separate and be cared for by the sexton of Calvary.

The cemetery is divided into four divisions, each named for an ancient Roman catacomb where Christians buried their dead and sometimes held secret services. Old Calvary (St. Callixtus tract) and New Calvary (tracts named for St. Agnes, St. Sebastian, and St. Domitilla) are slightly noncontiguous, separated by an eight-block stretch, which includes housing and a busy interchange of the Brooklyn-Queens Expressway and the Long Island Expressway.

A sought-after locale to shoot movies because of the Manhattan skyline backdrop, Calvary appeared in the funeral scene in Francis Ford Coppola's *Godfather* in 1972. This was considered too commercial and undignified, so the cemetery has refused permission for other movie directors to use its location for films.

Walking Trip Through Calvary

Take the L (BMT) subway to Lorimer Street; transfer to the Queensbound G (BMT) train to Greenpoint Avenue; transfer to the B24 Queensbound bus on Greenpoint Avenue over the J. J. Byrne Memorial Bridge crossing Newtown Creek three blocks to the Main Gate at Gale Avenue. Or, take the Queensbound #7 (IRT) subway to Hunters Point Avenue in Long Island City, Queens. Transfer to the Q67 bus on 21st Street, two blocks east of the subway station, which winds its way along Borden Avenue eastward to Greenpoint Avenue to the Gale Avenue gate.

Maps

A cemetery map is helpful and may be obtained by mail. Call the Calvary Cemetery office at Second Calvary, 718-786-8000, or write to them at 49-02 Laurel Hill Boulevard, Woodside, New York 11377. Maps may be picked up in person at the main office in Second Calvary, which is several blocks from First Calvary (Old Calvary).

Directions

In old cemeteries, some details get lost in the mists of time. Calvary's sections are neatly labeled on their maps and clearly posted along the roadsides. But some road signs do not appear on the cemetery's roads, and many of them cannot be clearly read on the maps. A few have names unknown even to the cemetery officials.

Hours

Cemetery hours are, daily, 8:00 a.m. to 4:30 p.m.
Office hours are, daily, 9:00 a.m. to 4:15 p.m.

> Enter the Main Gate at Gale Avenue and proceed past the life-size crucifix scene and the old redbrick office building (with public restrooms) on St. John's Avenue.

Section 10

On the left side of St. John's Avenue

The Malone monument, in the front row on the left, just one hundred feet past the crucifix, features a seated woman on the stone's top, eyes downcast, holding a cross in her hands. Next to it, facing the opposite direction, is the Lynch monument, showing a standing female figure staring down while draping her arms around a roughly hewn log cross. Both memorials are examples of nineteenth-century Romantic cemetery art, a generally nondenominational motif also found in many Protestant cemeteries. It stresses sad emotions through weeping angels or feminine figures. Also in the front row, fifty feet beyond the Malone monument, is the triumphalist Callahan compound, where statues of Mary and Joseph guard the entrance to a large memorial base flanked by angels and a forty-foot tower topped by a Sacred Heart of Jesus statue. In the same row, just across the paved pathway, stand very similar obelisks on bases for the Flynn and Dollard families. The Dollard stone has a Sacred Heart of Jesus statue on top, but the figure is missing from the Flynn memorial.

Section 9

On the right side of St. John's Avenue

This section contains many tall grey granite tombstones topped with white marble statues of angels, Jesus, Mary, or Joseph. Toward the road and

Calvary Cemetery

Calvary appeared in the funeral scene in Francis Ford Coppola's 1972 film *The Godfather.* The cemetery has refused permission for other movie directors to use its location for films.

1. Malone Monument
2. Lynch Monument
3. Callahan
4. Flynn and Dollard
5. J. Kennedy
6. Uelhof Monument
7. Johnston
8. Joseph Doelger
9. James Candler
10. Halloran
11. Soldiers Monument
12. Alsop Family
13. Cantore
14. Alfred E. Smith
15. St. Callixtus
16. Carroll
17. Cohalan
18. McAleenan
19. Palmeri
20. McColgan
21. Tierny

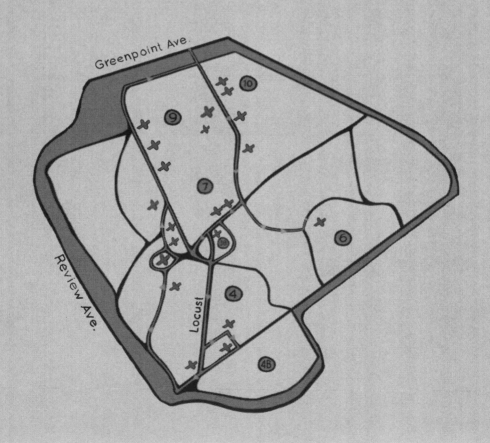

across from the Dollard obelisk is the J. Kennedy mausoleum, made of heavy grey ashlar blocks and pink granite columns in front. It has a granite statue of St. Joseph on top holding his traditional symbols: a stalk of lilies in one hand and a carpenter's square in the other. Two rows behind the J. Kennedy mausoleum is the Uelhof monument, which is engraved with an image of the communion host, the chalice, and a priest's stole. One of the nine family members memorialized on the front of the grey stone is Rev. Henry S. Uelhof, ordained in the Austrian Tyrol in 1886.

A detour on St. John's Avenue down the steep hill east toward the Brooklyn-Queens Expressway in Section 6 will lead you to encounter the enormous Johnston mausoleum, the largest in the cemetery. The Roman Revival structure, built of large grey granite ashlar blocks, towers over a dozen smaller mausoleums. The domed structure, topped by a statue of a standing Jesus holding a cross, is fifty-five feet high. The Johnston mausoleum also features four seated angels on a protruding platform below the dome and a badly weathered white marble pediment scene showing Jesus raising Lazarus from the dead.

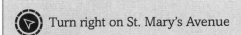 Turn right on St. Mary's Avenue

Section 7

On the right side of St. Mary's Avenue

A marble angel on top of the intricately carved Victorian obelisk in the front row memorializes Joseph Doelger. In front of the column are steep steps leading to the sealed entrance to the crypt below. Twenty feet farther along the road is a marble die on a granite base for James Candler featuring the bas-relief of a long, sleek sailing ship, indicating his occupation. His stone is part of a three-piece complex for James and Ellen Candler. The engraving for Ellen features her with her child in heaven.

Section 3-B
On the left side of St. Mary's Avenue

The large, bulky Halloran mausoleum incorporates both neoclassical elements, such as the massive Roman entries, with busy Victorian Gothic designs. It is built of granite blocks and topped with a heavy Maltese cross.

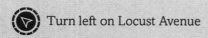 Turn left on Locust Avenue

Section 4
On the left side of Locust Avenue

Halfway down the curvilinear road, walk one hundred feet into Section 4 to see the Soldiers Monument, which honors Roman Catholics who fought in the Civil War. The central obelisk, decorated with garlands and starbursts, rises fifty feet and is topped by a bronze statue representing peace. Four life-size bronze soldiers on low pedestals, each dressed in a different regimental uniform, stand guard over the monument. It is city-owned and maintained by the Parks Department. The plaque reads: PLACED BY THE MAYOR, ALDERMEN, AND COMMONALITY OF THE CITY OF NEW YORK. Twenty-one Civil War soldiers are interred at this site.

Walk fifty feet down the hill toward Newtown Creek to arrive at the Alsop Family Burial Ground, a small Protestant enclave with thirty-one surviving tombstones with burial dates ranging from 1718 to 1889.

Alsop Family Burial Ground

This distinct graveyard, surrounded by a cyclone fence with two openings without gates, measures just thirty feet by forty feet. Its separate existence is guaranteed by the land deed in 1846. Seventeen of the thirty-one markers are made from fragile brownstone (soft, porous brown sandstone) and some have been rendered unreadable by weathering. Thirteen are marble, and the most recent memorial, an 1889 cross-topped monument erected for William Alsop (d. 1883) and Sarah Leaird Alsop (d. 1889), is made of dark grey granite.

It is interesting that in such a limited selection of gravestones, the evolution in Protestant, specifically Puritan, theology in America can be noted by a fundamental change in one of the most common designs. The winged death's head is used on the early brownstone markers for Richard Alsop (d. 1718), and the not-so-early Elizabeth Alsop (d. 1763), and another Richard Alsop (d. 1764). A winged angel's head is carved on the large brownstone marker for Hannah Alsop, almost certainly later than the others, though the date is worn off. Winged death's heads reflect fear of the stern God of Judgment Day, and winged angel's heads, usually commissioned after the Great Awakening beginning in the 1730s, display an optimistic belief in a benevolent God of love.

The View

One hundred yards south of the Alsop Family Burial Ground rises the new Kosciuszko Bridge, stretching from Maspeth, Queens, to Greenpoint, Brooklyn, over the Newtown Creek. A constant stream of trucks and cars passing overhead emit a muffled ambient rumble in what was a quiet agricultural community two centuries ago. Newtown Creek is now lined with oil storage facilities and a modern municipal sewage disposal plant. Blissville, the former village along Newtown Creek, has been displaced, though some of the neighborhood residents refer to the largely industrial area of eight square blocks in front of Old Calvary's main gate as Blissville. The bridge was named for Tadeusz Kosciuszko, a military engineer and Polish nationalist who fought for freedom and republicanism in Poland, France, and the United States. He served under George Washington as a colonel in the Continental Army.

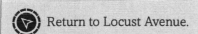 Return to Locust Avenue.

Corner of Section 4

At the intersection of Locust and Calvary Avenues

The large pink granite Cantore monument, faux vault cover in front, displays a life-size bas-relief of Mother Cabrini surrounded by a border of flowers and the Greek chi rho and alpha omega letters, symbolizing the name of Jesus. The inscription reads: MOTHER CABRINI PRAY FOR US. Mother Cabrini was the first American citizen to be proclaimed a saint by the Roman Catholic Church. She was born in Italy in 1850, and came to the United States with the Missionary Sisters of the Sacred Heart of Jesus in 1889. She became the patron of immigrants by establishing schools, orphanages, and hospitals throughout the country that served their needs. She died in 1917 and was canonized in 1946. Her body is enshrined within the glass-sided altar at the Shrine Chapel of St. Frances Xavier Cabrini in Manhattan's Washington Heights.

 Continue thirty feet west on Calvary Avenue; turn right on an Unnamed Avenue; and right on the next Unnamed Avenue.

Section 45

On the right side of the Unnamed Avenue, which borders the chapel

One hundred feet from the chapel and three rows into Section 45 is a simple low granite marker reading, ALFRED E. SMITH, GOVERNOR OF NEW YORK, BORN DECEMBER 30, 1873, DIED OCTOBER 4, 1944. This is the grave of New York state governor and 1928 Democratic presidential nominee Alfred E. Smith. As the first Roman Catholic presidential candidate, the Happy Warrior endured bigotry and hostility in many states during his campaign; and though he lost the presidency, he gained a special place in the hearts of American Catholics.

 Walk across the circular road to the chapel.

Chapel of St. Callixtus

The chapel is well known to motorists on the Brooklyn-Queens Expressway. From the highway elevated by the Kosciuszko Bridge, it appears as a bright white shrine on a knoll in the midst of greenery in the large cemetery filled with white and grey tombstones. From ground level, its central, elongated beehive tower looms majestically upward. The Chapel of St. Callixtus was patterned after the Church of Sacré-Coeur in Montemartre, Paris. Its white tile-covered dome rests on colonnettes rising over the red tile roof and is crowned by a life-size statue of the Sacred Heart of Jesus. The architecture is essentially Romanesque Revival, particularly recognizable in the rounded triple-setback arched entrance topped with a scene of Jesus surrounded by saints. The archway is inscribed with the words of Jesus: I AM THE RESURRECTION AND THE LIFE (John 11:25). The chapel's interior resembles a crypt with a vaulted ceiling and the preponderance of marble and granite. (Mass: Saturdays at 10:00 a.m.)

 At the front of the chapel, proceed (north) and walk along Central Avenue.

Section 46

On the right side of Central Avenue

Fifty feet from the chapel and two rows back stands the Carroll monument, topped with marble statues of the Holy Family. Next to it is an especially elaborate Celtic cross monument for the Cohalan family. The cross uses a traditional Irish rope design and incorporates medallions of Jesus and the animal symbols representing the four Gospels. In front of it, and partly hidden behind a large London plane tree, is the neoclassical McAleenan mausoleum, noted for its four plain Doric columns.

 Continue on Central Avenue as it merges into St. Rose Avenue.

Section 7
On the right side of St. Rose Avenue

The front-row Palmeri stone is a rough granite block dominated by a deep relief carving of the crucifixion scene over a profusion of lilies—symbols of the Resurrection. Two praying angels with particularly feathery wings flank Jesus. The Italian inscription reads: In Memoria del Mio Caro Figlio Frank Palmeri, 1898-1928, Riposa in Pace. Fifty feet past the Palmeri stone, the facade of the Sessa monument is presided over by a crowned Mary holding a crowned Infant Jesus. Below them clamor carved figures labeled "Souls in Purgatory" who are being comforted by angels as they reach upward.

Section 9
On the right side of St. Rose Avenue

Three rows from the road stands an eight-foot-high memorial resembling a rounded heap of stones, which serves as the monument for the McColgan family. Rough stones, tree stumps, or log crosses were used in the Romantic style to denote nature. Forty feet farther in the same row is the tall dark grey Tierny monument, topped by a full-bearded patriarchal statue of St. Patrick, patron saint of Ireland.

 Turn right on an Unnamed Avenue inside the fence along Greenpoint Avenue to return to the Gale Street Gate.

St. Raphael's Church (Roman Catholic)
Nearby at 35–20 Greenpoint Avenue, between Hunters Point Avenue and Borden Avenue (service road of the Long Island Expressway)
718-729-8957

Though it is a familiar landmark to drivers on the Long Island Expressway, few New Yorkers can identify by name the tall redbrick and sandstone church and steeple at the edge of the eight-lane highway. St. Raphael's Church was built in 1868 to serve mourners visiting the cemetery and to minister to German and Irish immigrants in the area. The exterior architecture is broodingly medieval, though the inside has refined French Gothic lines, bright stained-glass windows, and elaborate polychrome Stations of the Cross set in finial-laden Gothic frames. (Masses: 9:00 a.m. Sundays; 11:00 a.m. weekdays)

BROAD CHANNEL

Houses on a Set of Swampy Islands

Positioned tenuously on a group of four fused *pols* or *polds* (Old Dutch for marshy islands) near the middle of Jamaica Bay, this community is arguably the city's most isolated. Broad Channel takes the name of the waterway that separates it from the Rockaways. Colonial era fishermen and clammers arriving by boat put up shacks, though a permanent community was not established until 1880. The population now numbers about 2,500. The jerry-built summer-bungalow structures, many constructed on pilings or stilts, perched mostly along the edges of nine short inlets dredged by the city, were eventually enlarged and winterized. By 1916, fishing was prohibited because the waters were declared polluted, though by then the community had assumed an insular life of its own. During Prohibition, the settlement got a reputation as a haven for speakeasies and bootleggers, who called it Little Cuba, a story that is a matter of pride to some of the inhabitants.

In 1924, the Cross Bay Boulevard was constructed connecting the island to two parts of Queens: Howard Beach and Rockaway Peninsula. The IND subway line, using a causeway and trestle constructed earlier for the Long Island Rail Road, began service to the Rockaways and opened a station on Broad Channel in 1956. New York City, which owned all the land and had been leasing it to householders with ten-year renewable leases, privatized it in 1982, permitting residents to buy the property on which their homes were built. Housing styles are summer seaside with whimsical homemade additions. Most of the original wood surfaces have been covered with vinyl, aluminum, or wood shingles. There is a profusion of American flags and BEWARE OF DOG signs. Few institutional buildings are here, but the island possesses both an American Legion Hall and a

Veterans of Foreign Wars Hall. This is a community that likes to show its patriotism.

Because of low population and no place for more structures, most grocery shopping and gasoline purchasing must be done in Howard Beach or the Rockaways. There are just a few small mom-and-pop stores on Broad Channel. Children attend either the parochial school at St. Virgilius or Public School 47. After sixth grade, they are bused to Rockaway for middle school and high school.

Today the community is still happily isolated in the midst of Jamaica Bay, though the close proximity of busy JFK Airport, which originally opened as Idlewild Airport in 1948, and the takeoff noise of the big jets is a constant reminder that many things have changed since this little settlement began.

Brief notoriety came to the island as a result of some extremely poor choices made as part of the annual Labor Day Parade. The parade made television, radio, and print news in 1998 when a photographer made public photos of a group of white men parading in Afro wigs, blackface, and outlandish clothing, dribbling basketballs and throwing slices of watermelon to the onlookers. Behind their pickup truck, they dragged a mannequin representing the black man dragged to his death earlier that summer in Texas. Some residents claimed it was all in good fun, or, alternatively, an isolated incident. In previous years, the same group had entered the parade to mock Hasidic Jews, Chinese, and gays. Some who were public employees were suspended from their jobs. The shameful tradition ended after the negative publicity in 1998.

Walking Trip to the Wildlife Refuge: A Wide Spot in the Causeway

 Travel via A train toward Far Rockaway or Rockaway Park, or via Cross Bay Boulevard by car from the Belt Parkway.

The subway trip along the causeway is unique for its view of birds and fishing boats out the windows of both sides of the cars. The train runs on tracks set just a few feet above the water. As soon as you leave the train, you feel far removed from the city. Jamaica Bay is twenty-eight square miles of shallow waters flushed by Atlantic Ocean tides twice daily. The salty sea air, small houses, and slow-moving atmosphere evoke a southern coastal town, not the Borough of Queens. Streets are called roads in Broad Channel. Arriving by subway to the Broad Channel Station lets you off on West Road, the easternmost street on the island, where it intersects with Noel Road (squeezed in between East 7th and East 8th Roads). From there, head west to the center of the island.

St. Virgilius Church and School, which serves the largely Roman Catholic community, is on Noel Road along the way to Cross Bay Boulevard. The tiny church with beige shingles looks like a cottage. Next to it is the similarly diminutive white wooden Christ Presbyterian Church by the Sea. Across the street is an elongated garage, home of the Broad Channel Volunteer Fire Department. The FDNY serves Broad Channel, though there are no station houses on the island, so the volunteers serve a preventive as well as a social purpose. The corner of Noel and Church Road is pretty much the civic center of the settlement.

The Visitor Center of the Jamaica Bay Wildlife Refuge

Part of the National Park Service's Gateway National Recreation Area
718-318-4340

Built in 1971, the Visitor Center of the Jamaica Bay Wildlife Refuge is located at the island's far north end, about three quarters of a mile from the intersection of Cross Bay Boulevard and Noel Road. There you may hike along trails going around East Pond and West Pond to catch a glimpse of egrets, sandpipers, plovers, killdeers, oystercatchers, snipes, woodcocks, swallows, geese, and swans. Owls and hawks represent the raptors. Reptiles and amphibians can be spotted around the ponds. Remember to bring mosquito repellant, binoculars, and lunch. The surrounding bay's waters, marshlands, islands, and freshwater and saltwater ponds, located on a major migration route, give rest and sustenance to over three hundred species of birds. In fact, most visitors to Broad Channel come for the wildlife. (Tours of Jamaica Bay by private boat can be arranged from Sheepshead Bay in Brooklyn. Wildlife cruises of the bay are periodically sponsored by the American Littoral Society [718-634-6467] or Friends of Gateway [212-352-9330].)

Walking Trip from the A Train Station to View the South End of the Island

 From the station, walk west on Noel Road to Cross Bay Boulevard and turn left (south).

The island features miniature dwellings with roomy back decks, a few shops, some bait and tackle stores, a Chinese takeout restaurant, a pizzeria, a hot dog stand, and two bars. A small public library is next to the island's well-cared-for park between East 14th and East 16th Road, which offers tennis, racquetball, and basketball courts. Don't miss the long narrow wooden walkway one hundred feet off Cross Bay Boulevard at East 12th Road. It leads over a marsh to a set of seven especially isolated houses built high on stilts. It is a good place to observe waterfowl.

Boating, Fishing, or Crabbing

Smitty's Boat Rental and Bait and Tackle Shop
301 East 9th Road at Lanark Road
718-945-2642

Just around the corner from the subway station is the most convenient place to get outfitted for boating, fishing, or crabbing in Jamaica Bay. Bluefish, striped bass, porgies, fluke, flounder, blackfish, weakfish (sea trout), and blue crabs abound in the shallow waters. Crabbing can be done from a boat or the dock with either a long-handled net or a mesh crab trap with fish or chicken for bait. (Blue crabs from Jamaica Bay are just like blue crabs from Chesapeake Bay—the raw material for Maryland crab cakes or she-crab soup.)

Restaurant Recommendations

All American Deli
Cross Bay Boulevard at West 10th Road, near the subway station
718-945-5400

This sandwich shop and grocery store is a good place to stock up on provisions for hiking at the Jamaica Bay Wildlife Refuge, which sells no food or drink. Here you can buy soft drinks, chips, and the usual variety of deli sandwiches.

Grassy Point Bar and Grill

Cross Bay Boulevard at East 18th Road

A good place to meet locals, this is mostly a bar, though an active one. Food is served on special event weekends, where you can sample an island barbecue, fish fry, or chicken dinner. The bar sponsors horseshoe, softball, and dart leagues, and the adjoining lot is the scene of neighborhood parties.

On the Waterfront

At the end of Van Brunt Road, just east of Cross Bay Boulevard next to a bait and tackle shop off East 20th Road
718-474-7768

This oasis with a million-dollar view is located at the southern end of the island, just before the toll bridge to Rockaway Peninsula. Built out over the water, the cheerful restaurant has indoor facilities plus a windswept open-air bar and restaurant just a few feet from a broad pier where boats tie up. The bar serves everything, but tropical drinks are especially popular. The kitchen makes generous portions of traditional bar food plus a limited selection of Italian and seafood entrées.

FLUSHING

Flushing's founding English families chose to build their settlement on the flat wooded land just east of a narrow inlet of the East River. They sailed into Flushing Bay from New England in 1654, after securing permission from the irascible and intolerant Dutch governor Peter Stuyvesant to remain in the colony of New Netherlands but not the town of New Amsterdam. Many of the New Englanders were from Connecticut and Massachusetts, where they had been dissatisfied with the thin topsoil, stony farmland, and cold winters. New England's Puritan leadership seemed too sectarian for them, judging by the relatively tolerant society they established in Long Island.

The pioneers developed land that had been purchased from Algonquian-speaking Lenape American Indians and named it Vlissingen, in a nod to the New Netherlands authorities, after a Dutch port town. Locating close to the water guaranteed them access to trade and provided some semblance of safety in the unknown land. Living twenty miles from the Dutch authorities in New Amsterdam promised to provide some degree of autonomy for the new village. The village grew up along the east bank of the Flushing River, and near numerous springs and watercress-laden freshwater ponds.

Though the English were allowed to settle, they had not been made to feel welcome because the Dutch, already sandwiched between larger, more populous English colonies in New England and Pennsylvania, feared becoming a minority in their own colony. Stuyvesant's hesitant tolerance shifted to outright hostility when Flushing began to attract English Quakers (Society of Friends) in 1657. The governor, actually the director-general of the mercantile colony, had a poor track record regarding religion. Upon becoming governor in 1647, Stuyvesant forbade all public worship except in the Reformed Church, the official state religion of the Netherlands. When twenty-three Sephardic Jews from Brazil arrived in New Amsterdam,

Stuyvesant refused to allow them to settle and imprisoned the group. Stuyvesant's employer, the Dutch West India Company, which had Jewish investors, overturned his decision and the refugees were allowed to remain.

With Quaker meetings and missionaries active in his colony, Stuyvesant reneged on an earlier assurance of religious freedom for the village, and his council promulgated a law banning Quaker religious activity. At the time, Quakers often proselytized by verbally disrupting services of other Protestant denominations. After Henry Townshend was convicted and fined, thirty-one residents signed a 1657 petition, known as the Flushing Remonstrance, declaring their freedom of religion. A combination of religious and secular reasoning that flattered the United Provinces (Dutch Netherlands), it said in part:

> The law of love, peace and liberty in the states extending to Jews, Turks and Egyptians, as they are considered sons of Adam, which is the glory of the outward state of Holland, soe love, peace and liberty, extending to all in Christ Jesus, condemns hatred, war and bondage. And because our Saviour sayeth it is impossible but that offences will come, but woe unto him by whom they cometh, our desire is not to offend one of his little ones, in whatsoever form, name or title hee appears in, whether Presbyterian, Independent, Baptist or Quaker, but shall be glad to see anything of God in any of them, desiring to doe unto all men as we desire all men should doe unto us, which is the true law both of Church and State; for our Saviour sayeth this is the law and the prophets.[9]

Stuyvesant rejected the Flushing Remonstrance and suppression continued. John Bowne, a farmer, was arrested, imprisoned, and fined in 1662 for allowing Quakers to meet in his house. Not a Quaker himself, but married to one, he took the fight to the directors of the Dutch West India Company in Amsterdam. They sustained his position and ordered Stuyvesant to allow all Protestant worship and to tolerate Quakers as long as they did not disrupt services. Quakers prospered in Flushing and built a meetinghouse in the village center in 1694.

---

[9] "Document: The Flushing Remonstrance, 1657." Thirteenth, New York Public Media.

Flushing continued to attract Yankee settlers because it offered easy marine transportation, timber, rich fishing grounds, and fertile soil. *Spartina patens* (salt hay) grew along the sides of Flushing River and could be used as fodder. By 1700, it was a prosperous community of English colonists with a minority of Dutch and French Protestants. Many farm families owned household and field slaves.

The long colonial phase of Flushing's history created a comfortable village, the seat of town government, with a population overwhelmingly involved in agriculture and fishing. During the American Revolution, Flushing was occupied by British troops until the end of the war in 1783.

From the close of the war until New York State fully ended slavery in 1841, Flushing became a magnet for emancipated slaves in Long Island. Encouraged by the Quakers, who had become intrepid foes of slavery, blacks settled in the northern part of the village. Their reception was not uniformly positive, as many of Flushing's whites resented their presence. Henry D. Waller, in his 1899 *History of the Town of Flushing*, sympathetically described their bigotry:

> These negroes became so numerous, so aggressive, so lawless, that the peace and quiet of the community were greatly disturbed. They filled the streets at night; they held out-of-door dances and barbecues, which generally degenerated into drunken brawls. Town ordinances and the mild influence of the Quakers were without avail. The apprentices and other young men of the village took matters into their own hands. They formed a sort of vigilance committee and attacked with volleys of rotten eggs, these noisy gatherings which made sleep impossible.[10]

The nineteenth century saw an expansion of Flushing's economic base. Beyond marine transportation, timber, fishing, and farming, several new industries developed: furniture factories, iron foundries, metal factories, glassworks, and food processing plants. Agriculture increasingly revolved around apple orchards, dairy products, vegetable farms, and nurseries specializing in ornamental trees and bushes.

---

[10] Henry D. Wallace, *History of the Town of Flushing, Long Island, New York*. Flushing: J.H. Ridenour, 1899.

In the twentieth century, many companies connected with the automotive industry established themselves in Flushing. They brought with them shops selling automobile parts and supplies, muffler installation, vehicle repainting, engine rebuilding, carburetor and transmission repair, body shops, and auto graveyards. Other industries included photographic equipment, plumbing supplies, wholesale florists, construction contractors, printing, and binding. Computer companies, small investment corporations, geriatric centers, and medical and dental clinics are late-twentieth-century additions to the Flushing economy.

Great demographic changes occurred in the nineteenth century, and Flushing's population increased tremendously. Attracted by tolerant Quaker attitudes, free blacks continued to move into the village. German and Irish immigrants arrived in large numbers in the early decades of the nineteenth century. Religious institutions mirrored the population. St. Michael's Roman Catholic Church was organized in 1826 and joined other Christian denominations: Episcopal, Dutch Reformed, Congregational, Quaker, Baptist, Methodist, and African Methodist Episcopal. The first Jewish synagogue was formed in 1901. While roads gradually improved, it was the railroad that firmly connected Flushing with the other villages of Long Island and the booming market in New York City. The Long Island Rail Road, one of the country's oldest and now the largest commuter system, first ran through Flushing in 1836 and made commuting to Manhattan feasible. By 1890, the trolley had also extended to Flushing from western Queens and joined with a local trolley line running along Main Street to connect Roosevelt Avenue and College Point. Railroad and trolley connections began to transform the community into a suburb. Housing developments followed, especially to the south and east of Northern Boulevard and Main Street, the civic and business center of nineteenth-century Flushing.

Toward the close of the century-long Great European Migration, the source of immigrants shifted from northern and western Europe to southern and eastern Europe. Flushing attracted a sizable Jewish and Italian population. By the 1920s, the ethnic mix was English, Dutch, Irish, German, Jewish, and Italian. There were few farms left, and most of the area was filled with Victorian houses characterized by many architectural features. Clapboard and shingle houses predominated. A growing number of six-story apartment buildings were constructed during the boom years of the 1920s.

In 1917, the Interboro Rapid Transit elevated subway line extended to Main Street and Roosevelt Avenue, a move that further spurred development. The Whitestone Bridge was completed in 1940 and connected Flushing to the Bronx. Housing increased tremendously following World War II until all Flushing was filled with residential and commercial buildings. The maze of highways built by Robert Moses made it easy to get to and from Flushing from anywhere in Greater New York. The independent town's civic center along Northern Boulevard ceased to exist after the 1898 Consolidation of New York City, and the commercial center shifted a few blocks to Roosevelt Avenue and Main Street as the IRT (now #7 line) gained in importance. Highways also brought light industry to the edges of Flushing, especially along Flushing Bay and the remnants of Flushing Creek.

After World War II, a small but discernible Asian population began to set down roots in Flushing. Initially, immigrants came from China, but Koreans and Indians also began settling in the area, drawn by reasonable housing prices and good transportation. In general, Koreans predominate north of Northern Boulevard, and Chinese farther south. Indians have located in the far south of the neighborhood. In 2001, a Chinese American from Flushing became the first Asian American elected to the New York City Council. Flushing now has Hindu temples, Buddhist temples, Sikh gurdwaras, Daoist temples, and Islamic mosques.

A walk through today's Flushing highlights architectural treasures of its colonial beginnings as well as of the not-so-distant past—public spaces and an array of food shops, specialty stores, and restaurants unrivaled in diversity in all New York City. Flushing is not just a bedroom community for the city's center in Manhattan. It has modern hotels, international banks, and financial investment firms. For many new Americans from Korea and China, it is Flushing that is the center. The 2000 census put Flushing's Asian population at 52 percent of the total population in Flushing.

Fortunately and uniquely in a city that constantly razes the old and builds the new, the political, ethnic, commercial, and housing changes have not destroyed a number of important historical sites in Flushing. Remnants of each stage of Flushing's development from the seventeenth century remain intact.

Tour 1: Old Flushing Town Center Walking Trip

 From the Main Street Subway Station at Roosevelt Avenue, walk north along Main Street four blocks to Northern Boulevard.

St. George's Episcopal Church
Main Street, between 38th and 39th Avenues
718-359-1171

This restful 1854 Gothic church with a sharply pointed conical steeple is enclosed by a small grassy yard sprinkled with two-hundred-year-old gravestones. It now looks completely out of place on this strip of modern buildings sporting sleek neon signs in Korean and Chinese. After 1664, when New Netherlands became an English colony, the Anglican (now Episcopal) denomination was the established church in New York and attracted a disproportionate share of the colony's wealthy and politically active citizens. Because of the area's Quaker and Dutch Reformed roots, that status was less pronounced in Flushing than in other towns. St. George's Church serves as a visual gateway to several historic buildings grouped near the old town center.

China Buddhist Association
136-12 39th Avenue, just east of Main Street
718-460-4318

The ground-floor sanctuary, visible through the front window, is arranged facing an altar dominated by a glass-encased statue of Guanyin, the highly regarded and beloved Bodhisattva of Compassion. A bodhisattva is a Buddha-to-be who has chosen to stay in the Sentient Being Realm to help the inhabitants achieve higher states. Also on the front altar to the left is the Pure Land Buddha (also called Amitabha). Shakyamuni, the Historical Buddha, often at the front of temples, here is found among several bodhisattvas at the back. On the front altar are the traditional five offerings: flowers, fruit, oil, pure water, and fire (candles). The temple represents Mahayana Buddhism, the form prevalent in East Asia.

Turn right (east) one block on Northern Boulevard.

Friends Meeting House (1694)
137-16 Northern Boulevard at Linden Place
718-358-9636

The back of this 1694 Quaker meeting house faces the street and its dark-shingled facade and high-pitched roof lend it a brooding, medieval look. Inside, though, it is warm and open, with rough colonial-period pews characteristically placed on all four sides facing the open center. Congregants sit during generally silent worship facing one another with no altar to serve as a focal point. The sanctuary's simplicity creates a cozy atmosphere, leaving the visitor with a sense of entering a different time. This is the oldest building in Flushing and the oldest religious structure in New York City. The graveyard in the back, which had been the front facing a quiet lane in 1694, is marked by plain tombstones with rarely more than the name and dates of the deceased. George Fox formed the Society of Friends in England in 1649. (Sunday silent worship begins at 11:00 a.m. in winter, 10:00 a.m. in summer. Visitors are welcome to the hour-long meeting and to the coffee and cake social hour afterward.)

Flushing Council on Culture and the Arts (formerly Municipal Courthouse, originally Flushing Town Hall)
137-35 Northern Boulevard, at the corner of Linden Place
718-463-7700

To the west of Flushing Greens (now mostly covered by bricks) stands the former government center of Flushing, dating from when it was one of the first three towns in Queens County. Flushing had its own government, and the tall imposing Romanesque Revival structure built in 1864 shows community pride. It functioned as the town hall until 1898, when Consolidation united all government entities in Manhattan, Brooklyn, the Bronx, Staten Island, and Queens and eclipsed the individual town governments within the five boroughs. Today the Town Hall building functions as a busy theater and gallery specializing in Flushing-related exhibits and performances by area residents. The gallery and gift shop are

the nineteenth century. Once affiliated with the Dutch denomination, it now is a nondenominational community church reflecting the ethnic richness of Flushing. Its motto is appropriately multicultural: "A diversified fellowship for a diverse community."

 Proceed right (west) two blocks on Roosevelt Avenue to the Main Street Subway Station.

Tour 1 Restaurant Recommendations

Kum Gang San Korean Restaurant

138-28 Northern Boulevard, between Union Street and Bowne Street
718-461-0909

This is a lively traditional Korean restaurant with an expansive dining room and large rear window featuring a wide backyard waterfall and a rustic bridge. The fare covers the usual offerings: scallion pancakes, spicy and pungent kimchi (hot fermented cabbage or other vegetables), panchan (Korean tapas), every imaginable fish entrée, and tabletop barbecues for grilling meat, mostly short ribs and steak.

Joe's Shanghai Restaurant (Chinese)

136-21 37th Avenue, between Main Street and 138th Street
718-539-3838

Crowds pack this modern well-lit efficient eatery with waiters smartly attired in green polo shirts. Diners come to sample a wide variety of dumplings, especially the delicate soup dumplings, and steamed buns, turnip shortcakes, scallion pancakes, drunken crabs, salt-baked prawns, and Shanghai lion's head (a meatball draped in shredded cabbage). While waiting for their orders, small children gather around the enchanting four-hundred-gallon fish tank stocked with several colossal goldfish. Joe's has a popular branch in Manhattan's Chinatown at 9 Pell Street.

Tour 2: Contemporary Main Street Walking Trip

 From the Main Street Subway Station and Roosevelt Avenue, walk south along Main Street two short blocks to 41st Road.

41st Road

A two-block stretch between Main Street and College Point Boulevard

This picturesque side street, used in movies and advertisements, looks as if it could have come right out of a provincial Chinese town. Its tiny stores in three-story buildings are filled with merchandise and shoppers hunting for bargains. On the ground floor are Chinese pharmacies, hardware stores, clothing shops, butcher shops, grocery stores, and shops specializing solely in dried items (fish, vegetables, fruit). The second and third floors are filled with nail salons, travel agencies, and insurance brokers. All shops sport large colorful Chinese and English language signs advertising their wares. Lanes in Shanghai and Beijing similar to 41st Road are disappearing as the wrecking ball destroys old neighborhoods in favor of skyscrapers.

Queensboro Hill Public Library

1 Library Plaza, at the corner of Main Street and Kissena Boulevard
718-359-8332

Constructed of mottled black granite and green tinted glass, the library is one of the largest buildings on the street. The 76,000-square-foot building opened in 1998 and was the fourth public library to occupy this corner. The modern five-story building is furnished with blond desks, chairs, and bookcases. After school, it fills with diligent, focused children reading, working on the computers, and completing homework assignments.

The Free Synagogue of Flushing

41-60 Kissena Boulevard at Sanford Avenue, around the corner from the library, one block east of Main Street
718-961-0030

Built in 1927 on a very sharp corner, this tall, neo-Baroque structure with a high front stairway and stately portico columns is flanked by a set of two bronze menorahs. Jews began moving to Flushing in large numbers after World War I and, along with the Irish, soon composed the largest ethnic groups. This was the neighborhood's second synagogue.

 Continue walking south on Main Street five blocks to Elder Avenue at Kissena Corridor Park.

This walk takes you past many Chinese and Indian restaurants, as well as grocery and spice shops.

Tour 2 Restaurant Recommendation

New Shere Punjab (Indian)

42-87 Main Street, between Blossom and Cherry Avenues
718-358-2299

Specializing in the Punjabi cuisine of northern India, Shere Punjab has a relaxed, cheerful ambiance with a plush dining room, comfortable furniture, and attentive waiters. There are several tandoori oven specialties marinated in a spicy red sauce and baked at a hot temperature. Though many vegetable dishes are listed, the emphasis here is on meat platters. The choices include curry (mixed spices), masala (onion, green pepper, and tomato sauce), shaag (spinach), dopiaza (tomato base), rogan josh (ginger and garlic), mughlai (nuts and tomatoes), and vindaloo (fiery hot curry sauce) served with goat, mutton, chicken, fish, or shrimp.

Tour 3: Hindu Temple Walking Trip from Main Street

 Continue south on Main Street one block past Cherry Avenue to Elder Avenue; turn left (northeast) three blocks to Kissena Boulevard; then right (southeast) one block to Holly Avenue.

Hindu Center

45-52 Kissena Boulevard at Holly Avenue
718-358-6726

The brightly painted modern exterior exhibits general Hindu architectural motifs, though no detailed carvings or statuary. Inside are five heavily decorated traditional statues of prominent deities at the front of a very plain sanctuary. Sunday services begin at 5:30 p.m.

 Continue (northeast) on Holly Avenue three short blocks to Bowne Street; turn left (northwest) and walk one hundred feet.

Hindu Temple of North America (1977)

45-57 Bowne Street, between Holly Avenue and 45th Avenue
718-460-8484

Fascinatingly ornate, this large temple dedicated to the deity Ganesh is built to resemble richly carved South Indian houses of worship with scores of carvings adorning the grey stonework. The six towers on the roof are constructed to resemble mountains, because the gods are believed to be attracted to mountains. Under the central roof tower is an enormous hollowed-out black granite block, a garbhagriha, or womb chamber, shipped in one piece from India. This holds the flower-bedecked statue of the elephant god Ganesh, first son of gods Shiva and Parvati. Ganesh, the one who removes obstacles, is associated with prosperity, success, and wisdom. On the god's birthday each September, the statue is removed from the temple, placed on a chariot, and becomes the focus of a celebratory procession around the block. (Call the temple office for exact festival date and time.) Other statues include Vishnu, Shiva, Parvati, and Lakshmi. There are also representations of the Nine Planets (Navagrahas) underscoring the importance of astrology in Hinduism. Saturday and Sunday services begin at 9:00 a.m.

Return to Main Street Subway Station by walking nine blocks (northwest) on Bowne Street to Roosevelt Avenue, then turn left (west) and go two blocks on Main Street.

Tour 3 Restaurant Recommendation

Dosa Hutt (Indian)

45-63 Bowne Street, off Holly Avenue next to Hindu Temple of North America

718-961-6228

Next to the temple, this inexpensive little café offers just a few very simple south Indian vegetarian specialties, including several varieties of dosa (crepe), uthappam (Indian-style mini-pizza), vada (doughnut), and iddly (steamed lentil patties).

STATEN ISLAND

ST. GEORGE

Home to the Staten Island Ferry
Terminal and Borough Hall

Staten Island was the place each early European explorer saw first upon passing through the narrows that separate it from the western end of Long Island (Brooklyn) and lead into the Inner Bay. Giovanni da Verrazzano, an Italian sailing for France in 1524, Henry Hudson, an Englishman sailing for the Netherlands in 1609, and Adriaen Block, a Dutchman in the service of his own country in 1614, were the first recorded European visitors. Though he barely took a look, Verrazzano got the narrows named for him as well as the suspension bridge in 1964. Hudson, who carefully mapped the river that now bears his name, was ultimately well rewarded by New Yorkers. Block, who was stranded in Manhattan in the spring of 1614 when his ship burned at anchor, and surely got to know the entire region better than the other explorers, has had nothing local dedicated to him. (Block's surname was eventually attached to an island off the coast of Rhode Island 135 miles to the east.)

Seen from the sea, Staten Island's center rises majestically above the low-lying coast. The spine of the island is a terminal glacial moraine left by the Wisconsin ice sheet, which receded ten thousand years ago. The deposits of rock form a range of hills, which have been given separate names. Fort, Ward, Grymes, Emerson, Todt, and Lighthouse Hills are high only in comparison with the coastal plain. The highest is Todt Hill, 409 feet above sea level.

Staten Island was bought from Lenape (Munsee) American Indians in 1630 for a trove, which included kettles, axes, hoes, and awls. Native Americans in the land that became the five boroughs of New York City and its surrounding area were the Lenape, eastern woodland Indians who spoke a dialect of the Algonquian language. Their area, Lenapehoking, the land of the Lenape, encompassed the coastal region drained by the lower

Hudson, Raritan, and Delaware Rivers. Today, that would be New York City, Nassau County, southern New York State, New Jersey, eastern Pennsylvania, and eastern Delaware.

Henry Hudson is credited with giving the island its name. Staten Island, English for Staaten Eylandt, is derived from the Staaten General (Estates General), the governing body of the Dutch West India Company, which owned all the territory of New Netherland. After the English conquest in 1664, the island was renamed Richmond, to honor the Duke of Richmond, King Charles II's illegitimate son. For more than two centuries, both names were used. After the 1898 Consolidation, Richmond remained the county name and Staten Island was used as the borough name.

In 1639 and 1649, abortive attempts were made to plant colonial settlements in Staten Island. Failure may have been caused by Native American hostility, or by the Dutch attempt to impose the patroon system on New Netherland. Patroonships were feudal-like estates where tenants labored on the land held by a landlord for a set number of years. The system was unworkable in a large open country where tenants could disappear and move deeper into the wilderness.

The first settlement, of which almost nothing is known and nothing is left, came in 1660, when nineteen Dutch, Walloon, and French Huguenot pioneers established a community close to the sea called Oude Dorp. It was somewhere in the northern part of South Beach, near the present location of Fort Wadsworth and Arrochar. In 1666, former governor-general of the Dutch West India Company Peter Stuyvesant, who had been peacefully removed from his position when the English took control of the colony in 1664, referred dismissively to the Staten Island settlement.

> It is inhabited only on the South side, behind the hill, and consequently out of sight of the fort, by 10–12 men but so and so able to bear arms, who, in order to be protected against a sudden attack of the Savages, did, about a year ago, erect a small, slight wooden Block-house, about 18 x 20 feet square, in the centre of their houses, and borrowed from one Cornelis Steenwyck a small piece capable of discharging a one-pound ball, and from the

Director and Council a little iron swivel; its garrison consisted of 6 old soldiers, unfit to accompany the others against the Indians.[11]

The English changed the name of the hamlet to Dover. Under the English, some settlers arrived erecting houses in widely disparate areas of the island. Two outstanding examples are extant. The Christopher Billopp House, now called Conference House, was built on a hill overlooking Raritan Bay (Tottenville) in 1680. The Voorlezer's House was erected in Richmondtown in 1695 for Hendrich Cruser, voorlezer (lay reader and schoolmaster) of the Dutch Reformed congregation.

Staten Island grew slowly and was, from the beginning, economically dependent on Manhattan. Population statistics show that only 727 free people and slaves lived on the island at the close of the seventeenth century. At the beginning of the republic, a century later, the free and enslaved population numbered 4,600.

The primary economic pursuits of Staten Islanders until the middle of the nineteenth century were related either to the sea (fishing and ship building) or to agriculture. Farmers raised dairy and beef cattle, hogs, corn, vegetables, and fruit. The island was dotted with apple, peach, cherry, plum, and pear orchards. Markets for these goods were primarily in Manhattan. There were few cultural, social, or economic distinctions among a population almost uniformly composed of independent agriculturalists and fishermen.

Specialization began in the nineteenth century when Staten Islanders entered new economic pursuits, many related to the Industrial Revolution: wood shingles, lumber, paper mills, bricks, terra-cotta, iron foundries, breweries, and factories producing furniture and guns. In 1860, a steam railway opened from Vanderbilt's Wharf in Stapleton to Tottenville. Trolleys along the north and east shores followed. The summer tourist industry centered around big beach hotels and bungalow colonies, was

---

[11] Peter Stuyvesant, "Memorial of Ex-Director Stuyvesant to the States-General, Praying That the Documents and Answer Submitted by Him to the States-General May Be Considered Sufficient for His Justification, &c., and That He Be Permitted to Return to New Netherland." Edited by E. B. O'Callaghan. Compiled by John Romeyn Brodhead. In *Documents Relative to the Colonial History of the State of New-York; Procured in Holland, England, and France*, 443. Vol. 2. Albany, NY: Regents of the University, 1856. Accessed March 25, 2019.

dependent on sea and rail transportation. Immigration increased as new job opportunities opened. By the 1898 Consolidation, sixty thousand New Yorkers lived in Staten Island.

Cornelius Vanderbilt (1794–1877), Staten Island's most financially successful son, is usually associated with enormous railway trusts and his spectacular creation, Grand Central Terminal. But Vanderbilt spent most of his life involved with the shipping industry. In 1812, at age eighteen, he was captain of a ship ferrying passengers and hauling freight, mostly farm produce, across New York Harbor. As a result of dependable transportation, some wealthy Manhattan families began building summer homes in St. George and New Brighton. Vanderbilt eventually ruled over a worldwide shipping empire. Though he had several homes, he returned to Staten Island to construct a mansion near the place he grew up in Stapleton. When he died, he left a $100 million fortune to his heirs. The mansion no longer exists.

Daniel D. Tompkins, governor of New York State (1807–1813) and vice-president of the United States during the administration of James Monroe (1817–1825), was a major landowner and developer. In Manhattan, Tompkins owned a wide swath of land from 2nd Avenue to the East River. Tompkins Square Park in the East Village was posthumously named for him. He also developed Tompkinsville, Staten Island, and in 1817 established a scheduled ferry service between Staten Island and Manhattan from the foot of what is now Victory Boulevard in Tompkinsville. Fascinated by new technology, Tompkins used a steamboat for his ferry.

Staten Islanders voted for inclusion into New York City to take advantage of Manhattan's enormous tax base, which would assure that they would get coveted city services (police, fire, sanitation, streets, schools) at bargain rates.

Three bridges were constructed in a short period of time in the interwar years and helped the island break out of its isolation. They were the first bridges built connecting Staten Island to any other landmass. The Goethals Bridge, named for General George W. Goethals, chief engineer of the Panama Canal, uses a cantilever design and opened in 1928, connecting Staten Island to Elizabeth, New Jersey. The Outerbridge Crossing—named for Port of New York Authority chairman Eugenius H. Outerbridge, not in regard to its isolated location—is a cantilevered bridge built in 1928, which spans the Arthur Kill to Perth Amboy, New Jersey.

The Bayonne Bridge, built in 1931, is a long steel archway over the Kill Van Kull to Bayonne, New Jersey. The three bridges greatly increased commerce, and Staten Island's population began to increase. They connected Staten Island with New Jersey, not the other four boroughs of New York City. Staten Islanders had to depend on ferries to travel to Manhattan or across the Verrazzano Narrows on the 69th Street Ferry to Bay Ridge, Brooklyn.

Following World War II, new prosperity and the internal combustion engine made it possible for New Yorkers to move progressively farther out from more crowded sections of the city. Staten Island drew people who desired an escape from the physical congestion of the other boroughs, and who were intrigued by the nearness of the sea and a relatively bucolic setting of hills and dales punctuated by meadows and woods. The population at the end of the war stood at 180,000.

A bad break for Staten Island was the city's decision to transport garbage from the other four boroughs to its western end. Reeking garbage always gave New York's streets an awful smell and appearance. Poor neighborhoods fared worse. Charles Dickens, after visiting the Five Points part of Manhattan in 1842, then an Irish slum (now Chinatown), reeking from refuse, remarked, "All that is loathsome, drooping, and decayed is here." In 1881, the Department of Street Cleaning was organized to keep the streets clean and to collect garbage. It changed its name in 1929 to the Department of Sanitation. In 1934, the United States Supreme Court outlawed ocean dumping, though it continued for six more decades. In 1948, a gigantic 2,200-acre dumping facility was established in Fresh Kills, Staten Island. Beyond the odors, the telltale sign was thousands of seagulls looking for a meal hovering over the mountains of garbage. Mount Trashmore—or Mount Garbage, as it was sometimes called—received ten thousand tons of garbage daily. It was closed in 2001, much to the relief of Staten Islanders.

Garbage disposal presents contemporary New York with expensive options for collection and disposal. Laws, and common sense, prohibit dumping any refuse in the ocean or burning it (which would emit toxic smoke in the air); so since the closing of Fresh Kills Landfill, it is hauled from curbsides in neighborhoods by twelve-ton capacity garbage trucks to sixteen smelly, slippery transfer stations, weighed, unloaded, compacted, and put in tractor trailers or railroad boxcars, and shipped to poorer rural areas in Upstate New York, Connecticut, Pennsylvania, Virginia, and West Virginia, which accept it in gigantic dumps. Two billion dollars of New York City tax money is used yearly to ship garbage and to pay towns to bury it.

Continued unwillingness by New York City to close Fresh Kills, until the administration of Rudoph Giuliani made good on a campaign promise, had fostered a secession movement in the 1980s and 1990s. Though secession would have been economically unfeasible for Staten Islanders because it would have meant giving up city services subsidized by Manhattan's enormous tax base, it showed the depth of frustration caused by the Fresh Kills dump. Closing the garbage facility largely ended talk of secession.

An optimistic note is that ambitious plans are being made by several city agencies and nongovernmental groups to convert the four mountains of Fresh Kills into a park. Open green space, woodlands, sports fields, golf courses, even ski slopes are possibilities. Some say it will take thirty years for the garbage to decompose, while others claim more than a century will need to pass before the dump is stabilized. The mountains of buried garbage, 180 feet high, are shrinking two feet per year. The decaying mass emits polluted water and methane gas. The water is drained to a purifying facility and pumps extract the methane, which is sold by the Sanitation Department to a power company for heating gas. Because it has been covered by a thick plastic liner and eighteen inches of soil, Fresh Kills no longer smells like rotting garbage. At some point several decades into the future, the hilly open space, now covered with grass, a few bushes, and scrub trees, may become a very large park. When it does, it will be three times the size of Central Park.

After 1964, when the Verrazzano Bridge connected Staten Island to Brooklyn, the population of Staten Island increased rapidly. It seemed possible to many newcomers, mostly from Brooklyn, that they really could escape urban decay and poor schools, buy a single-family or two-family house, have a backyard, and own an aboveground backyard pool. Architectural historian Norval White characterized the resulting building frenzy on the island as producing "banal monotony and vulgarity." It also had the effect of fusing the distinct villages and settlements within the borough by filling up the open spaces with housing. You can still discern the various village centers by a few older buildings clustered together, which is one of the island's charms, but there are no longer clear borders between former villages.

The population of Staten Island soared from 200,000 in 1970 to 450,000 in 2000. Most of the newer buildings are three-story houses, as it has become obvious that almost all the open land is gone and construction has nowhere to go but up. In the initial period after the Verrazzano Bridge was completed, the white population was composed largely of Italians, Irish, Germans, Jews, and Scandinavians.

The 2000 United States Census showed that in the previous decade, each major racial group increased its numbers in Staten Island, but by widely different percentages. The increase for whites was 5 percent, blacks 17 percent, Hispanics (of any race) 38 percent, and Asians 66 percent. Primary Asian groups include East Asians (Chinese and Koreans) and South Asians (Indians, Pakistanis, Bangladeshis).

Staten Island changed tremendously in the twentieth century. There are, however, a few remaining small-town aspects. Some of the streets still resemble winding country roads without sidewalks. A car ride along Amboy Road on the east side of the island's interior will take you past numerous nineteenth- and early twentieth-century houses mixed with newer buildings. Staten Islanders support a thriving local newspaper, the Staten Island Advance, a borough-wide paper with a daily readership of eighty-five thousand.

Walking Trip Through St. George

Take the Staten Island Ferry from the Battery in Manhattan. (Cars are not permitted.) Or, by automobile from the Verrazano Bridge, take the Clove Road exit on the Staten Island Expressway (US 278); turn right (north) on Vanderbilt Avenue; turn left on Bay Street, which becomes Richmond Terrace at the Ferry Terminal.

This ferry is the best deal in town. For most of the twentieth century, the fare was frozen at five cents each way. It was raised to twenty-five cents from 1976 to 1989, and to fifty cents from 1989 to 1991. In what many New Yorkers thought was an understandable payback to Staten Islanders,

Staten Island: St. George

Increased population fused the distinct villages on the island by filling up open spaces. You can still discern the various village centers by clusters of older buildings.

1. Borough Hall
2. Curtis High School
3. House No. 103
4. House No. 125
5. St. Peter's Church
6. House No. 1–5
7. House No. 2
8. Ambassador Apartments
9. House No. 117
10. Ganas Community
11. Brighton Heights
12. Farmers Greenmarket

who were angry enough to agitate for secession, a Republican mayor who received the vast majority of votes in the Republican borough ordered the fare to the outlying island be reduced to zero. No one complained because everyone got to benefit.

The view is a 360-degree panorama complete with sea breeze and salt air. From the ferry, the harbor comes alive with tugboats, freighters, tankers, fishing boats, pleasure craft, and an occasional ocean liner or warship. The large orange ferryboats, with names like *American Legion, John F. Kennedy*, and *The Gov. Herbert H. Lehman*, have three levels and swiftly careen across the harbor, deftly cruising through a maze of vessels. The ferry's horn blows when a witless weekend skipper fails to appreciate the hulk coming toward him. From the open decks, the view north of the skyscrapers in downtown Manhattan is spectacular, and the ferry passes Governors Island to the east and Ellis Island and Liberty Island to the west. Staten Island, the Island of Hills, slowly comes into focus to the southwest.

St. George Ferry Terminal in Staten Island
At the tip of St. George

Cavernous and crowded with a mix of sixty-one thousand Staten Islanders and tourists each day, the recently renovated St. George Ferry Terminal has amenities in the waiting room (a news stand, a historical society gallery, a doughnut shop, a pizzeria, a fast-food outlet) and more across the hall (two delis, a photography shop, and a postal station). The waiting room has its quirky charms, and one of them is people-watching. Another is observing the pigeons fly in and stay around to pick up dropped popcorn and other items of food. Most tourists ride the ferry to get an unparalleled view of Ellis Island and the Statue of Liberty. Regrettably, when the twenty-five-minute, 6.2-mile trip is over, they disembark the ferry, go into the waiting room, and take the next boat back to the Whitehall Ferry Terminal in Manhattan. Stay and visit Staten Island! The connections to the train, buses, and taxis are well marked and just outside the terminal.

 Walk to the Staten Island Yankees Stadium just beyond the west end of the Ferry Terminal.

Staten Island Yankees Stadium (officially Richmond County Bank Ballpark at St. George)

On Richmond Terrace at the west side of the Ferry Terminal
718-698-9265

Next to the Ferry Terminal is the new stadium, built in 2001, for the single-A affiliate Yankee farm team. The eight-thousand-seat stadium affords each fan a clear view of the baseball field and a very impressive harbor panorama. The orange and blue brick stadium with a porthole motif is surrounded by a large parking lot.

> Walk across Richmond Terrace from the Ferry Terminal or the Staten Island Yankees Stadium to Nick La Porte Place. Begin at Nick La Porte Place and Richmond Terrace, walking uphill.

Borough Hall

Richmond Terrace at Nick La Porte Place

The civic headquarters housing the borough president's office was finished in 1906. The handsome brick building with marble trim perches on a steep hill and is a welcoming symbol of Staten Island to visitors who arrive by ferry. Its ample mansard roof has two levels of dormer windows and a square clock tower. After the 1898 Consolidation, individual town governments were abolished and all island politics centered here or in City Hall in Manhattan. The old county seat in centrally located Richmondtown was disestablished and moved to St. George. (West of the Borough Hall on Richmond Terrace is the Roman Revival Richmond County Courthouse.)

> Turn right (north) two blocks on Stuyvesant Place; turn left (west) up the hill on Hamilton Avenue two blocks; turn right (northwest) on St. Mark's Place two blocks to Westervelt Avenue.

Buildings Along St. Mark's Place
Curtis High School

105 Hamilton Avenue, at the corner of St. Mark's Place

Built in 1904 on the crest of a hill where nineteenth-century luxury resort hotels once stood, the sprawling leafy Curtis High School campus is a collection of several additions built on to the original structure. Educational Gothic is the style and crenellated cornices, carved quatrefoils, and finials adorn the complex. George William Curtis was a nineteenth-century journalist, editor, and social reformer who maintained a summer house on Staten Island.

House Number 103
This looming shingle-style house with rounded corners was built in 1890. It has several other distinguishing features: a large central stained-glass window, a double chimney, and a spindle-bordered widow's walk.

House Number 125
A dark squat shingled cottage with shadow-casting overhanging eaves and an immense front circular tower capped with a cone roof and a weather vane, this 1895 building struts its individuality on the somnolent block. The squinting half-eyelid windows in the conical roof are a unique feature.

St. Peter's Church (Roman Catholic)
49 St. Mark's Place, between Nicholas Street and Westervelt Avenue
718-727-2672

The easily recognized neo-Romanesque church with large Cardinal's Tower (to honor Cardinal John Farley) was finished in 1901. (Cardinal Farley started his ecclesiastical career as assistant pastor at St. Peter's.) Its hillside perch makes it a landmark across the harbor. The cross-topped tower, once Staten Island's tallest man-made landmark, is now surpassed by nearby apartment complexes. This was the first Roman Catholic parish in the county, and this church replaces an earlier wood structure built in 1839 and destroyed in the 1890s.

House Number 1-5
This 1860 Queen Anne two-family house is an eclectic creation. The shingled edifice has a peaked corner tower like a witch's hat and large dormers. The Gothic concoction is made more memorable by wavy bands of shingles and latticework over the porches.

From St. Mark's Place, turn left (south) on Westervelt Avenue a fraction of a block; veer left (southeast) on Hamilton Avenue two blocks; veer right (south) on Daniel Low Terrace five blocks to Corson Avenue.

Buildings Along Daniel Low Terrace
House Number 2

This dark and sullen brick barn-like house has a distinct gambrel roof and front bay window. Though built well after the Dutch period, probably in the 1860s, it calls to mind the simple gambrel-roof farm structures that Dutch colonists favored.

Ambassador Apartments

30 Daniel Low Terrace

Though it was constructed during the Great Depression, this 1932 art deco apartment house spared no expense in decorating with metal, polychrome terra-cotta, and variegated brickwork. A whimsical double-sun and water fountain scene enlivens the facade.

House Number 117

Commanding a high hill on the corner of Fort Place, this 1885 neo-Gothic castle sports complementing shades of red in its brickwork, terra-cotta tracery, and roof shingles. It stands aloof on its perch, displaying its colorful red color scheme and eye-catching gables and dormers.

Turn right (west) three blocks uphill on Corson Avenue.

Ganas Community

135 Corson Avenue, between Westervelt Avenue and Jersey Street
718-720-5378

This 1960s-style intentional community focusing on environmentalism, group living, and feedback learning was formed in 1979. The group is semicommunal and describes itself as a bonded, caring, hardworking, fun-loving extended family. Ganas occupies nine buildings and has seventy-five residents. They operate five area resale stores called Every Thing

Goes, and own a seventy-acre upstate conference center, campground, and country hotel. (Visits arranged by appointment.)

 Turn back (east) on Corson Avenue to the end of the block; turn right (south) two short blocks on Westervelt Avenue; left (east) four blocks on Victory Boulevard to St. Mark's Place. Continue one long block to Hyatt Street.

Brighton Heights Reformed Church (Reformed Church in America)
320 St. Mark's Place, at the corner of Hyatt Street
718-448-0165

A reminder of the seventeenth-century preponderance of Dutch Reformed Protestants in Staten Island, this new corner church was built in 1999, a replacement of an 1866 structure demolished by fire. The Dutch Reformed Church was the original name of the Reformed Church in America. It was the official religion of New Netherland from 1625 until 1664. The Anglican Church (Church of England), now called the Episcopal Church in the United States, became the established church under English rule. Even during the Dutch colonial period, the Dutch were a minority, so their established church exerted influence primarily through the government of the Dutch West India Company.

Farmers Greenmarket
St. George Municipal Parking Lot, at the corner of St. Mark's Place and Hyatt Street

Lively conversation and bantering between buyers and sellers punctuates this pleasant atmosphere where city and country meet over tables offering freshly harvested onions, garlic, scallions, cucumbers, squash, sweet corn, new potatoes, and a variety of berries. Some farmers also bring in baked goods: pies, cakes, brownies, and breads. There are no farms left on Staten Island; these farmers drive in from New Jersey. (Saturdays in summer, 8:00 a.m. to 2:00 p.m.)

Turn right (east) on Hyatt Street-Nick La Porte Place three blocks to return to Ferry Terminal.

Restaurant Recommendation

Lakruwana (Sri Lankan)

668 Bay Street, between Broad and Thompson Streets in Stapleton
347-857-6619

Lakruwana presents the cuisine of the island nation of Sri Lanka, located just south of India. Decorations mix Buddhist and Hindu motifs with demon masks on the walls and rustic tables and chairs made partly from rope and wood. Food is served on traditional plates and you may eat with your hands. There are many mild and spicy curries on the menu: fish, seafood, vegetable, and a choice of meats—lamb, goat, and chicken. Biryani, fish cutlets, and deviled shrimp are also popular. On weekends, Lakruwana offers an all-you-can-eat buffet.

Return to the Ferry Terminal. Take the SI51 or SI76 bus along Bay Street about one and one-half miles from the St. George Ferry Terminal to Thompson Street in Stapleton, or the Staten Island Railway from the Ferry Terminal two stops to Stapleton.

TOTTENVILLE

New York City's Most Southerly Neighborhood

Built on Raritan Bay, Tottenville is one of Staten Island's oldest settlements and its most isolated outpost. Early ferry service connected Tottenville with Perth Amboy, New Jersey. The town was a center for commercial clam and oyster boats, which plied the waters of Raritan Bay and the Arthur Kill, the narrow strait barely separating Staten Island from New Jersey. Numerous boatyards lined the Arthur Kill. Some of Tottenville's residents worked in the brick and terra-cotta industry two miles north of town. The settlement was originally called Bentley Manor, though it was also known as Bentley Dock, Billop's Point, and Totten's Landing. Tottenville became affixed to the town in 1862 when many members of the Totten family resided there.

Housing in Tottenville ranges from tiny cottages to large Victorian homes in the older town center around Main Street and north of Amboy Road. Some houses possess complex and whimsical gingerbreading and several varieties of the white picket fence. The area is picturesque, though slightly shabby. The town center is a working-class neighborhood, while the newer area south of Amboy Road resembles a generic middle-class suburb. Tottenville has so little traffic that families set up portable basketball hoops in the streets.

Tottenville is a commuter suburb now, and automobiles, buses, and the Staten Island Railroad (part of the MTA subway system) have conspired to strangle viable commerce on Main Street. So the former movie theater and bank are closed. The shops are either empty or house ephemeral businesses trying to compete with well-stocked shopping malls only a few minutes away.

Walking, Car, Bus, or Staten Island Railroad Trip

Take the Staten Island Railroad to Tottenville Station, or S78 bus from Ferry Terminal. Upon arrival on the Staten Island Railroad, exit the front of the train at Bentley Street; turn left (south) on Bentley Street to the end of the block; turn left (east) on North Avenue one block; turn right (south) on Main Street to the Tottenville Masonic Temple.

Or, by car, from the Verrazzano Bridge, take the Bay Street-Hylan Boulevard exit from the Staten Island Expressway (U.S. 278) progressing south on Hylan Boulevard to Satterlee Street; or from the Ferry Terminal, drive on Bay Street south to Hylan Boulevard to Satterlee Street.

Arriving by S78 bus, begin by walking north to the Tottenville Masonic Temple.

Tottenville Masonic Temple

236 Main Street, between Craig Avenue and Amboy Road

This unexceptional two-story marble and reddish-brown brick building has muted elements of Greek Revival in its design. It resembles many fraternal group headquarters throughout the United States. Above the second-floor windows is a bit of color, a polychrome terra-cotta Masonic symbol. The building shows that Tottenville once had the same small-town superstructure found from coast to coast. The Masonic Order originated in Europe and drew its inspiration from both the guild system and the Enlightenment. The contemporary worldwide organization traces its roots to 1717 when four like-minded builders' guilds in London merged. Freemasonry was established in the United States in 1730. In the early days, it was associated with Freethinkers, and many of its members held Voltaire and Locke in high regard. Numerous leaders of our early republic were active in Masonic lodges, including George Washington, Samuel Adams, Paul Revere, Benjamin Franklin, John Hancock, and Lewis and Clark. Fourteen United States presidents and nine signers of the Declaration of Independence were Freemasons. Their secret rituals bothered some Americans, and an Anti-Masonic Party was organized in 1825 and remained active for two decades. Freemasons, as they are called, use builders' tools to symbolize moral truths. They profess a nondenominational belief in God and in the brotherhood of Mankind.

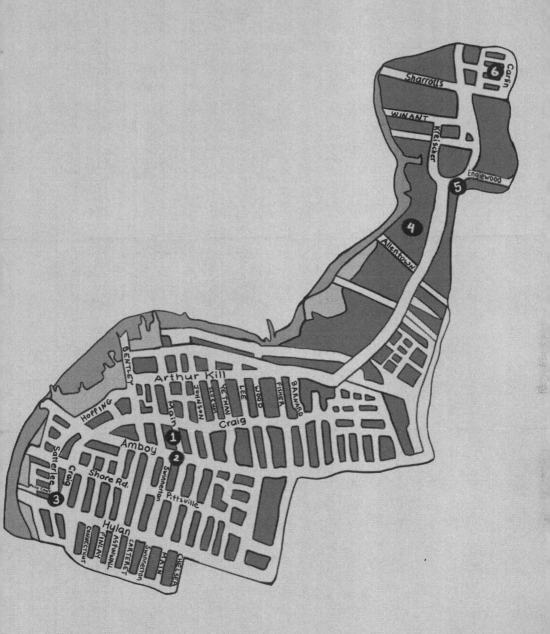

Staten Island: Tottenville

The Tottenville Masonic Temple resembles the many of the fraternal group's headquarters throughout the United States.

1. Masonic Temple
2. St. Paul's Church
3. Conference House

4. Charleston
5. Kreischer House
6. Clay Pit Ponds

Though nonsectarian and nonpolitical, the group has a quasireligious nature and begins and ends meetings with a prayer. In the United States, the organization ultimately took on a completely nonideological nature, becoming a fraternal group, which raises funds for a number of charities, including senior citizen homes, hospitals for handicapped children, orphanages, and blood banks. There are three million Masons in the United States and two million more in foreign countries. There has been some slippage in membership and activities in recent decades. Each lodge does not have its own building in New York City. Masonic Hall on West 24th Street and 7th Avenue in Manhattan is where ninety metropolitan lodges meet in twelve elaborately decorated two-story chambers in a building with eighteen floors. The building in Tottenville still functions as a Masonic Hall, though the first floor is rented out to the community office of the Richmond County district attorney.

 Turn right (west) one block at Amboy Road.

St. Paul's Church (United Methodist)

7558 Amboy Road, between Main and Swinnerton Streets
718-227-2485

Organized in 1859, St. Paul's Methodist congregation built this plain brick church in 1861. At the time, it was the largest structure in Tottenville. Orange bricks and white wood trim set off the restrained Greek Revival structure. Its only architectural conceit is the eye-catching inverted scalloping of the wood cornice around a pediment interrupted by a recessed central window. The plain boxlike interior mirrors the diffident mood of small-town Protestant architecture. The slightly elevated chancel has a low, curved kneeling bench for communion. A small table with an open Bible to serve as an altar is at the center of the chancel, a pulpit is to one side, and four large deacon's chairs face the congregation. The narrow stained-glass windows reach almost to the roof. Their floral and geometric patterns are broken only at the tops, where small trefoils contain even more diminutive symbols common in the Methodist faith: a crown and cross, an anchor, and the three crosses of Calvary.

Follow Amboy Road west seven short blocks; left (south) on curving, rural-like Satterlee Street six short blocks to Philip Court.

Conference House

Satterlee Street, between Philip Court and Hylan Boulevard with 7455
Hylan Boulevard as its street address
718-984-6046

On a hill overlooking Raritan Bay (the confluence of the Raritan River and Arthur Kill) sits the 1680 stone house of British naval officer Christopher Billop. The house experienced a few hours of fame on September 11, 1776. Just as the American Revolution was beginning, three noted patriots met with Admiral Lord Richard Howe to see if the two sides could resolve their issues and stop the fighting. Howe, who commanded the large British naval fleet anchored off Staten Island in the Outer Harbor, had been authorized to act as a peace envoy. He had suggested the meeting by letter delivered to the Congress, who were meeting in Philadelphia. Most representatives were suspicious, especially John Adams; but on the strong urging of Edward Rutledge, the Congress chose three members, including Adams and Rutledge, to meet with Howe.

Benjamin Franklin, John Adams, and Edward Rutledge represented the Americans and traveled through New Jersey toward Staten Island. It took two days to reach Perth Amboy, where the Americans were met by a British naval barge to take them to Staten Island. Conference details had been arranged by Christopher Billop, a British loyalist and great-grandson of the mansion's original owner, who often entertained Redcoat officers in his home. Billop and Howe put the Americans at ease and provided them with a sumptuous lunch of ham, beef tongue, and mutton. Conference House had been decorated with moss sprinkled over the wood floors, and its walls and windows were trimmed with leafy green tree branches.

The afternoon conference went nowhere. The two sides never progressed beyond their opening demands. Howe offered amnesty to any American who swore allegiance to George III, King of England. He had no authority to offer any other concessions. Rutledge suggested to Howe the advantages to Britain of recognizing American independence, forming an alliance, and carrying on profitable trade. But Howe had not been authorized to negotiate anything substantive. The meeting adjourned as a failure, and the Americans crossed the Arthur Kill by ferry and made their way back to Philadelphia. The American Revolution continued from 1776 until 1783, when the two sides signed the Treaty of Paris and the British withdrew from the colonies.

According to a dubious but persistent local Staten Island legend, Christopher Billop, the original owner of the house, was responsible for Staten Island's being part of New York. When the British captured New Amsterdam from the Dutch in 1664, two colonies claimed Staten Island. Lord Berkeley and Lord Carteret, royal proprietors of New Jersey, claimed the large hilly island barely separated from New Jersey by the narrow strait called the Arthur Kill. (*Kill* means stream in Dutch.) The governor of New York also claimed it. To settle the matter, the Duke of York (brother of the King of England) sponsored a unique competition: the island would go to whichever colony whose resident could circle the island in a boat within twenty-four hours. Christopher Billop, a former sea captain, won for New York.

Billop had been granted 932 acres at the south end of Staten Island in 1675. Later, he increased his landholdings to 1,600 acres. In 1709, he began ferry service from his land in Staten Island across the Arthur Kill to Perth Amboy, New Jersey. (The Tottenville area was once called Billop's Point. Billop Avenue in Tottenville is named for him.)

Charleston & Port Socony Continuation

Arthur Kill Road, twisting in a north–south direction between Bentley Street to Sharrotts Road and continuing north to Rossville, where it heads inland (east) to Richmondtown

Return to Main Street. Take the S74 bus from Main Street (in front of the Police Station) along Arthur Kill Road to Sharrotts Road; or drive or hike along winding Arthur Kill Road to Sharrotts Road.

The southern section of Arthur Kill Road resembles a spiraling rural two-lane highway in the American South. The quiet is punctuated by a periodic speeding car or pickup truck. If you walk, be aware that there are no sidewalks. You may need to ward off barking dogs and dodge discarded appliances, burned car hulks, and strewn garbage. Surprisingly, this, too, is New York City. In colonial times, the big industry was oyster gathering in the river. Clay pits, brickworks, and terra-cotta production took over in the nineteenth century and into the twentieth. Today, there are a lot of weed-filled empty lots, tumbled-down houses, two dry docks, and a prison.

Kreischer House
4500 Arthur Kill Road near Englewood Avenue

Located on a hill above the forgotten back end of Staten Island, the home of Balthazar Kreischer's son, Charles, proudly possesses the highest ground in the area. The large white Victorian residence with cupola and gingerbread latticework was built in 1885 for the brick baron who had founded the Kreischer Brick and Terra-cotta Works in 1854. His employees worked in the nearby clay pits and brick kilns and lived in a company town. Charleston was called Kreischerville until 1927.

Turn right (east) two blocks on Sharrotts Road to Carlin Street. Turn left (north) on Carlin Street. The entrance to the Clay Pit Ponds State Park Preserve is one hundred yards down the secluded Carlin Street.

Clay Pit Ponds State Park Preserve
Enter one hundred yards down the secluded Carlin Street two blocks east of Arthur Kill Road, with an address of 83 Nielsen Avenue off Sharrotts Road
718-967-1976

Numerous walking paths and horse trails reticulate 260 acres of woodland, wetland, bog, sandy barren, and meadow habitats in this New York state park preserve. Now a haven for hikers and birders, it was once the source of clay for Staten Island's former brick industry. In 1854, Balthazar Kreischer opened the first brick factory; several others started along Arthur Kill Road during the late nineteenth century. The park's five ponds, which appear natural, were once clay pits that filled up with rainwater, transforming them into clay pit ponds. The park authorities sponsor many activities from their ramshackle century-old headquarters in a former farmhouse. They host birding walks and lectures on gardening, canning, paper production, and animals of the region. Many animals live in the park, including screech owls, raccoons, lizards, box turtles, and numerous songbirds.

Restaurant Recommendation

Killmeyer's Old Bavarian Inn & Beer Garden (German)

4254 Arthur Kill Road at Sharrotts Road
718-984-1202

While most old beer gardens did not survive the twentieth century, Killmeyer's remains alive and well. In fact, the present restaurant has been in business only since 1995, but the building had been a series of inns, beer gardens, and bars since 1855. South German decor abounds in this place of gemütlichkeit. It includes heraldry, beer steins, paintings, wildlife taxidermy, romantic paintings, and a stained-glass portrayal of Mad King Ludwig II's Neuschwanstein Castle in Bavaria. Killmeyer's has indoor seating and an outdoor garden with picnic tables to enjoy hardy Bavarian favorites, like the combination called *Wurstteller mit allem Drum und Dran* (sausage with everything), a sampling of sausages, and other favorite dishes: pork shank, duck, and roast chicken. The bratwurst (pork sausage) and Jägerschnitzel (breaded pork cutlet) are particularly juicy and are served with three varieties of sauerkraut, one of them sweet and sour. Along with hefty portions of meat, the accompanying potatoes or spaetzle (dumplings) and vegetables make the table groan. They stock three hundred varieties of domestic and foreign beers. A three-piece oompah-pah band serenades weekend diners. Outside, the sidewalk is made from bricks embossed with the Kreischer name from the neighboring clay pit.

SNUG HARBOR CULTURAL CENTER

S ailor's Snug Harbor, a retirement home for sailors, opened its doors in 1831. The complex of Greek Revival temple buildings constructed between 1833 and 1892 provided for "aged, decrepit, and worn-out sailors" and was funded by Robert Richard Randall, a wealthy merchant. The former retirement facility for sailors solved the societal problem of how to handle single men too old to work on ships. Many drank heavily and had no families. The facility opened with twenty-seven residents, numbered one thousand in 1900, and had only 150 when it left Staten Island.

Sailor's Snug Harbor was essentially a prison to keep impoverished, potentially rowdy sailors off the streets and out of sight. The sailors were compelled to wear uniforms, follow a strict schedule, and attend church services. There was a no-drinking rule, and inmates needed written permission to leave the premises, which were surrounded by a high fence and guarded gates.

The retirement facility moved to Sea Level, North Carolina, in 1975, and in 1976, the buildings on Richmond Terrace became the site of the Snug Harbor Cultural Center. The complex of twenty-six large and small Greek Revival buildings on an eighty-acre site just one and a half miles from the ferry includes galleries, museums, studios, concert spaces, gardens, and a gift shop. The facility also contains painting and lithographic studios for artists and rooms to host lectures and show films.

Re-created buildings and rooms pertaining to the original historical mission of the complex include the chapel, the restored library once used by the residents, and a reconstructed bunkroom with sparse furnishings for the old salts: a single bed, a desk and chair, a dresser, and a small locked strongbox for personal items.

 From the Ferry Terminal, travel along Richmond Terrace to Snug Harbor Cultural Center.

Take S40 bus from Ferry Terminal, or walk one and one half miles west on Richmond Terrace.

Snug Harbor Cultural Center

1000 Richmond Terrace, between Tysen Street and Kissel Avenue
718-448-2500

Since the retirement facility moved to North Carolina, the Snug Harbor Cultural Center emerged on the grounds. It now constitutes Staten Island's premier cultural center and has several main sectors, most of them recently restored. They include the Staten Island Children's Museum, Music Hall for public concerts, John A. Noble Collection of Marine Paintings and Lithographs, and Newhouse Center for Contemporary Art ranging from paintings to sculpture.

The Botanical Garden has several components: Main Garden, Glass House, Pond Garden, Herb Garden, Rose Garden, English Perennial Border Garden, Heritage Farm Project, and NYC Compost Project. The Chinese Scholar's Garden opened in 1999. It is a series of courtyards that were constructed in a style appropriate for a very wealthy member of Old China's scholar-gentry class. The compound overlooks a twenty-acre pond and contains within its walls courtyards, portals, bridges, ponds, and pavilions based on yin-yang (dialectical) principles. Of special interest is the carved woodwork, elaborate window tracery, ceramic roof tiles, calligraphy plaques, the seventy-eight varieties of garden plants, and eighteenth- and nineteenth-century Chinese furniture.

There are other buildings as well: a Gothic Revival church, the Great Hall for special musical and theatrical performances, a Discovery classroom, an outdoor stage, and three Victorian houses once occupied by the former institution's governor and three of his assistants. Snug

Harbor is a vibrant and worthwhile facility, an architectural treasure, and a good place to meet Staten Islanders.

Restaurant Recommendation

Adobe Blues (Mexican)

63 Lafayette Avenue at Fillmore Street, two blocks south of Richmond Terrace
718-720-2583

Homemade juicy fresh salsa with the distinct flavor of cilantro is served with all dishes at Adobe Blues. The menu has all the usual northern Mexican specialties. Combination plates are very filling; each presents three different selections from the following: enchiladas, tacos, tostadas, and burritos. Rice and red beans are the usual accompaniments.

ABOUT THE AUTHOR

For five decades, historian Bob Swacker has led tours through the neighborhoods of New York City. His tours combine decades of historical research in libraries, cemeteries, and historical societies; interviews with borough residents; and many miles traveled on foot in the field. He has taught at Saint Ann's School in Brooklyn since 1970 and for many years he has taught courses on New York City at Saint Ann's and at New York University. Dr. Swacker is the co-author, with Leslie Jenkins, of *Irish New York* (Rizzoli Publishing, 2006). He lives in Stuyvesant Town.